Tourism Events in Asia

T0289963

The roles and impacts of planned events within tourism are of increasing importance for destination competitiveness. *Tourism Events in Asia* is a unique contribution to the understanding of the impacts of events in the development planning, promotion and marketing of destinations in the rapidly growing tourism market of Asia.

Balancing theory and practical examples, the book analyses the tools and techniques of branding, marketing and media involvement as well as visitor motivations for successful tourism events in Asia. It reviews a range of different event types from dark tourism festivals, film tourism festivals, cultural heritage tourism festivals, food tourism festivals, business events, sports events; and meeting, incentives, conferences and exhibitions (MICE) and much more.

Written by an international team of authors, this book is essential reading for anyone interested in the Asian tourism events market and will be a valuable resource for students and researchers of events, tourism, marketing and branding.

Azizul Hassan is a member of the Tourism Consultants Network of the UK Tourism Society and is currently working towards a PhD at Cardiff Metropolitan University. His main areas of research are technology-supported marketing in tourism; innovative marketing dynamics; destination branding in tourism; cultural heritage tourism; heritage interpretation; and sustainable management/marketing alternatives for cultural heritage industries. He is a regular reviewer of Tourism Analysis, the International Journal of Human Resource Management, the International Journal of Ecotourism, the eReview of Tourism Research (eRTR) and the International Interdisciplinary Business-Economics Advancement Journal.

Anukrati Sharma is Associate Professor in the Faculty of Commerce and Management, University of Kota, Kota, Rajasthan, India. In 2015, she received Research Award from the UGC, New Delhi, on *Analysis of the Status of Tourism in Hadoti and Shekhawati Region/Circuit (Rajasthan): Opportunities, Challenges, and Future Prospects.* Her doctorate was on tourism marketing from the University of Rajasthan. Her core research areas are tourism, strategic management, law, general management and international business management. She is member of several professional bodies. She attended and presented papers in many national and international conferences.

Routledge Advances in Event Research Series
Edited by Warwick Frost and Jennifer Laing
Department of Marketing, Tourism and Hospitality,
La Trobe University, Australia

For more information about this series, please visit: www.routledge.com/
Routledge-Advances-in-Event-Research-Series/book-series/RAERS

Tourism Events in Asia

Marketing and Development

Edited by Azizul Hassan
and Anukrati Sharma

 Routledge
Taylor & Francis Group

LONDON AND NEW YORK

First published 2019
by Routledge
2 Park Square, Milton Park, Abingdon, Oxon OX14 4RN

and by Routledge
605 Third Avenue, New York, NY 10017

First issued in paperback 2021

Routledge is an imprint of the Taylor & Francis Group, an informa business

Publisher's Note
The publisher has gone to great lengths to ensure the quality of this reprint but points out that some imperfections in the original copies may be apparent.

British Library Cataloguing-in-Publication Data
A catalogue record for this book is available from the British Library

Library of Congress Cataloging-in-Publication Data
A catalog record for this book has been requested

Typeset in Times New Roman
by Apex CoVantage, LLC

ISBN 13: 978-1-03-224165-4 (pbk)
ISBN 13: 978-1-138-47691-2 (hbk)

DOI: 10.4324/9781351105743

Printed in the United Kingdom
by Henry Ling Limited

Contents

Figures

Tables

Contributors

Ahmad R. AlBattat is an Assistant Professor and Post Graduate Coordinator (Hospitality, Events, and Tourism) in Post Graduate Centre, Management and Science University, Selangor, Malaysia. He is a visiting Professor and external examiner in Medan Academy of Tourism (Akbar Medan), Indonesia. He holds a Doctoral degree in Hospitality Management from University Sains Malaysia (USM). He worked as an Assistant Professor, Ammon Applied University College, Amman, Jordan; as a Senior Lecturer and Research Coordinator in School of Hospitality & Creative Arts, Management and Science University, Shah Alam, Selangor, Malaysia; and, as a Researcher at Sustainable Tourism Research Cluster (STRC), Pulau Pinang, Malaysia. He has been working for the Jordanian hospitality industry for 17 years. He has participated and presented research papers in academic conferences held in Malaysia, Taiwan, Thailand, Indonesia, Sri Lanka, and Jordan. He is a scientific committee member and reviewer of *Journal of Tourism Management*; *Journal of Hospitality Marketing and Management (JHMM)*; *Current Issues in Tourism (CIT)*; *Asia-Pacific Journal of Innovation in Hospitality and Tourism (APJIHT)*; *International Journal of Economics and Management (IJEAM)*; *AlmaTourism*; *Journal of Tourism, Culture and Territorial Development*. His latest works are published in refereed international journals, books, and conference proceedings.

Dimah Ajeeb is a visiting lecturer at the University of Greenwich and a reviewer at the *International Journal of Tourism Cities (IJTC)*. The author's publications and research interests fall within the following topics; urban policy and strategy, town planning, spatial planning, urban governance, decentralisation, devolution, multi-level governance, localism, policy-making and implementation, urban design, community development, urban regeneration and renewal, gentrification, prosperity, tourism policy and planning, local economic development, architecture "designs, principles, history and heritage, and regulations".

Shruti Arora is a freelance writer. She did her PhD research from the University of Kota, Kota, Rajasthan, India. Her PhD topic was 'Growth and development of event management sector in Rajasthan – an evaluation'. She has research interests in event tourism and festival tourism. She has published four research papers in impact factor journals. Among those, two papers were social media marketing; the third was titled "The Impact of Events on Rajasthan Tourism with Reference to Different Fairs and Festival" in *Transteller Journal* that brought her the Best Paper Certificate and the last paper was titled "Shift in Marketing Trends in the Current Competitive Scenario".

Afreen Choudhury is an Assistant Professor in the Department of Marketing, Faculty of Business Studies, University of Dhaka. She completed BBA and MBA major in Marketing from the same institute as the topper of the batch and as an acknowledgement of her academic credential achieved the UGC (University Grant Commission) Merit Scholarship–2010. She has always forwarded her innovative ideas in different leading research publications. Her area of research interest includes sustainable innovation, blue ocean strategy, green branding, corporate social responsibilities, and social media marketing.

Bekir Bora Dedeoğlu, PhD is Assistant Professor at the Department of Tourism Guiding at Nevsehir HBV University, Turkey. His research interests include tourism marketing, social media marketing, destination marketing, destination branding, tourist behaviour, and hospitality marketing. He is author of articles in journals such as *Journal of Destination Marketing and Management, International Journal of Contemporary Hospitality Management* and *Journal of Travel and Tourism Marketing*. He has also served as reviewer for top tourism and hospitality journals such as *Tourism Management, International Journal of Hospitality Management, Asia Pacific Journal of Tourism Research, Total Quality Management & Business Excellence, Journal of Hospitality Marketing & Management* etc.

Desloehal Djumrianti is a Senior Lecturer in Tourism Department of State Polytechnic of Sriwijaya, Palembang Indonesia. With her educational background in marketing, Internet studies, and tourism, she also has a large number of experiences as a guest lecturer in the business schools of both private and public universities in Indonesia, and speaker in national conferences, seminars and symposiums of e-marketing tourism. Several of her publications and books are related to tourism, marketing, events, culture and education. Furthermore, Djumrianti has research interests around areas of the use of Internet-based communication in the tourism and cultures context, critical discourse analysis, e-marketing tourism, and postcolonialism. Her current researches are related to the representation of destinations on the official websites and roles and functions of social media as promotional tools.

Azizul Hassan is a member of the Tourism Consultants Network of the UK Tourism Society, and is currently working towards a PhD at Cardiff Metropolitan University. His main areas of research are: technology-supported marketing in tourism; innovative marketing dynamics; destination branding in tourism; cultural heritage tourism; heritage interpretation; and sustainable management/marketing alternatives for cultural heritage industries. He is a regular reviewer of *Tourism Analysis*, the *International Journal of Human Resource*

Management, the *International Journal of Ecotourism*, the *eReview of Tourism Research (eRTR)* and the *International Interdisciplinary Business-Economics Advancement Journal*.

Karabi Kabir (e-mail: karabishapnil@gmail.com) is a Lecturer in Tourism and Hospitality Management at University of Dhaka, Bangladesh. Her research interests include sustainable tourism development, tourism policy development, event management and socio- cultural impact of tourism.

Kemal Gürkan Küçükergin is an Assistant Professor in the Tourism and Hotel Management at Atılım University, Turkey. He holds Master and PhD degree in tourism management from Gazi University. His research areas are destination marketing, tourist behaviour, Partial Least Squares-Structural Equation Modelling and tourist emotions.

Karen Miranda-Fernandez is the Vice President for Research and International Affairs and Dean of the College of Hotel, Restaurant and, Tourism Management of Imus Institute of Science and Technology, Philippines. She is also the Vice President for Education and Accreditation of Asia Pacific Institute for Events Management (APIEM), United Kingdom. She has been appointed as Visiting Professor in Malaysia: Olympia College, Management and Science University, and Universiti Teknologi MARA; Indonesia: Sahid Tourism Institute of Surakarta and Bandung Institute of Tourism; Thailand: Maha Sarakham University, Naresuan University, North Bangkok University, Burapha University, and National Institute of Development Administration; and Taiwan: Ming Chuan University and Chung Hua University. She became a postdoctoral scholar at School of Events, Tourism and Hospitality in Leeds Beckett University, United Kingdom. She holds a doctoral degree in Business Management specialised in Hospitality with a major in Hotel and Restaurant Management, both earned at Philippine Women's University, Manila. Dr. Fernandez is the book author of "Guide to Event Management's Best Practices" and Editor-in-Chief of the *International Journal of Sustainable Tourism and Hospitality Management*.

Amir H. Moghaddam is an Iranian PhD Student in Anthropology, Hacettepe University, Ankara, Turkey. He has research interests in tourism and terrorism, racism and ethnocentrism in tourism, identity and tourism and tourism in Afghanistan. Moghaddam is editor in chief of a book in Persian language by title of 'Anthropology of tourism' (2012 and 2017). He also wrote some articles on cultural and security impacts of tourism in Persian language and contributed in 'The encyclopedia of tourism' in 2016.

Nor Aida Abdul Rahman currently serves as a Head of Aviation Management at Universiti Kuala Lumpur, Malaysian Institute of Aviation Technology, in Subang, Selangor, Malaysia. She has worked as internal and external trainer in management, supply chain, Halal logistics and postgraduate research. She has written three books on postgraduate research. Her research work has appeared in several reputable academic journals, book chapters and refereed conference proceedings. She earned a PhD in Management (supply chain management) from Brunel University, London, UK. She is also serving as Academic Advisor in college, a chartered member for Chartered Institute of Logistics and Transport Malaysia (CILTM), HRDF Certified Trainer, Chairman (Academic Committee) for Malaysian Association of Transportation, Logistics and Supply Chain Schools (MyATLAS), Vice President (Research Journal) for Institute for Research in Management and Engineering UK (INRME), JAKIM Halal Certified Trainer, and is a member of Academy of Marketing, UK.

Haywantee Ramkissoon is an Associate Professor at Curtin University, and Monash University, both in Australia. She also holds a Senior Research Associate position at the University of Johannesburg. She was honoured with the Emerging Scholar of Distinction award by the Fellows of the International Academy for the study of Tourism in recognition of her contribution to innovative and ground-breaking tourism research. She holds two Doctoral degrees, in Applied Environmental Psychology and in Tourism. Her postdoctoral focused on societal innovation and behaviour change. She has published widely in reputable journals such as *Tourism Management, Annals of Tourism Research, Journal of Sustainable Tourism, Journal of Travel Research* and *Journal of Hospitality Marketing & Management* and sits on several editorial boards of prestigious journals and on international scientific committees. She is the book review editor for *Current Issues in Tourism*, and Research Note Editor for the *Journal of Hospitality Marketing & Management*. She is a reviewer for over 50 peer-reviewed journals. Dr Ramkissoon has served as Director of Research (Tourism), and on judging panels of International Research & Development Grant Councils. She works closely with industry partners and academic institutions and organisations, and disseminates her work through conferences, workshops and seminars. She has been a visiting professor and scholar at several reputable international universities and research councils in North America, Asia, Europe, Africa and Australasia, and has been a contributor as keynote speaker, panellist and presenter at national and international academic and industry events.

Samik Ray is ex-faculty of Department of Folklore, University of Kalyani; Travel and Tourism Management in MPTI (Kolkata); and WTCC School of Trade and Commerce. He is also ex-trainer and faculty of Regional Level Guide (RLG) Training (Govt. of India, Department of Tourism). Ray is presently working as RLG (Govt. of India, Department of Tourism), and Editor of 'Tourism Theory and Practice'. He is the author of several essays on tourism studies and management, social science, and literary criticism.

Saadia Shabnam is a Doctoral Researcher at the Curtin University, Australia. She received the Australia Awards, 2014 for pursuing her PhD research in Marketing. Her research interest is in the area of tourism management and marketing, ecotourism development, service supply chain, corporate social responsibility and responsible consumption. She has published research articles in several international peer-reviewed journals and conference proceedings.

Anukrati Sharma is currently Associate Professor in the Faculty of Commerce and Management, University of Kota, Kota Rajasthan, India. Dr. Sharma has worked as an internal trainer and teacher in the management arena. Her doctorate degree was from the University of Rajasthan, India where the dissertation research explored tourism promotion and prospects in Rajasthan. Her core research areas are: tourism, strategic management, and international business management. She is serving as the editorial board member of twenty-six reputed national and international journals. Also, she has written/edited ten books on different subjects.

Shikha Sharma is an Assistant Professor at Chandigarh University, India. She has research interest in tourism marketing and management, managing visitors impacts at heritage sites, destination planning and development, sustainable tourism and community participation towards destination development, niche tourism and emerging concepts in tourism. Dr. Sharma has presented over 20 research papers at national and international conferences and seminars. She has published over ten articles in various journals/edited books.

Muhammad Shoeb-Ur-Rahman is an Assistant Professor, Department of Tourism and Hospitality Management, University of Dhaka, Bangladesh. At present, Rahman is doing his doctoral study in tourism management at Lincoln University, New Zealand. His main areas of research interests concentrate on tourism management, sustainable tourism development, tourism planning and policies, destination development, cultural tourism, and medical tourism.

Salam Tadros is a lecturer at Ammon Applied University College, Amman, Jordan. She holds a master's degree in Hospitality Management from Glion Institute of Higher Education. She started her career in hotels and then moved to academia. She has a solid ground in education and training, and has joined many projects with USAID. Her areas of interest include hospitality management, customer service, front office operations and housekeeping management.

Elena Egorovna Totonova holds a PhD in Geography and is an Associate Professor at the Institute of Foreign Philology and Regional Studies, North-Eastern Federal University, Republic of Sakha (Yakutia), Russia. She is the Head of the master's programme in 'Tourism, Cultural Heritage and the Environment'. She graduated from the Graduate School of Geography of the Moscow State University, Lomonosov with specialty in 'Economic, Social and Political Geography' and Doctoral studies from the Institute for Economic Research of the Far Eastern Branch of the Russian Academy of Sciences, specialising in 'World Economy'. Her main areas of research are: the problems of economic development in the northern territories of Russia and Canada, tourism, and the development of entrepreneurship in the North. She is the author of eighty scientific works, two of which are monographs and two textbooks. Dr. Totonova is a full member of the National Academy of Tourism, the Russian Society for the Study of Canada, the Association of Russian Geographers of Social Scientists, and an associate member of the Center International for the Study of Indigenous Peoples at Laval University, Canada.

Introduction

Azizul Hassan and Anukrati Sharma

Tourism events are an important reason for tourism that supports the planning, promotion and development of marketing of a particular destination. The influences of tourism events are increasing across Asia. This book aims to provide theoretical and practical content for academicians, researchers, students, event planners, destination managers and other stakeholders of the event, tourism and hospitality industry. In doing so, the book covers the concept of events, tourism, destination branding, destination marketing, social media marketing, digital marketing, sustainable tourism development, accountability of media, dark tourism festivals, film tourism festivals, cultural-heritage tourism festivals, food tourism festivals, business events, sports events, MICE and much more. It includes case studies and examples of tourism events to bring the factual position and the role of marketing strategies in event promotion.

The book argues for the rapid and continuous growth of tourism events in Asia, which may work as a powerful and fundamental source that can help in many ways. The overall image of an event can be transformed by adopting the strategies and tactics of branding and marketing. The book also imputes how psychological factors impact the visitor's choice while choosing a certain event. The book has a specific focus on Asian tourism events aligning with case studies and presently accommodates fourteen chapters excluding this book introduction chapter.

The **first chapter** addresses theoretical debates of event tourism on the lens of Getz's remarkable works between 1989 and 2008. In this chapter, Ray critically presents arguments that tourism and events are interrelated from the historic era. Tourism events hosting and promoting are important in the Asian economy. Tourism events are able to interact with the latest marketing strategies. Countries in Asia are mostly successful and make significant contribution in this regard.

In the **second chapter**, Rahman, Kabir and Hassan profiled diverse traditional tourism events in South Asia in line with the Getz's (2008) framework for understanding and creating knowledge about event tourism. This chapter is a classic example that visualises the conceptual framework of event tourism in practice. Tourism events are having effects in the South Asian culture. A brief summary of major tourism events in South Asia with cultural and ritual aspects is also presented.

In the **third chapter**, Sharma identifies different events of the Hadoti region of Rajasthan, India. Sharma argues that tourism events in this region are not only creating a positive image but are also supportive in generating income, beneficial changes, social wellbeing and socio-economic development. The chapter analyses the effects of these traditional tourism events and suggests how innovative approaches can have better effects on tourism promotion in this particular region.

In the **fourth chapter**, Shabnam, Ramkissoon and Choudhury focus on 'Pohela Boishakh', the largest festival of its kind in Bangladesh. This is recognised as the 'Intangible Cultural Heritage of Humanity' by UNESCO. On the understanding of Getz et al. (2007), the authors explored festival stakeholder relationships and resource dependency issues, in particular. The authors deliberately advance stakeholder theory application to festival tourism, festival management and marketing in an integrated manner in this chapter.

In the **fifth chapter**, Sharma outlines the way through which specific events help to re-position and re-define the identity of Malana of India as a place with touristic value. This chapter views religious, social, economic and environmental features followed by importance analysis of these festivals.

In the **sixth chapter**, Sharma with Arora highlight the diversities and goodness that information technology can bring in promoting tourism events. For doing this, the authors explore the role of information and communication technology in marketing and promoting tourism events of Rajasthan, India. The application and successful utilisation of information technology in event tourism can help to attract tourists, and spot factors to motivate destination choice.

AlBattat, Tadros and Miranda-Fernandez in the **seventh chapter** show the significance and capacities of social media in promoting tourism events in Jordan. The authors present three important and relevant examples supporting their claims. Social media supports events to promote tourism activities in Jordan. This chapter identifies affirmative roles of social media and tourism events in profiling host cities, attracting visitors, delivering economic benefits, and creating jobs.

In the **eighth chapter**, Dedeoğlu and Küçükergin write on social media sharing in tourism. The authors observe that events where individuals would most likely immortalise the moment, through sharing of photographs and videos with their friends and families, were not examined in detail in the literature. Their study was conducted to make theoretical proposals to fill this gap in the Turkish context.

Djumrianti in the **ninth** aims to investigate how the social media is used in promotional cultural events; social media used as a source of information to gather the **chapter** events; and the roles of Twitter, Instagram and Facebook in the promotion of traditional cultural events of three different cities of Indonesia.

In the **tenth chapter** Rahman discusses the popular and innovative tourism events of four territories (i.e. South, North, East and Central region) in Peninsular Malaysia. Based on analysis, this chapter identifies key strengths of each of these territories. From practice context, the author affirms that findings and suggestions of this chapter are beneficial for both fellow researchers and also for managerial and policy planning bodies.

In the **eleventh chapter**, Hassan analyses the 'Omor Ekushey February' (the 21st of February) 1952 as an arguably dark tourism event in Bangladesh. This day is recognised by UNESCO and celebrated as the 'International Mother Language Day'. This chapter suggests a theoretical reshaping of dark tourism terminology that should not limit focus on death and disaster. The chapter concludes that a conceptual shift of dark tourism festival is necessary to focus inquiry not on death per se but peoples' perception about it.

In the **twelfth chapter**, Moghaddam shows that the rate of venerability and importance of an event in Iran plays the main role in the acceptance or resistance of the tourists by hosts. Diverse areas of anti-tourism against the commodification of culture are given emphasis in this chapter on the ground of Varf Chal (Pour Snow in Pit)/Zan Shahi (Kingdom of Women) Ceremonies in the North of Iran.

In the **thirteenth chapter**, Ajeeb examines the extent to which The Municipal Administration Modernisation (MAM) project was successful in its proposed strategies, practices and outcomes in tourism marketing and events. To that end, she utilises a comparative case study approach through which it will look into different international contexts where the European Union and equivalent national bodies have developed similar projects of cultural tourism in old city centres in Syria.

The **fourteenth chapter** is written by Totonova from the Asian tourism setting of Russia. This chapter aligns the European and North American perspectives where the author explains the diverse level of economic and social development of territories of Canada and Arctic regions of the Republic of Sakha. The chapter mainly discusses general economic status of these territories with special attention to tourism events and related activities.

This book expects to balance theory and experimentation, providing a thorough explication of the tools and techniques of branding, marketing, and media involvement for tourism events in Asia. Countries in Asia are going to be major players in the global tourism market with millions of inbound and outbound tourists. Thus, this book should be a unique contribution towards understanding events in Asia.

1 Event tourism in Asian context

Samik Ray

Introduction

Broadly, an event is a social/cultural/economic/political/scientific happening of personal/local/regional/national/global significance that changes the state that existed before happening. An event could be accidental, unplanned, chance directed or planned and organised. The present chapter will focus on the latter type and refer it by general term 'event' instead of 'planned and organised event'. Racing games or sports events like Olympics, gathering for surplus produce exchanges, pilgrimages and festivals are examples of the early intercultural organised events though the earliest form was marked in gatherings for primitive hunting or food gathering.

Travelling is perpetually imperative to event participation but the relationship between tourism and event had been accepted only with a planned event's emergence as tourism motivator (Getz, 2008) or major driver of destinations' identities, attractiveness, competitiveness, promotion and development. Such mutualism triggered the perception of tourism-oriented event or event-dependent tourism, thus event tourism practice. Subsequently event tourism management including marketing has emerged as a specialised professional field within tourism.

International Congress and Convention Association's (ICCA) survey on the cities hosting international meetings indicated that in 2014 Singapore, Beijing, Seoul and Hong Kong were placed among world's top twenty hosts of international meetings (ICCA, 2018). In terms of international overnight visitors' volume six Asian cities together received more than 80 million tourists in 2016 and positioned among top ten destinations (CNN Travel, 2017). MasterCard's Global Destination Cities Index predicts seven out of top ten most visited destination cities in 2017 will be from the Asian continent, namely Bangkok, Dubai, Singapore, Tokyo, Seoul, Kuala Lumpur, and Hong Kong by raising total volume of overnight visitors to 95 million or more (MasterCard, 2017; World Economic Forum, 2017). According to UNWTO (2016), Asia and the Pacific became the second most visited region next to Europe in 2016 with 303 million international arrivals which will grow annually by 5.1 per cent in 2010–2020 and 3.7 per cent in 2020–2030 on average in business travel sector. Those facts, figures and predictions specified Asia's emergence as the most promising destination of the 21st century with respect to international tourist arrival, overnight visitors, international business travel and meetings, event tourism development, and event hosting.

Event tourism studies

2.1 Trends

Relation between tourism and event is a long-established fact. Independent growth of tourism and event research is only a post-world war phenomenon. Those researches hardly combined two fields where notable exceptions are Hawkins and Goldblatt (1995) and Getz's (2005) effort. Study and research on event tourism is merely a few decades' story. The volume of researches done on event tourism within this span indicates its growing importance though practices spread faster than researches. Researches pay more attention to general discussion, impact studies, taxonomy and analysis of certain types emphasising developed countries' events.

General studies

Among general studies management, marketing, planning, designing, evaluation and concept building receive much attention. The earliest reference of planned event is found in Boorstin's (1961) work. Festival and convention's importance in tourism's context was noted by Greenwood (1972) and Gunn (1979) without perceiving events' role as an attraction. Syme et al. (1989), Getz (1998, 2002, 2007), Rittichainuwat et al. (2001), Weed (2005), Mackellar (2006), Bowdin et al. (2011), and Krajnović (2016) made significant effort to introduce the concept of event tourism systematically. Getz's (2000b, 2005) contributions led the way to event management studies and scopes of its researches. Contributions on event management education (Hawkins and Goldblatt, 1995), evaluation of management effectiveness (Getz, 1989), risk management (Berlonghi, 1990; Tarlow, 2002), and media management at sport events (Getz and Fairley, 2004) enriched management studies further. Aspects like convention strategies in destination planning (Getz et al., 1998), bidding on events (Getz, 2004), event design (Berridge, 2006), marketing and communications (Hoyle, 2002; Masterman and Wood, 2006), and service quality evaluation (Getz et al., 2001) are few among many that draw attention on planning and marketing research.

Impact studies

Socio-cultural and economic impact studies on festival and sports events got much importance. Most noteworthy are economic impact studies on festival visitors (Scotinform Ltd., 1991), evaluation and impact assessment (Mossberg, 2000), hallmark events to contest tourism seasonality (Ritchie and Beliveau, 1974), mega events' impact on tourism (Getz, 1999), event tourism's economic impact analysis (Della Bitta et al., 1978; Vaughan, 1979; Crompton and McKay, 1994; Bond, 2008), expositions' economic impact on tourism (Ritchie, 1984), mega-events' role in generating tourism (Bos, 1994), resident perceptions of event impacts (Fredline and Faulkner, 2002) on social impact scale (Fredline, 2006), and hosts' perceptions over social impacts of sport tourism events (Ljudevit et al., 2012). Contribution on impact of event tourism from an anthropological approach (Greenwood, 1972) is important too.

Type studies

Type-specific studies focus largely on business, MICE, festival and sports event tourism. While Lee and Back (2005) dealt with varied aspects of MICE tourism events, contributions on festival events in tourism perspective are made by Getz (2000a), Allen et al. (2011), Getz (2007), and Quinn (2009). Researches of Getz (2003), Supovitz and Goldblatt (2004), and Ljudevit et al. (2012) on aspects of sports event and tourism are acclaimed notably by event tourism academics. Getz (1989, 1991, 2000b, 2002), Hall (1992), Formica (1998), and Goldblatt (2007) delved into special event tourism aspects.

Events of Asia till 20th century: trends in changes

Trend in general

Instances of Asia's credentials in dealing and hosting diverse events were evident centuries before the quantitative facts supported comprehension about it. Festivals, fairs, competitive racing and games with ball, stick and horse were the earliest common events hosted locally across Asia. Conferences are considered as a modern event, though its origin could be traced back to 400 BCE when first Buddhist council at Rājgir was attended by 500 spiritually enlightened monks. Significance of those events was far reaching within contemporary Asian socio-cultural fabric. Asia's appearance as potential host of event is neither accidental nor sudden happening; rather it evolved through transformation within the paradigm of event since early years. Transformations gradually made Asia to become an important event hosting destination of the day.

Changes: early perspective

The earliest transformation became apparent with perception of events by socio-cultural, entertainment and trade values instead of primitive hunger compulsion. Events in Asia then emerged as an agent of socialisation, offering opportunity to the multitude to be socialised and to be creative. Eventually involvement in event was regarded as a dignified, glorious and esteemed social act to Asian elites and fun, entertainment, pilgrimage and necessity to common people or sometimes an act to oblige immediate hierarchy, existed within contemporary societal power structure.

Asian events were largely a combination of entertainment, trading and social gathering. The significance of livestock fairs was located primarily in their trade value but socio-cultural, religious and entertainment value appeared to be important as a parallel to trading; there were folk music festivals, dances, magic shows, races, jugglery, fire-eating, sword-swallowing, stilt-walkers, gambling, wrestling, animal fights, and pilgrimage to sacred lake or confluences, altogether leading to socialisation. Primary focus of India's 'Kumbha' and 'Gangasagar' fair is pilgrimage leading to moderate entertainment, local business opportunity, and scope for socialisation. Bhutan's Tshechu is apparently a national event for religious cause but functionally a socio-cultural gathering leading to create an opportunity for socialisation, social bonding across the country and local trading.

Transformation: accessibility perspective

Improvement of cross-country road transportation and on-road safety between the 12th and 18th centuries under Islamic military and traders' hegemony was another turning point as it led to increase people's mobility from cross section and cross boundary towards events' participation. The construction of more roads, bridges and railways as colonial military and commercial strategic initiative made travelling for events' participation cost-effective, less time-consuming and less hazardous. Development in terms of accessibility made Europeans curios about oriental cultural events. Their participation either as curious visitor or trader of merchandised items or as scholar added global flavour to Asian events. It happened mainly in British and French colonies in Asia.

Changes: Event infrastructure perspective

Asian events rotated periodically in association with life stream and took place at permanent venues set aside for event, thus getting social sanctions. Changes in venue, though not common, occurred sometimes to accommodate socio-economic or political compulsions as is found in shifting of the 'Harihar Kshetra' fair from Hajipur to Sonpur by Mughal emperor Aurzangzeb, or changes of lantern festival venue at Chinese emperors' will. Initiatives to provide event infrastructure like well digging; security picket posting; building of structures for trading, selling and storing of produce or for religious rites; and construction of new styled accommodations with food, fun and security provisions (inns, serāī, traven, pānthasālā, dharamsālā) were evident. All those together turned market-cum-fair and festivals to be an important institution within medieval and colonial urban fabrics of Asia and made some internationally significant as they were attended by common visitors, pilgrims, inquisitives, merchants and producers across boundaries.

A group of internationally eminent market-cum-fair was lying on silk- cotton routes of Asia as in Baku, Bukhara, Kashgar, Khurasan, Merv, Samarkhand, Xinjiang and more. In Sultan and Mughal India livestock fairs of Pushkar and Sonpur rose into prominence by scale and significance due to immense cross-national consequences over the host's economy as were attended by military, state, cattle breeders, and traders across Asia towards trading of finest livestock. Even after Mughal decline the military of rising princely states and subsequently colonial rulers sustained the similar demand for those. With the introduction of better road-rail transportation and infrastructure during the colonial era, 'Kamba' and 'Gangasagar' fairs happened to be significant by the scale and nature of gathering as attended by millions of Hindu pilgrims, merchants, missionaries and curious Europeans.

Changes: Local control to state support

A shift from local control to state support was clearly evident at Pushkar and Sonpur fairs in Sultan and Mughal India, at Kumbha fair in British India, and in Chinese annual lantern festival. In British India colonial government was officially involved in some grand scale fairs and festivals to look after public health, security and other infrastructure management. Further events became commercial pursuits in medieval India, as in Kumbha fair 'sādhus' of 'ākhḍās' earned a huge amount as management tax from all visitors but in western perception it was not conceptualised before the industrial era.

20th-century perspective

However, it appeared that by the end of the 19th century Asian events were set with basic 5As (Accessibility, Accommodation, Attraction, Activity, Amenity) which endorse sanction for modern day tourism, though the concept of organised tourism, initiated at the behest of Grand or Cooks' tour in Europe, was absent. Since the beginning of the 20th century Asia witnessed power conflicts over control of resources, trade, and territory; independence struggles and revolutions for decolonisation and emergence of peoples' regimes. The tradition of hosting events came to a halt, but successful hosting of Asian games and five Olympics in the midst of struggle and socio-economic devastation indicates that Asia will be a promising destination for any mega events in future.

Event tourism: conceptualisation

Concept and nature

It has already been explored that events hosting depends on 5As of tourism. Conversely events are considered as one of the major motivators of present day tourism and an important driver for destination imaging. So relation between the two is logically marked by mutual dependency but neither of the two fields perceived the fact prior to New Zealand's Tourist and Publicity Department's acceptance of the term 'Event Tourism' in 1987 or construction of structured frame towards event tourism planning by Getz (1989). It was stated that all sorts of events, irrespective of type, nature and focus come under event study and its practice but tourism takes interest only in planned events having profit orientation, commercial value, greater socio-cultural bearings, prospect of public gathering, and tourist motivating capacity. Growing demand for specialised services towards managing those planned events triggered mutualism between tourism and event, thus to the emergence of event tourism.

By and large it is a sub-area of tourism like sports, business and cultural tourism. The distinction between event tourism and those subareas is not clearly specified and rationalised. Observing sizeable similarities among those a question was raised: do event tourism and sports or cultural tourism belong to same type (Fredline et al., 2003)? Primarily it seems that event tourism overlaps those forms by common key area of interest and offer planned events and event experience. While event tourism focuses on all planned events including sports, culture and business events, sports tourism deals with any kind of sports including sport events or cultural tourism largely in hosts' culture including cultural events. Unlike event tourism, those forms do not focus only on events.

Indeed, event is the principal motivator for event tourism and main attraction to event tourists while for other forms it is not. Further nature and types of event tourism market and event tourist differ from the markets of other forms. Corporate, industry, guilds of traders, federations or associations of professionals or employees, clubs, societies, regional or international leagues and many more individual tourists interested to participate or visit the events, together form the periphery of event tourist, thus the target market of event tourism. Event experience, either through direct participation or as an observer-spectator-witness, is the main attraction for event tourists. Only MICE sector ensures 100 per cent direct participatory experience. Overnight stay mainly revolves round event duration. Usual spending capacities of event tourists are higher than the normal travellers and most spend are done for event-related activities.

In terms of portfolio approach and model (Getz, 2008; Oklobdžija, 2015) demands in international and domestic event markets vary from high to low according to the types, nature and significance of events. A onetime event generates value-dependent demand, either high or low. Periodic and occasional events draw either high or medium demand. Mega or hallmark types attract both international and domestic tourists at a high scale. Major local celebrations mainly attract domestic tourists, local visitors, and occasionally a few curious international tourists. Minor local events draw attention of local visitors. In an Asian context theoretically Tokyo (1964) and Seoul (1988) Olympics, FIFA world cup (2002), Kuala Lumpur's Asian Games (1998) and New Delhi (2010) Commonwealth Games, Pushkar and Kumbha fair of India, Singapore's Arts Carnival, Cantonese Opera Festival etc. belong to either mega or major event types, and thus drew millions of international and domestic tourists and visitors. Chinese lantern festival, Bengal's Durga festival, Chariot festival of Odisha, Nagaland's Hornbill festival, Thimpu Tsechu, Thaipusam of Malaysia etc. are local festivals but draw a large number of domestic and a moderate quantity of international tourists.

Categories

Economic returns from event tourism vary according to an event's demand and value; its geo-political extension, magnitude and significance, importance in tourism, extended spectrum of attraction for tourism etc. Accordingly, effort to develop a typological division was made and similar scholastic attention was evident within event studies. Varied parameters are used to categorise both event and event tourism.

According to nationality of attendees till late 20th-century, Asian festivals and carnivals were largely local with few exceptions, sports sometimes turned to be interregional, and fairs were primarily local but appeared as international too. In the 21st century newly created festivals, trade shows, specialised fairs, and a good number of MICE events are considered to be international.

In terms of nature tourism events are classified into religious and sacred celebrations, carnivals and cultural celebrations, commercial, sports competition, or political meetings (Ritchie, 1984; Hall, 1992). In Asian context Kumbha and Gangasagar festival of India or Thaipusam of Malaysia may belong to sacred religious celebration, Chingay Singapore parade to cultural category, Asian games to sports competition class, and the summit between Kim Jong-Un and Donald Trump in 2018 at Singapore is the latest example of political meetings.

Variation in magnitude, demand, value and significance made tourism events divided as mega, hallmark, major and local (Getz, 2005; Allen et al., 2011). Mega events involve complex organisational activity, vast international exposure, high level involvement of public finance, large-scale tourism, huge infrastructure development, wide media coverage, and an enormous economic and socio-cultural effect on host destination and community. Tokyo (1964), Seoul (1988), Sapporo (1972), and Nagano (1998) Olympics and FIFA World Cup (2002) are examples of Asian mega events.

A hallmark event is special in terms of its touristic importance and attractiveness; it becomes synonymous to the spirit of host destination, community and its tradition; turns local pride to international recognition; affects destination and community economically by increasing tourism revenue; and contributes to destination imaging and positioning with competitive advantage. Pushkar and Sonpur fairs of India, Sapporo snow festival, and Harbin International Ice and Snow Sculpture festival of China may belong to hallmark type.

Major events are large-scale events in terms of attraction, arrival of tourists or visitors, and profitability; and have a strong destination imaging, marketing and branding role. All Formula One Grand Prix of ASIA, beginning from Malaysia (1999) to Azerbaijan (2016), are major events. Attractions of local events are socio-cultural festivals, sports competitions, religious celebrations, and entertainment of local significance. It creates feeling of togetherness and awareness about local traditions within the host community. It encourages tolerance and unity within a multi-cultural, multilingual and multi-ethnic fabric of destinations as is found in Asia. It draws attention of domestic tourists with little or moderate visit of international visitors and moderate media coverage e.g., Nagaland's Hornbill festival, Kolkata's 'Durga' festival, and Vietnam's 'Hoi An' lantern festival.

Getz (2008), by extending the spectrum, prepared a set of more complete and logical classes: cultural, political, art and entertainment, business, science and education, sporting event, recreational and private. Hernández et al. (2011), based on endogenous resource type, categorised event tourism into religious, nature, food, music, festivals and cultural classes.

Asia's event-oriented tourism, contrived since early state, could be categorised into socio-cultural, business-trade, political-state, sport competition, and recreational. Events are primarily directed to trade and economic value, while socio-cultural and sometimes political value is perceived largely in non-specific fairs, trade shows, carnivals, sport events, festivals and conferences. Thus classification cannot be done in an absolute sense as overlapping in nature, theme, focus, participants' character, and value is quite common in most events to date except in specific and sample fairs. Accordingly, events which are heterogenic by nature, focus, value, and participants' character could be classified as a separate category and termed as mixed.

Event tourism management

Concepts

Attractions that motivate people to travel to a place are varied. Nature, culture, heritage, business and manmade structures for leisure activity are most common and largely accepted attractions for travel but inclusion of an event in the set of attractions is fairly contemporary (Getz, 1991; Swarbrooke, 1994; Crouch and Ritchie, 1999). In relation to other attractions events, whether temporary or permanent by nature and one-time or periodical by occurrence, play a significant role to attract visitors at a high scale (Lee and Back, 2005) and subsequently increase spending and length of stay, provide a unique experience, draw increased investment (Thrane, 2002; Ponce, 2007), improve infrastructure (Kim and Petrick, 2005), create destination image by identifying with the soul and tradition of host destination and community or organising mega happening, and altogether contribute decisively to the development of a better positioning and competitive advantage for destination and its tourism economy.

Like other special-interest travel, event tourism management can be perceived from both demand and supply sides (Getz, 2008). Demand side ascertains events' value in context of destinations' positive imaging; evaluates points of event marketing in overall destination marketing; and locates co-branding prospects with destinations. Supply side leads a destination to promote events towards increase of tourist arrival, improvement of infrastructure and tourism capacity, urban regeneration, building positive imaging etc.

Event tourism management as a sub-area of tourism utilises similar management mechanisms including marketing, promotion, and development, which tourism devises. It differs from other fields of tourism primarily in two ways. First, it focuses only on all kinds of planned events. Second, it is project-oriented and includes recurring and non-recurring, small and big, local and global event projects. Principally it comes under the destination promotion programme where both event and tourism separately and together in the form of event tourism play a role of major drivers of 21st-century destinations' identities, attractiveness and competitiveness, specifically in Asia. Thus the first step involves planning, infra-structure development, and promotion initiatives including unique propositions to project a destination as a competent place for events hosting. Th second step is market survey and identification of the target market and initiatives of marketing. The third step involves operation management to make a particular project suc-cessful. Tourism stakeholders' involvement becomes important when operation of hosting begins. Event tourism management thus involves promotion, branding, marketing, devising event concept, planning, product development, infrastructure development, coordination among event, media, sponsor and support service, coordinating technical aspects etc. of a particular event.

Only an effective management device including promotion and marketing can make event tourism projects beneficial to a destination. National tourism board (NTB), destination management/marketing organisation (DMO), convention and visitors' bureau (CVB), tourism promotion board (TPB), tourism authority, tour-ism and event organisations or agencies are involved in the state of the art of event tourism. The spectrum of event tourism stakeholders also includes the host com-munity at large, and all the other beneficiaries from the service sector. A common concern of those stakeholders is better economic benefits, though they differ in aims and perceptions.

Asian context

So far, step one is concerned DMO, CVB, TPB, NTB and other national tourism organizations (NTO) of 21st-century Asia act as a catalyst for event tourism indus-try developments, and engage actively in formulating and implementing plan and policy towards event-oriented tourism development and promotion. Growth and success varies a lot. While Japan, Korea, China, Singapore, Hong Kong, Thailand, and Malaysia grew significantly, India shows slow progress, and other south Asian countries' performance is remarkably low. Initiatives vary according to the focus, nature of activity, and destination resources. Most common initiatives in this regard are policy support, publicity and propaganda, event creation and regenera-tion, infrastructural development, marketing support, technological and human resource supply support, support to the growth of professionals etc.

Perceiving the importance of plan and policy, new emerging economies of Asia put effort on devising event promotion policy for destination imaging, develop-ment and subsequent economic gain. Thus, formation of promotion board or departments under the government gets priority in post-world war Asia. Singapore Exhibition & Convention Bureau (SECB), Singapore Tourism Board (STB), Bei-jing Municipal Commission of Tourism Development, Beijing Convention and Visitors Bureau, Seoul Convention Bureau, Hong Kong Tourism Board, Japan National Tourism Organization (JNTO),Thailand's Ministry of Tourism and Sports (MOTS),Tourism Authority of Thailand (TAT), Thailand Convention and Exhibi-tion Bureau (TCEB), Philippine Department of Tourism (PDOT), Philippine's Tourism Promotions Board (TPB), Malaysia Convention & Exhibition Bureau (MyCEB), Malaysia Tourism Promotion Board, Malaysia's Ministry of Tourism,

Art, and Culture (MOTAC) etc. play significant role in destination promotion by encouraging events and event tourism. For example, Singapore Tourism Board (2014) in 'MICE 2020 Roadmap Report' and Malaysia Convention and Exhibition Bureau (2018) in 'Malaysia's Business Events Roadmap: Charting Malaysia's Journey to 2020 and Beyond' mapped out business events' future. Malaysia laid the groundwork for collaboration and support to host events energising organisations like Business Events Industry Council and Malaysian Association of Convention and Exhibition Organisers and Suppliers (MACEOS). The Second National Tourism Development Plan (2017–2021) of MOTS (2017) sets a vision for Thai efforts towards destination promotion targeting high potential segments such as MICE, festivals and sports tourism. Similar endeavours are apparent in PDOT and JNTO's policy approaches.

As we belong to e-age destination promotion and publicity organisations or boards in Asia develop their websites with a section for events that provides information about past and forthcoming events like Vegetarian Food Festival (Thailand) or 2020 Tokyo Summer Olympics; event hosting locations and its infrastructural capacity and resource availability; competence in sponsorship arrangement and media coverage; hospitality expertise; and success stories. Some NTOs provide information about their policy, plan and future initiatives to attract potential markets e.g., website of Thailand's Ministry of Tourism and Sports (Thailand Ministry of Tourism and Sports, 2018). Websites are made to be available in major search engines despite web crawler's use and have to be linked with major social media for quick and better publicity, promotion and marketing within competitive situations through virtual interaction leading to develop social network relationships with individuals and corporations. Staging overseas trade shows and exhibitions, publications of promotional literature in print media or presentation in media like TV do exist as destination awareness, marketing and promotion initiatives parallel to web publicity in Asia. JNTO's support to Sapporo snow festival through web, print and audio-visual media publicity is a notable example in this context.

Asia's destination promotion organisations typically use event tourism to attract visitors in the off-peak season and increase total volume of arrival in peak season. Thus planned events of any kind are considered to be potential. A traditionally existing event becomes crucial to them as it is ready to be utilised for immediate economic gain, destination regeneration, destination imaging and to substantiate the destination's ability to host events. Simultaneously emphasis on creating new events eases competitive bidding and generation of new markets. Accordingly, to lure visits during the off-season Thailand organises regular events like annual music festival, Tastes of Thailand, and other special events across the country during low seasons. Hundreds of events take place every year all over Asia to cater to locals only but miss out on opportunities to attract regional or international tourists due to absence of effective promotion strategy. Some events are identified with the traditional spirit of the destination and its community and thus have potential to destination imaging. Many efforts to turn such local festivals to events of international attraction are found. Bhutan Tourism Council's effort to regenerate centuries' old Thimpu Tshechu as an event of international attraction is quite fascinating as it makes 35 per cent of total international arrivals at Bhutan to be attracted to this festival (Bhutan Tourism Monitor, 2017). Another example is JNTO's support to promote Sapporo snow festival in the international market by posting information about the event and its access, accommodation, facilities, amenities in web media; publicising the event through overseas offices; infrastructural development; and media coverage is important too. JNTO's market report too helps the event organisers there to know SWOT's position and act accordingly. Thus a humble effort of a few school students turns to an event of over three million across the globe by now. Joining of Self Defence Force in the event (1955), international media coverage during1972 Sapporo Olympics, beginning of International Snow Sculpture Contest in 1974 contributed to its rise as a global event too. Bangkok Entertainment Fest, a government initiative in public-private partnership model, is also a noteworthy example of effort to new event creation. Let's look at Dhaka's International mother language day festival, which began out of a protest march against language discrimination at Dhaka in 1952 and grew into a celebration of millions under Bangladesh government's patronage, spreading across nations by attracting interest well beyond Bangladesh as it captured the mood of struggle for mother language and received international recognition by UN resolution in 2008.

A destination's success in promoting event hosting or event-oriented tourism depends largely on availability of required infrastructural facilities. Manila, Bangkok, Dubai, Singapore, Tokyo, Sapporo, Seoul, Kuala Lumpur, and Hong Kong are facilitated by world class facilities to host any kinds of events. Beside world class accommodation, amenities and rapid transit access facilities those destinations endeavoured to increase event-oriented infrastructure facilities, particularly construction of permanent world class event venues. Beside government initiatives, public-private partnership endeavours and sole private efforts with technical, administrative and bureaucratic support of government are found. While Seoul aims to expand current meeting capacity from 64,000 sqm to 103,000 sqm and develop a MICE complex in Southeast of Seoul by 2028 (Seoul Metropolitan Government, 2018a, 2018b, 2018c), Beijing expanded exhibition facilities to 0.7 million sqm and increased capacity to host fifty large-scale exhibition events in 2011–2015. Kuala Lumpur built world-class meeting and convention venues with minimum 16,000 sqm of event space e.g., Kuala Lumpur Convention Centre, Sime Darby Convention Centre, Putra World Trade Centre, Genting International Convention Centre featured by high-tech facilities, and Matrade Exhibition & Convention Centre complex, an architectural icon. Philippines' competitive advantage is her event venues. Manila's CCP Complex, an architectural landmark with displayed paintings of Filipino master artists, has a plenary hall of over 3500 seats with reception, exhibit areas and meeting rooms. SMX, a privately run world-class venue, combines events with recreation, shopping and entertainment facilities. World Trade Centre Metro Manila is another world-class venue covering 8,300 sqm space. Cebu International Convention Centre, a provincial government's initiative, has 28,000 sqm constructed floor space on 3.8 hectares land.

Leading event hosting countries of Asia launch targeted marketing for major tourist origins like ASEAN, America, Australia, Japan and Europe. It involves targeted advertising and packages suitable for each origin including loyalty pro-gramme. Governments encourage joint marketing in public and private partnership models to increase marketing effectiveness across stakeholders by co-developing regional tourism strategy and sharing relevant data among regional peers, and by enhancing tourism connectivity among sub-regional groups of states like CLMVT (Cambodia, Laos, Myanmar, Vietnam, Thailand sub-regional cooperation), BIM-STEC (Bay of Bengal Initiative for Multi-Sectoral Technical and Economic Coop-eration), and SAARC (The South Asian Association for Regional Cooperation). Like PDOT and TPB some southeast Asian counties' marketing strategy also involves coordination between the international clients and the local event hosting organisation; assistance in matching the international organisation's requirements with suitable Philippine facilities and services; and locating and endorsing their accredited and professional MICE suppliers.

Technological and human capital is vital to the growth of event-oriented tourism in Asia. Southeast Asian destinations emphasise the use of new technological resources. Thailand in this regard made a major development introducing modern app facilities to provide a nationwide integrated data base, booking and payment scope to the travellers. The integrated app system aims to facilitate online trip bookings, journey planning and navigating around the country through maps and directions in 3D; put emphasis on travellers' preference; ease payment and receiv-ing system; and develop direct relation between provider and receiver of services.

To develop industry oriented human capital south-east and eastern Asian coun-tries made major and effective attempts. During the last fifty years Korea, man-dated by its Higher Education Act, took initiatives to the growth of tourism education and training towards generating a quality workforce balancing academ-ics, technology, and vocational skill and involving government and public-private partnership endeavours (Cho and Soo, 2005). Singapore is considered as one of the best centres of tourism workforce development in Asia. Like Korea, MOTAC and Malaysia's Higher education department together with private collaboration turned the country into a centre for tourism educational excellence in Asia-Pacific region Ministry of Tourism, Arts and Culture Malaysia (2018). MOTAC patronises skill-based training e.g., tourist guide training, think tourism, Eco-host training programmes. Thailand too followed similar models introducing tourist guide courses, spa training, travel and tours management and enhancement courses.

In order to catch potential markets, Asian nations place their emphasis on both horizontal and vertical growth of event tourism, putting equal importance on b2b (CeBIT and Hong Kong Electronics Fair), b2c (Calcutta Book Fair), and mixed shows (International Jewellery Dubai). To provide best possible exposure, partner-ship with overseas global cities and associations representing the market segment are encouraged. Cooperating media partnership with professional journals, web groups, TV channels, and news agencies are common in Asian context towards events' publicity. The industry-specific concepts require specialists on the side of the organisers. Thus governments and event tourism organisers offer attractive packages to encourage those skilled professionals to join the industry.

Conclusion

Growth of event tourism within emerging economies of Asia is fairly new. Conditions that made it possible are parallel growth of industrial, information technology, and other service sectors; rapid increase of market-oriented economic systems and intensified international trade; differentiation in market segments, necessity of destination promotion and imaging, ascendency of lifestyle experience paradigm in tourism, and requirement of specialisation in event hosting. Asia's success in event hosting and event tourism came out of transformation in perception and the resulting initiatives devised towards promotion and development of this sector. Shift is perceived primarily in conceptual swings from traditional to new meaning of planned event, thus considered to be a specialised area of creative exchanges and experiences within the state of tourism art and creativity instead of mere socialisation and trading. The resulting initiatives that led to success are found in devising pragmatic policy and its effective implementation to support all stakeholders involved in hosting events and promoting event tourism for destination imaging, development and subsequent economic gain by formation of promotion board or departments; mapping out future potential and targets of event business; launching targeted marketing; enhancing connectivity and cooperation in tourism, trade, and technology within sub regions; sharing technological, tourism, economic and trade information and expertise within regions; exporting event concepts to growth market; introducing partnership with global cities, regional states, and associations representing the market segment; developing cooperating media partnership; constructing world class event hosting facilities and amenities supported by neo-technological facilities and expertise; putting emphasis on training and education to supply best possible skilled, specialised experts etc. The initiatives are persuaded in the public-private partnership model, sole state effort, and foreign collaboration. Indeed, it becomes possible due to liberalisation of market economy within new emerging economies of Asia, particularly liberalisation of the Chinese market. As a whole the changes in perception and initiatives taken in the last few decades by Asian countries led the event tourism industry to positive growth, and thus turned Asia into the most promising destination of 21st century events.

References

Allen, J., O'Toole, W., Harris, R. and McDonnell, I. (2011). *Festival and special event management*. Brisbane: John Wiley & Sons.

Berlonghi, A. (1990). *The special event risk management manual*. Dana Point, CA: Self-published.

Berridge, G. (2006). *Event design*. Oxford: Butterworth-Heinemann.

Bhutan Tourism Monitor. (2017). *Home*. Retrieved from: www.bhutan.travel (accessed: the 19th May, 2017).

Bond, H. (2008). *Estimating the economic benefits of event tourism: A review of research methodologies*. Retrieved from: www.liverpool.ac.uk/media/livacuk/impacts08/pdf/pdf/Impacts08-HBond_Oct_2008_Econ_Benefits_of_Event_Tourism.pdf (accessed: the 14th June, 2018).

Boorstin, D. (1961). *The image: A guide to pseudo-events in America*. New York: Harper & Row.

Bos, H. (1994). The importance of mega-events in the development of tourism demand. *Festival Management and Event Tourism*, **2**(1), pp. 55–58.

Bowdin, G., Allen, J., O'Toole, W., Harris, R. and McDonnell, I. (2011). *Events management*. Oxford: Butterworth-Heinemann.

Cho, M.-H. and Soo, K.K. (2005). Past, present, and future of tourism education. *Journal of Teaching in Travel & Tourism*, **5**(3), pp. 225–250.

CNN Travel. (2017). *Home*. Retrieved from: https://edition.cnn.com/travel/article/most-popular-citiesinternational. . ./index.html (accessed: the 10th June, 2018).

Crompton, J. and McKay, S. (1994). Measuring the economic impact of festivals and events: Some myths, misapplications and ethical dilemmas. *Festival Management and Event Tourism*, **2**(1), pp. 33–43.

Crouch, G. and Ritchie, J.R.B. (1999). Tourism, competitiveness and societal prosperity. *Journal of Business Research*, **44**, pp. 137–152.

Della Bitta, A., Loudon, D., Booth, G. and Weeks, R. (1978). Estimating the economic impact of a short-term tourist event. *Journal of Travel Research*, **16**, pp. 10–15.

Formica, S. (1998). The development of festivals and special events studies. *Festival Management and Event Tourism*, **5**(3), pp. 131–137.

Fredline, E. (2006). Host and guest relations and sport tourism. In H. Gibson (ed.) *Sport tourism: Concepts and theories*. London: Routledge, pp. 131–147.

Fredline, E. and Faulkner, B. (2002). Variations in residents' reactions to major motorsport events: Why residents perceive the impacts of events differently. *Event Management*, **7**(2), pp. 115–125.

Fredline, E., Jago, L. and Deery, M. (2003). The development of a generic scale to measure the social impacts of events. *Event Management*, **8**(1), pp. 23–37.

Getz, D. (1989). Special events: Defining the product. *Tourism Management*, **10**(2), pp. 135–137.

Getz, D. (1991). *Festivals, special events, and tourism*. New York: Van Nostrand Rheinhold.

Getz, D. (1998). Event tourism and the authenticity dilemma. In W. Theobald (ed.) *Global tourism*. Oxford: Butterworth-Heinemann, pp. 409–427.

Getz, D. (1999). The impacts of mega events on tourism: Strategies for destinations. In T. Andersson, C. Persson, B. Sahlberg and L. Strom (eds.) *The impact of mega events*. Ostersund, Sweden: European Tourism Research Institute, pp. 5–32.

Getz, D. (2000a). Festivals and special events: Life cycle and saturation issues. In W. Garter and D. Lime (eds.) *Trends in outdoor recreation, leisure and tourism*. Wallingford: CABI, pp. 175–185.

Getz, D. (2000b). Developing a research agenda for the event management field. In J. Allen, et al. (eds.) *Events beyond 2000: Setting the agenda, proceedings of conference on event evaluation, research and education*. Sydney: Australian Centre for Event Management, University of Technology, pp. 10–21.

Getz, D. (2002). Event studies and event management: On becoming an academic discipline. *Journal of Hospitality and Tourism Management*, **9**(1), pp. 12–23.

Getz, D. (2003). Sport event tourism: Planning, development, and marketing. In S. Hudson (ed.) *Sport and adventure tourism*. New York: Haworth, pp. 49–88.

Getz, D. (2004). Bidding on events: Critical success factors. *Journal of Convention and Exhibition Management*, **5**(2), pp. 1–24.

Getz, D. (2005). *Event management and event tourism*. New York: Cognizant Communication Corp.

Getz, D. (2007). *Event studies: Theory, research and policy for planned events*. Oxford: Elsevier.

Getz, D. (2008). Event tourism: Definition, evolution, and research. *Tourism Management*, **29**(3), pp. 403–428.

Getz, D., Anderson, D. and Sheehan, L. (1998). Roles, issues and strategies for convention and visitors bureaux in destination planning and product development: A survey of Canadian bureaux. *Tourism Management*, **19**(4), pp. 331–340.

Getz, D. and Fairley, S. (2004). Media management at sport events for destination promotion. *Event Management*, **8**(3), pp. 127–139.

Getz, D., O'Neill, M. and Carlsen, J. (2001). Service quality evaluation at events through service mapping. *Journal of Travel Research*, **39**(4), pp. 380–390.

Goldblatt, J. (2007). *Special events: The roots and wings of celebration*. New York: Wiley.

Greenwood, D. (1972). Tourism as an agent of change: A Spanish Basque case study. *Ethnology*, **11**, pp. 80–91.

Gunn, C. (1979). *Tourism planning*. New York: Crane Russak.

Hall, C.M. (1992). *Hallmark tourist events: Impacts, management and planning*. Belhaven: London.

Hawkins, D. and Goldblatt, J. (1995). Event management implications for tourism education. *Tourism Recreation Research*, **20**(2), pp. 42–45.

Hernández, J., Campón, A. and García, J. (2011). Proposals for the development and commercialization of bird watching tourism in Extremadura. *Cuadernos de Turismo*, **28**, pp. 93–119.

Hoyle, L. (2002). *Event marketing: How to successfully promote events, festivals, conventions, and expositions*. New York: Wiley.

ICCA. (2018). *2014 statistics*. Retrieved from: www.iccaworld.com/npps/story.cfm?nppage=4852(accessed: the 14th June, 2018).

Kim, N. and Petrick, J. (2005). Residents' perception on impact of FIFA World Cup: The case of Seoul as a host city. *Tourism Management*, **26**, pp. 25–38.

Krajnović, A., Buškulić, A. and Bosna, J. (2016). *The role of the tourist boards in the development of event tourism of Zadar County*. Retrieved from: https://bib.irb.hr/datoteka/836868.Krajnovic_Buskulic_Bosna.pdf (accessed: the 14th June, 2018).

Lee, J. and Back, K. (2005). A review of convention and meeting management research. *Journal of Convention and Event Tourism*, **7**(2), pp. 1–19.

Ljudevit, P., Lidija, P. and Liljana, C. (2012). Host population perceptions of the social impacts of sport tourism events in transition countries: Evidence from Croatia. *International Journal of Event and Festival Management*, **3**(3), pp. 236–256.

Mackellar, J. (2006). Conventions, festivals, and tourism: Exploring the network that binds. *Journal of Convention and Event Tourism*, **8**(2), pp. 45–56.

Malaysia Convention and Exhibition Bureau. (2018). *Malaysia's business events roadmap*. Retrieved from: www.myceb.com.my/about-us/malaysias-business-events-roadmap (accessed: the 20th June, 2018).

MasterCard. (2017). *MasterCard's global destination cities' index*. Retrieved from: https://newsroom.mastercard.com/. . ./2016/. . ./FINAL-Global-Destination-Cities-Index (accessed: the 11th August, 2017).

Masterman, G. and Wood, E. (2006). *Innovative marketing communications: Strategies for the events industry*. Oxford: Butterworth-Heinemann.

Ministry of Tourism, Arts and Culture Malaysia. (2018). *Policy*. Retrieved from: www.motac.gov.my/en/profile/policy (accessed: the 20th July, 2018).

Mossberg, L. (ed.). (2000). *Evaluation of events: Scandinavian experiences*. New York: Cognizant Communication Corp.

Oklobdžija, S. (2015). The role of events in tourism development. *BizInfo Journal*, **6**(2), pp. 83–97.

Ponce, M. (2007). Turismo de reunions en la ciudad de Murcia, Un enfoque desde el tejido empresarial involucrado. *Cuadernos de Turismo*, **19**, pp. 105–131.

Quinn, B. (eds.). (2009). *Festivals, events and tourism in the SAGE Handbook of Tourism Studies*. London: Sage Publications.

Ritchie, J.R.B. (1984). Assessing the impacts of hallmark events: Conceptual and research issues. *Journal of Travel Research*, **23**(1), pp. 2–11.

Ritchie, J.R.B. and Beliveau, D. (1974). Hallmark events: An evaluation of a strategic response to seasonality in the travel market. *Journal of Travel Research*, **14**, pp. 14–20.

Rittichainuwat, B., Beck, J. and LaLopa, J. (2001). Understanding motivations, inhibitors, and facilitators of association members in attending international conferences. *Journal of Convention and Exhibition Management*, **3**(3), pp. 45–62.

Scotinform Ltd. (1991). *Edinburgh festivals study 1990/91: Visitor survey and economic impact assessment final report*. Edinburgh: Scottish Tourist Board.

Seoul Metropolitan Government. (2018a). *The Seoul Metropolitan Government report 2016*. Retrieved from: english.seoul.go.kr/seoul-launches-global-digital-seoul-2020/ (accessed: the 25th July, 2018).

Seoul Metropolitan Government. (2018b). *Seoul master plan*. Retrieved from: english. seoul.go.kr/policy. . ./urban-planning/. . .planning/1-2030-seoul-basic-urban-pla. . . (accessed: the 25th July, 2018).

Seoul Metropolitan Government. (2018c). *Seoul city unveils "Masterplan" for large-scale meetings industry development*. Retrieved from: www.miceseoul.com/webzine/201311/e_ sub1_1.html (accessed: the 20th July, 2018).

Singapore Tourism Board. (2014). *Home*. Retrieved from: www.stb.gov.sg (accessed: the 25th July, 2018).

Supovitz, F. and Goldblatt, J. (2004). *The sports event management and marketing handbook*. New York: Wiley.

Swarbrooke, J. (1994). The future of the past: Heritage Tourism into the 21st century. In A. Seaton (ed.) *Tourism: The state of art*. Chichester: Wiley, pp. 222–229.

Syme, G., Shaw, B., Fenton, D. and Mueller, W. (eds.). (1989). *The planning and evaluation of hallmark events*. Aldershot: Gower.

Tarlow, P. (2002). *Event risk management and safety*. New York: Wiley.

Thailand Ministry of Tourism and Sports. (2018). *Home*. Retrieved from: www.mots.go.th (accessed: the 20th July, 2018).

Thrane, C. (2002). Music quality, satisfaction, and behavioral intentions within a jazz festival context. *Event Management*, **7**(3), pp. 143–150.

UNWTO. (2016). *Tourism towards 2030*. Retrieved from: www.e-unwto.org/doi/ book/10.18111/978928441402 4 (accessed: the 10th July, 2016).

Vaughan, R. (1979). Does a festival pay? A case study of the Edinburgh festival in 1976. *Working paper 5*. University of Edinburgh: Tourism Recreation Research Unit.

Weed, M. (2005). Sports tourism theory and method: Concepts, issues and epistemologies. *European Sport Management Quarterly*, **5**(3), pp. 229–242.

World Economic Forum. (2017). *These are the world's most visited cities*. Retrieved from: www.weforum.org/agenda/2017/10/these-are-the-worlds-most-visited-cities (accessed: the 20th July, 2018).

2 Tourism events in South Asia
Brief profiling with cultural celebrations

*Muhammad Shoeb-Ur-Rahman, Karabi Kabir
and Azizul Hassan*

Introduction

The rapid growth of events over the last 20 years make these a significant part of the tourism industry as well as a major area of tourism research (Getz, 2013; Gupta and Lehmann, 2003; Pike and Page, 2014; Schreiber and Lenson, 1994). Getz and Frisby (1988) find that festival tourism is "an emerging giant". Together with mega events other smaller events are also gaining popularity day by day. The contribution of these events and festivals toward the tourism industry is noteworthy. Focus on these events and festivals is intended to extend the tourist season, raise market awareness and re-position destinations, as well as encouraging investment, generating revenue and boosting the local economy. This chapter provides an overview of typical South Asian events corresponding to such tourism prospects.

Events remain one of the most important 'motivator' components of tourism. An event can play a pivotal role in the development of marketing and promotional strategies of a particular tourist destination. The roles and impacts of planned events within tourism have been well documented, and are of increasing importance for destination competitiveness.

Defining events

Events can be defined in many ways. Here we have focused on some important definitions of events given by different authors. The standard definition of planned events is that provided by Getz (2008:404) who asserts

> planned events are spatial – temporal phenomenon, and each is unique because of interactions among the setting, people and management systems – including design elements and the program. Much of the appeal of events is that they are never the same, and you have to 'be there' to enjoy the unique experience fully; if a person misses it, it's a lost opportunity.

This simply indicates the exclusiveness of 'event' in terms of its arrangements and timing.

Similarly, The National Task Force on Tourism Data of Canada (1986a) emphasises the time dimension of event and defines 'special event' as "a celebration or display of some theme to which the public is invited for a limited time only annually or less frequently". However, special events can be distinguished from other types of attractions based on a set of criteria, namely: special events are open to the public; their main purpose is celebration or display of some theme; they occur once a year or less frequently; there are predetermined opening and closing dates; permanent structures are not owned by the event; the programme consists of one or more separate activities; and all activities take place in the same community or tourist region (Getz, 1989).

Burns and Mules (1986) have identified four key characteristics of special events: first, the major demand generated by the special event is, for the most part, not the demand for the event itself but demand for a range of related services – typically accommodation, food, transport and entertainment. Second, this demand is condensed into a relatively short period of time, from a single day to a few weeks and, as services cannot be produced ahead of time and stored, this leads to the typical 'peaking' problems experienced in the main service industries mentioned. Third, peaking influences both the level and the distribution of benefits received. Fourth, the net impact of redirecting local funds towards special events is relatively small; the major benefits arise from the attraction of new funds from outside the region by way of the export of goods and services, especially services.

The standard definition of hallmark events is that provided by Ritchie (1984:2) who defined such events as

> Major one-time or recurring events of limited duration, developed primarily to enhance the awareness, appeal and profitability of a tourism destination in the short and/or long term. Such events rely for their success on uniqueness, status, or timely significance to create interest and attract attention.

Defining event tourism

The term 'event tourism' was coined in the 1980s, and it formalised the link between events and tourism (Getz, 1997). Event tourism, which is not a recent phenomenon, has been defined as "the systematic planning, development and marketing of festivals and special events as tourist attractions, catalysts and image builders" (Getz and Wicks, 1993:2). The first Olympic Games were held in 776 BCE and religious events and festivals have been held throughout the ages. What is new is the scale of event tourism, with many cities seeking to specialise in the creation and hosting of special events due to the economic benefits they bring (Lynch and Veal, 1996).

According to Janiskee (1994:10), "this is the age of special events". Described as a one-time or infrequently occurring event of limited duration that provides consumers with a leisure and social opportunity beyond everyday experience (Jago and Shaw, 1998), observation and anecdotal evidence suggest that the number of special events has increased substantially over time (Getz, 1997; Getz and Wicks, 1993; Janiskee, 1994). Special event tourism is one of the fastest growing segments of the tourism industry influencing both day trip and overnight visitation (Backman et al., 1995). This is due to the ability of events to contribute to a city's range of tourist attractions, facilitate media coverage for the destination, and promote awareness of the destination for future visitation.

Typology of event tourism

A typology of the main categories of planned events based primarily on their form – that is, obvious differences in their purpose and programme has been identified as shown in Figure 2.1 (Getz, 2005). Some are for public celebration (this category includes so-called 'community festivals' which typically contain a large variety in their programming and aim to foster civic pride and cohesion), while others are planned for purposes of competition, fun, entertainment, business or socialising. Often they require special-purpose facilities, and the managers of those facilities (like convention centres and sport arenas) target specific types of events. Professional associations and career paths have traditionally been linked to these event types.

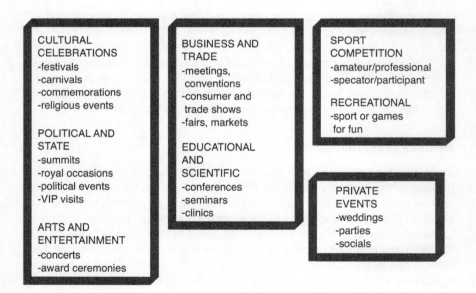

Figure 2.1 Typology of planned events
Source: Adapted from Getz, 2005

Event tourism has been further categorised by its characteristics by Hall (1989) as in Figure 2.2:

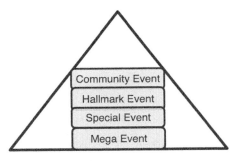

Figure 2.2 Characteristics of short-term staged events dimension
(Source: adapted from Hall, 1989)

In this research, the authors focus on the similarities among the different cultural celebrations of south Asian events which can be targeted as a promotional tool for extended touristic experiences in this particular region. The South Asian region comprising eight countries (Afghanistan, Bangladesh, Bhutan, India, Maldives, Nepal, Pakistan and Sri Lanka) is one of the most densely populated and poorest regions in the world. It extends south from the main part of the continent to the Indian Ocean. The principal boundaries of South Asia are the Indian Ocean, the Himalayas, and Afghanistan. The Arabian Sea borders Pakistan and India to the west, and the Bay of Bengal borders India and Bangladesh to the east. The western boundary is the desert region where Pakistan shares a border with Iran (Berglee, 2012).

South Asian regional events in brief

From a wide range of events and festivals, we put emphasis on those particular events which have enormous potential to attract tourists. By analysing the pattern and theme of these events, it has been identified that proper promotion and planning can create a huge 'buzz' among the tourists leading to repeat business through 'word of mouth'. A possible marketing implication encompasses targeting specific common events within the region which can attract tourists to experience the cultural diversities on offer. In fact, such a phenomenon can balance the tourists' movement throughout a planned period of time and eventually lead to sustainable destination management.

Events of Afghanistan

As a war prone country tourism has not been yet flourished as a successful industry. This land of Afghanistan has its own rich cultural and religious heritage. They observe their traditional events with great enthusiasm.

i   'Nau Roz' (New Year Festival): Nau Roz is the largest and best-known festival in Afghanistan, particularly in Mazar e Sharif, where it is called 'Gul e Sorkh'. 'Buzkashi' matches are held. People play music and dance. Farmers express their joy for the produce.

ii   'Mushaira' (Orange Blossom): This festival is held on April 13 every year in Jalalabad. Picnics and music concerts are held under the orange trees and near the shrines.

(Afghanistan Festivals, 2018)

Events of Bangladesh

i   'Pahela Baishakh': The advent of Bengali New Year (Pahela Baishakh; April 14 of each year) is the most cheerful, colourful and amazing public holiday that is immensely observed throughout the country. It is presumed that the tradition of Pahela Baishakh started about 600 years back. On this auspicious day, Bangladeshi people irrespective of their religion, caste and status attend the traditional procession usually known as 'Mangal Shob-hajatra'. This procession has received recognition of the "Intangible Cultural Heritage of Humanity" from the United Nations Educational, Scientific and Cultural Organisation (UNESCO) in 2016. UNESCO (2018) noted

> The Mangal Shobhajatra festival symbolises the pride the people of Bangladesh have in their folk heritage, as well as their strength and courage to fight against sinister forces, and their vindication of truth and justice. It also represents solidarity and a shared value for democracy, uniting people irrespective of caste, creed, religion, gender or age.

ii   'Dubla Rash Mela': This is the biggest fair in not only Bagerhat, but also the entire country of Bangladesh. This has become a grand occasion for many foreign tourists visiting the Sundarbans. In the Bangla month of 'Agrahayan' every year, the fair continues for five to seven days during the full moon.

iii   'Shakrain Festival': Celebrated especially in Old Dhaka, 'Shakrain Festival' (also known as Kite Festival) is observed at the end of the Bengali month Poush or January 14 or 15. This is day is also known as 'Poush Shang-kranti'. The major attraction of this festival is that people of all ages gather around their rooftop with their kites in the afternoon.

iv   'Baisabi Festival': This festival is commonly celebrated as 'Biju' by the Chakma and Tanchyanga, 'Shangrai' as Marmas and 'Baisuk' or 'Baisu' by Tripuras – is the main social festival of the tribal people in the hill districts of Rangamati, Bandarban and Khagrachhari. The Marinas celebrate Shangrai for four days.

v   'Kothin Chibor Dan Utsab': This is the greatest religious festival of the Buddhist community where 'Viksus' are given 'Chibor' or cloth to wear which the Buddhists believe as the best of all gifts. Chibor, the cloth that

Viksus wear, may be of any six colours: those of a tree's roots, trunk, bark, dry leaves, fruit or flower.

vi 'Fair of Ghoshbila': This fair, also known as Baruni fair, is organised in the village Ghoshbila under Alamdanga upazila of Chuadanga district to commemorate the day of goddess Ganga's arrival in a ghat. The legend says that the goddess Ganga appeared on that ghat which is considered as a holy place by the Hindus.

vii 'Langalbandh Mela': Every year on the eighth day of the lunar month that falls in the Bengali month of Chaitra, thousands of Hindu devotees from home and abroad assemble on the banks of the old Brahmaputra River for the 'Astami snan', a ritual bath in the river. On the occasion, a three-day fair is held in this place, starting before the day of Ashtami snan and ending a day after the bathing ceremony.

viii 'Shib Chaturdashi Mela': This fair continues for three consecutive days following the religious rituals where thousands of devotees gather in a Shiva temple at night on fourteenth Falgun. The Shiva has a history dating back a thousand years. The temple stands at the top of Chandranath hill located at Sitakunda in Chittagong. This fair is one of the oldest fairs in the entire subcontinent.

ix 'Gurpukur Mela': Every year the last day of the Bengali month of 'Bhadra' is the occasion for worshipping the snake goddess (Monsha Puja), and a fair is held on the occasion at Shatkhira in a place named Gurpukur.

x 'Golakandail Mela': From the first day of the Bengali month of Magh, a fair is held in Golakandail village of Rupganj upazila under Narayanganj district for seven days under a big banyan tree. Nobody knows the origin of the fair but it has continued for ages and is full of fun and festivity.

xi 'Fair of Adinath': Moheshkhali is an island under Cox's Bazar district not very far from the mainland. There, the Adinath temple at the top of Mainak hillock is a place of worship for Hindu devotees. A landlord named Nur Mohammad Shikdar donated 200 acres of land to reconstruct the age-old Adinath Temple. The fair associated with the temple started from that time.

xii 'Lalon Mela': Lalon Shah is one of most acclaimed and prominent philosophers from Bangladesh. Every year on the first week of April, a fair is organised following Lalon Shah's birth anniversary by the devotees. The fair is held at the 'Akhra' (the place where Lalon lived) situated in Kushtia (Visit Bangladesh, 2018).

Events of Bhutan

i 'Tshechu': This is a religious event celebrated on tenth day of a month of the lunar calendar corresponding to the birthday of 'Guru Rimpoche' (Guru Padmasambhava). Two of the most popular Tshechus in the country are the 'Paro' and 'Thimphu Tshechus' in terms of participation and audience. Besides the locals many tourists from across the world are attracted to these unique, colourful and exciting displays of traditional culture.

ii   'Nomad festival': The annual nomad festival is held in Bumthang in central Bhutan. Bumthang is about an eight-hour drive from the capital city of Thimphu. This annual gathering brings together the nomads of the north-eastern and northwestern Himalayan frontiers in an unforgettable celebration of their unique cultures and traditions. The festival is an ideal platform to witness and experience the unique traditions and way of life of different highlander communities in the country.

iii   'Sakteng festival': Sakten valley is situated in eastern Bhutan under Trashi-gang Dzongkhag at an altitude of 3000 metres. It is inhabited by a semi-nomadic people known as the Brokpas. Living close to nature in this pristine wilderness, the Brokpas' way of life has remained virtually unchanged through the years and they still mainly depend upon yak rearing and animal husbandry for their livelihoods. Sakteng valley remains untouched and unspoiled by the influence of the outside world.

iv   'Ura yakchoe': Ura valley in Bumthang is known for the famous dance known as the Ura Yakchoe. The dance is performed during a festival that is held every May. During the festival a sacred and important relic is put on display so that the people can receive blessings from it.

v   'Dochula Druk Wangyel festival': The Dochula Druk Wangyel Festival was established in 2011 in commemoration of His Majesty the Fourth Druk Gyalpo and the Armed Forces' victory over Indian insurgent forces residing in southern Bhutan in 2003.

vi   'Chorten Kora festival': The Chorten Kora Festival is set in Trashiyangtse, the easternmost district of Bhutan. Dakpa Kora is held on the fifteenth day of the third month corresponding to February 28, and Drukpa Kora (circumbulation by the Bhutanese) is held on the thirtieth day corresponding to March 15 every year.

vii   'Haa Summer festival': Set among pristine lakes and high alpine valleys, the Haa summer festival is a lively and uplifting celebration of traditional living-culture, nomadic lifestyles, unique Bhutanese cuisine, traditional sports and religious performances.

viii   'Matsutake festival': This festival celebrates the start of another mushroom season alongside the people of Ura. The season brings with it the opportunity to not only to sample some truly delicious meals but to cultivate a deeper insight into the rhythms of Bhutanese village life.

(Tourism Council of Bhutan, 2018)

Events of India

i   'Mamallapuram dance festival': Once the ancient port of the Pallavas, Mamallapuram plays host to a vibrant festival of dance.

ii   'Pongal': A celebration of the harvest, Pongal is observed for three days in January, in Tamil Nadu.

iii   'Vasant Panchami': The ceremonial welcome to spring when people, colourfully attired, especially in bright shades of yellow, dance, sing and make merry. In West Bengal, 'Saraswati' – the goddess of learning is worshipped. The festival is celebrated with great fervour in the university town of Santiniketan.

iv 'Surajkund crafts Mela': A delightful handloom and handicrafts fair is held annually at Surajkund. Skilled artisans from all over the country display the rich crafts tradition of India in the typical setting of a rural Indian marketplace.

v 'Nagaur fair': Nagaur bustles with life during its annual cattle fair which is one of the largest in the country. Exciting games and camel races are part of the festivities.

vi 'Kerala village fair': Every year, in the lush villages around Kovalam (18 km from Thiruvananthapuram), mid-January is the time for cultural events. The traditional thatch houses are decorated during this ten-day long festival and are the venue for folk dancers, music and festivities.

vii 'Bikaner festival': Dedicated to the indispensable 'ship of the desert', the festival starts off with a magnificent procession of bedecked camels. There are displays and competitions together with all the colour, music and rhythm unique to a fair in Rajasthan.

viii 'Shivratri': All over the country, Shivratri is observed as the night when Lord Shiva danced the 'Tandav' – his cosmic dance.

ix 'Holi': In March, during spring, comes Holi – the festival of colours. Celebrated all over North India, Holi is a time to make merry. People smear each other with coloured powder. Singing and dancing add to the gaiety of the occasion.

x 'Gangaur': The most important local festival in Rajasthan, Gangaur celebrations last for eighteen days. It is dedicated to Gauri, a manifestation of goddess Parvati. The festival is celebrated by girls and married women throughout Rajasthan.

xi 'Urs': The Urs are held every year at the Dargah of the Sufi Saint Khwaja Moinuddin Chisti, commemorating his symbolic union with God. Pilgrims from all over the world gather here to pay homage. Qawalis and poems are presented in the saint's honour.

xii 'Hemis festival': The courtyard of Hemis – the biggest Buddhist monastery in Ladakh – is the stage for the famous 'Hemis' Festival, which celebrates the birth anniversary of Guru Padmasambhava.

xiii 'Rath Yatra': This spectacular chariot festival is held at the famous Jagannath Temple at Puri. Images of Lord Jagannath, the Lord of the Universe; his sister Subhadra and brother Balbhadra are taken out in procession in three immense chariots.

xiv 'Janmashtami': The birth of Lord Krishna is celebrated with great fervour all over the country.

xv 'Teej': This swing festival welcomes the advent of the monsoon. Swings are hung from trees and decorated with flowers. Women, colourfully attired, swing on them and sing songs in celebration.

xvi   'Dussehra': Celebrated to mark the defeat of Ravana by Lord Rama, Dussehra symbolises the triumph of good over evil. The Ramlila – an enactment of the life of Lord Rama, is held during the nine days preceding Dussehra. On the tenth day, larger than life effigies of Ravana, his son and brother – Meghnath and Kumbhakarna, are set alight.

xvii   'Ka Pomblang Nongkrem': The most important festival of the Khasis in Meghalaya. This five-day long festival, held annually near Shillong, is an occasion for thanksgiving for a good harvest and the time to pray for peace and prosperity.

xviii 'Kurukshetra festival': The festival coincides with Gita Jayanti, signifying the birth of the Srimad Bhagvad Gita. Pilgrims gather here to take a dip in the sacred tanks of Brahma Sarovar and Sannehit Sarover. Week-long Bhagwad katha, dance, dramas and 'deep daan' are part of the religious festivities.

xix   'Baisakhi': The Hindu New Year finds expression in this exuberant festival, celebrated throughout India. Baisakhi celebrations in Punjab are spectacular, as this is a very special day for the Sikhs. It was on this day that Guru Gobind Singh founded the Khalsa. Robust revelry and feasting mark the celebrations and dancers perform the vigorous Bangra to the rhythmic beat of the drums.

xx   'Mahavir Jayanti': The birth anniversary of Lord Mahavira, the founder of Jainism, is observed by the Jain community. Special prayers are offered at temples and shrines.

xxi   'Ramanavami': The anniversary of Lord Rama's birth is celebrated as Ramnavami by the Hindus. The epic 'Ramayana' is read for eight days preceding the festival.

xxii   'Onam': Kerala's most important festival is celebrated in the honour of the ancient Asura king Mahabali. The occasion also heralds the harvest season. The decorating of houses with carpets of flowers, a sumptuous lunch and songs in praise of the golden reign of Mahabali, mark the ten-day long festivities. The major attractions of the Onam celebrations are the famed snake boat races along the backwaters at Champakulam, Aranmula and Kottayam.

xxiii 'Amarnath Yatra': In the month of Shravan, thousands of pilgrims make an arduous trek up to the Amarnath cave in the Kashmir Himalayas. They come to worship the sacred ice lingam – a symbol of Lord Shiva, which is a natural phenomenon.

xxiv   'Ganesh Chaturthi': This day is dedicated to the Lord Ganesh, the elephant-headed god of all good beginnings and success. Held annually, this festival is a ten-day long event. The images of Lord Ganesha are installed and worshipped and on the last day these are taken in processions to be immersed in flowing water. The sea front at Mumbai, packed with people, is a spectacular sight.

xxv   'Muharram': Commemorates the martyrdom of the Prophet Mohammed's grandson, Imam Hussein. Tazias, glittering replicas of the martyr's tomb, are carried in procession through the streets. The tazias of Lucknow and Hyderabad are noted for their splendour.

xxvi 'Diwali': This festival of lights is the prettiest and the most eagerly awaited occasion in India. It celebrates the return of Lord Rama, the hero of the epic Ramayana, to Ayodhya after a fourteen-year exile.

xxvii 'Sonepur Mela': Asia's biggest cattle fair is held at Sonepur, on the banks of the River Ganga. During this month-long fair, cattle, decorated for the occasion, throng the venue.

xxviii 'Pushkar Mela': Tranquil Pushkar is transformed into a spectacular fair ground for twelve days in the month of Kartik. Trading of cattle, camel races and dazzling displays of bangles, brassware, clothes, camel saddles and halters are the major attractions of this colourful event. Devotees come in their thousands to take a ritual dip in the lake on the day of the Kartik Purnima and to worship at the Brahma temple.

xxix 'Hampi festival': The magnificent ruined city of Hampi, once the capital of the Vijayanagar Empire, comes alive once again during this lively festival of dance and music, held in the first week of November.

Events of Maldives

i 'Eid-ul Al'h'aa': This falls on the tenth day of Zul Hijja in the Islamic Calendar. While those who can afford it are at pilgrimage at the holy Ka'aba in Mecca, for those who stay behind it is a time for celebrations and feasting.

ii 'Prophets birthday': As with all Muslims, Maldivians celebrate the Prophet's birthday. The Prophet's birthday is the twelveth day of Rabee-ul Awwal in the Islamic Calendar. Families invite one another to their homes to share the special dishes prepared for the day.

iii 'Kuda Eid': This is the first day of the month of Shawwal in the Islamic Calendar. This follows the end of Ramadhan and it is a period of feasting.

iv 'Independence day': Independence Day is celebrated on July 26. The high-light of the day is the official celebrations held in the evening at the Republic Square. The event begins with a march by the National Security Service and the National cadet corps. This is followed by drills, traditional dances and modern drills performed by hundreds of schoolchildren in colourful attire.

v 'Republic day': On November 11, 1968 the Maldives became a republic for the second time. The day is celebrated every year with parades and marches.

vi 'National day': This day is celebrated for the great victory of Mohamed Thakurufaanu over the Portuguese in 1573.

(The Maldives, 2018)

Events of Nepal

Nepal is a diverse country with its varying landscape, rich bio-diversity and even more diverse culture of the people residing in it. Each community holds their own unique cultures and traditions which they have been following for centuries. Each has their own set of beliefs and their own festivals to celebrate.

i   'Dashain and Tihar': The biggest and most popular festivals based on religion are Dashain and Tihar. Dashain, a celebration of Goddess Durga's victory over evil Mahisashur, has symbolic meaning deeply rooted in Nepalese society. Tihar, a celebration of lights and colour dedicated to Goddess Laxmi, also unfolds social joy throughout the nation.

ii   'Ghode Jatra' (the horse parade): This is celebrated during Chaitra (March–April), is another festival that unites all the people of the valley. Though there is no religious background for the parade, it is believed that a demon spirit was buried under Tundikhel and the horse parade ensures that it does not return from the burial site.

iii 'Gai Jatra': This is one of the most popular festivals generally celebrated in August–September. Even though Gai Jatra has presence throughout the country, it has most strongholds in the Newari community of Kathmandu valley. This festival has its roots in the belief that the god of death, Yamaraj, must be feared and hence worshipped.

iv   'Teej': This is a celebration of fasting in which women pray for marital bliss, wellbeing of their spouse and children and purification of their own body and soul. It takes place in August and September. In the present context, the festival has connotations with rights for women.

v   'Fagun Purnima': Allegedly named after the mythical demoness 'Holika', this is a day when the feast of colours is celebrated. The ancient Holi festival falls in late February or early March. It has growing popularity among Nepalese even today and it is enthusiastically celebrated throughout the nation.

vi   'Indrajatra': This falls in August and September. Both Hindus and Buddhists unite to celebrate the festival with great enthusiasm. 'Indrajatra' has historic significance in Nepal as well.

(Himalayan Glacier, 2018)

Events of Pakistan

i   'Basant': With the advent of spring 'Basant' festival is celebrated with pomp and show in mid-February every year in Lahore. In other words, this is the spring festival.

ii   'Sibi festival': This festival falls in last week of February at 'Sibi'. Traditional sports, handicrafts exhibition, folk music and dances.

iii 'Mela Chiraghan' (Festival of lamps): This is a mega event for the people of Punjab and especially for Lahorites, where it is celebrated with traditional fervour and activities at the shrine of the renowned Sufi Shah Hussain.

iv   'Shandur Polo festival': Traditional polo tournament between the teams of Chitral and Gilgit is held on the highest polo ground of the world – The Shandur Pass (Chitral district). Allied activities include folk music, folk dances and other competitions. A tent village along Shandur Lake is set up in cooperation with the local administration.

v   'Utchal': This event is celebrated by Kalash people in Kalash Valleys, Chitral. It is celebrated to mark the harvest of wheat and barley. The celebration lasts for two days with dancing, singing and feasting being its main features.

vi 'Lok Mela': The festival presents a unique opportunity to watch the culture and craft of the whole country at one place. This Folk Festival is held for one week at Islamabad. It includes folk music, songs, music contests, folk dances, craftsmen at work, exhibition and sale of handicrafts.

Events of Sri Lanka

i 'The Duruthu Perehera' (procession): This is celebrated on the first visit of the Buddha to Sri Lanka in January at the sacred temple of Kelaniya near Colombo attracting hundreds of thousands of devotees and visitors. The colourful pageant comprising of caparisoned elephants, along with dancers, drummers and musicians playing traditional wind instruments begun with the firing of cannon. The Randoli Perehera, the magnificent finale, is held the day prior to the January full moon.

ii 'The Navam Perehara': This culminates on the February full moon; it is a spectacle that has the certain participation of more than 100 caparisoned elephants brought from all over the island.

iii The new year festival: This festival of the Sinhalese Buddhists and Tamil Hindus in Sri Lanka coincides with the end of harvest. The New Year dawns with the transition of the sun from the house of Pisces to that of Aries, according to the Vedic Solar Calendar.

iv 'Vesak': This is the main Buddhist religious festival in Sri Lanka, on the full moon in May. Thus, Vesak is the first month of the Buddha Nirvana calendar. The Buddhists celebrate the triple anniversary of the important events in the life of the Buddha.

v 'Esala Perehara in Kandy': On the full-moon day of August each year, the sacred tooth relic of the Buddha, encased in a golden casket, is taken in procession on the back of the temple elephant. The magnificent procession is in all probability the most spectacular torch-lit parade in all of Asia.

vi 'Katharagama Esala festival': The Kataragama Shrine in the Deep South honours the God Katharagama worshipped by Buddhists and Hindus with equal fervour and devotion. During the two-week festival, thousands of Hindu devotees bear chariots, pierce their flesh with hooks, and commit acts of penitence mostly to honour vows beseeching the benevolence of the God Skandha.

vii 'Adivel festival': This is a Hindu Religious festival in honour of Lord Murugan. The festival is held each year sometime between the months of May and August; the auspicious date for the festival is usually announced 45 days prior to the event.

viii 'Deepawali festival': This is the most picturesque Hindu festival, celebrated in November. The Festival of Light, the triumph of good over evil, is marked by illuminations in the form of clay and brass lamps and making figures out of sugar known as Misri.

(Jetwing Travels, 2018)

Country Name	Cultural Celebration			
	Festivals	Carnivals	Commemoration	Religious Events
Afghanistan	i. NauRoz ii. Mushaira			
Bangladesh	i. Pahela Baishakh ii. Shakrain Festival iii. Kothin Chibor Dan Utsab	i. Fair of Adinath ii. Dubla Rash Mela iii. Fair of Ghoshbila iv. Langalbandh Fair v. Shib Chaturdashi Fair vi. Gurpukur Fair, vii. Golakandail Fair	i. Lalon Mela	i. Baisabi Festival
Bhutan	i. Nomad festival ii. Sakteng festival iii. Ura yakchoe iv. Haa summer festival v. Gomphu kora festival		i. Dochula druk wangyel festival	i. Tshechu ii. Chorten kora festival
India	i. Mamallapuram Dance Festival ii. Pongal iii. Vasant Panchami iv. Bikaner Festival v. Teej vi. Ka Pomblang Nongkrem vii. Baisakhi viii. Hampi Festival	i. Surajkund Crafts Mela ii. Nagaur Fair iii. Kerala Village Fair iv. Pushkar Mela v. Sonepur Mela	i. Hemis Festival ii. Kurukshetra Festival iii. Mahavir Jayanti iv. Onam	i. Shivratri ii. Holi iii. Gangaur iv. Urs v. Rath Yatra vi. Janmashtami vii. Dussehra viii. Ramanavami ix. Amarnath Yatra x. Ganesh Chaturthi xi. Muharram xii. Diwali
The Maldives			i. Independence Day ii. Republic Day National Day	i. Eid-ul Al`h`aa, Prophets Birthday ii. Kuda Eid

Figure 2.3 Typology of planned cultural celebration events of the South Asian region
(Source: the authors)

Country Name	Cultural Celebration			
	Festivals	*Carnivals*	*Commemoration*	*Religious Events*
Nepal	i. Ghode Jatra ii. Gai Jatra			i. Dashain and Tihar ii. Teej iii. Fagun Purnima iv. Indrajatra
Pakistan	i. Bassant ii. Sibi Festival iii. Shandur Polo Festival iv. Utchal	i. Mela Chiraghan		
Sri Lanka	i. Navam Perehara ii. New Year Festival iii. Katharagama Esala Festival			Duruthu Perehera i. Vesak ii. Esala Perehara in Kandy iii. Adivel Festival iv. Deepawali Festival

Figure 2.3 (Continued)

As a summary, typology of planned cultural celebration events of the South Asian region is presented above in Figure 2.3.

Conclusion and implications

This chapter systematically defines the term event, identifies the typology of events, and outlines South Asian cultural events. The observation has been made that South Asia remains one of the most vibrant, festival-loving regions in the world in respect of cultural celebrations. However, the authentic documentation of such events in correspondence with tourism phenomena has as yet not been attempted. Accordingly, the author has compiled and discussed a wide range of cultural events which have tourism potential. The research suggests that these events can turn into tourism products provided effective and efficient promotional strategies are implemented along with strategic planning orientation. There are commonalities in the described events meaning a common strategy can be taken at regional level under the leadership and supervision of regional organisations such as the South Asian Association for Regional Cooperation (SAARC). This will ensure the sustainability of the cultural heritage and tradition of this region; preservation and enrichment of these events are imperative.

This research can be a benchmark for future researchers who are interested to work on cultural tourism in South Asia. A broader marketing and management implication can be sought out aligning cultural event tourism. Besides, the policy-makers at regional level can promote the events to attract more tourists and spread the influx over a period of time to balance regional development. The current research has been challenged on the availability of quality data; the researchers predominantly focus on the available secondary sources of data. Future research can overcome this limitation by covering a considerable amount of time and collecting both primary and secondary data to increase validity.

References

Afghanistan Festivals. (2018). *Festivals in Afghanistan*. Retrieved from: http://afghanistan.saarctourism.org/festivals.html (accessed: the 05th January, 2018).

Backman, K., Backman, S., Uysal, M. and Mohr Sunshine, K. (1995). Event tourism: An examination of motivations and activities. *Festival Management & Event Tourism*, **3**(1), pp. 15–24.

Berglee, R. (2012). *World regional geography: People, places, and globalization*. Minneapolis, MN: University of Minnesota Libraries Publishing.

Burns, J.P.A. and Mules, T.L. (1986). A framework for the analysis of major special Events. In J.P.A. Burns, J.H. Hatch and T.L. Mules (eds.) *The Adelaide grand prix: The impact of a special event*. Adelaide: The Centre for South Australian Economic Studies, pp. 5–38.

Getz, D. (1989). Special events. *Tourism Management*, **10**(2), pp. 125–137.

Getz, D. (1997). *Event management and event tourism*. New York: Cognizant Communication Corp.

Getz, D. (2005). *Event management and event tourism*. New York: Cognizant Communication Corp.

Getz, D. (2008). Event tourism: Definition, evolution, and research. *Tourism Management*, **29**(3), pp. 403–428.

Getz, D. (2013). *Event tourism: Concepts, international case studies, and research*. New York: Cognizant Communication Corp.

Getz, D. and Frisby, W. (1988). Evaluating management effectiveness in community-run festivals. *Journal of Travel Research*, **2**, pp. 22–29.

Getz, D. and Wicks, B. (1993). Editorial. *Festival Management & Event Tourism*, **1**(1), pp. 1–3.

Gupta, S. and Lehmann, D.R. (2003). Customers as assets. *Journal of Interactive Marketing*, **17**, pp. 9–24.

Hall, C. (1989). The definition and analysis of hallmark tourist events. *GeoJournal*, **19**(3), pp. 263–268.

Himalayan Glacier. (2018). *The 10 major festivals in Nepal*. Retrieved from: www.himalayanglacier.com/blog/the-10-major-festivals-in-nepal.html (accessed: the 05th January, 2018).

Jago, L. and Shaw, R. (1998). Special events: A conceptual and differential framework. *Festival Management & Event Tourism*, **5**(1/2), pp. 21–32.

Janiskee, R. (1994). Some macroscale growth trends in America's community festival industry. *Festival Management & Event Tourism*, **2**(1), pp. 10–14.

Jetwing Travels. (2018). *Events and festivals*. Retrieved from: www.jetwingtravels.com/about-sri-lanka/travel-information/events-festivals/ (accessed: the 19th January, 2018).

Lynch, R. and Veal, A. (1996). *Australian leisure*. South Melbourne: Addison Wesley Longman Australia Pty Ltd.

The Maldives. (2018). *Maldives festivals*. Retrieved from: www.themaldives.net/culture/festivals/ (accessed: the 19th January, 2018).

The National Task Force on Tourism Data of Canada. (1986). *Project team on festivals and special events*. Unpublished.

Pike, S. and Page, S.J. (2014). Destination marketing organizations and destination marketing: A narrative analysis of the literature. *Tourism Management*, **41**, pp. 202–227.

Ritchie, J.B.R. (1984). Assessing the impact of hallmark events: Conceptual and research issues. *Journal of Travel Research*, **23**(1), pp. 2–11.

Schreiber, A. and Lenson, B. (1994). *Lifestyle and event marketing: Building the new customer partnership*. New York: McGraw-Hill.

Tourism Council of Bhutan. (2018). *Home*. Retrieved from: www.tourism.gov.bt/ (accessed: the 05th January, 2018).

UNESCO. (2018). *Mangal Shobhajatra on Pahela Baishakh*. Retrieved from: https://ich.unesco.org/en/RL/mangal-shobhajatra-on-pahela-baishakh-01091 (accessed: the 21st April, 2018).

Visit Bangladesh. (2018). *Traditional*. Retrieved from: http://visitbangladesh.gov.bd/things-to-see/fair-festivals/traditional/ (accessed: the 05th January, 2018).

3 Creating new event opportunities and re-creating old events in an innovative way

Case study of Hadoti region

Anukrati Sharma

Introduction

In the present era events are working as a source of tourism. Many destinations of the country are in demand because of events, whether it is a local fair, festival, cultural event, religious event, business event, or a sports event. The most important role these events are playing is of increasing the demand of tourism to a particular destination. According to Getz (1997) the local festival is a tourism endorsement instrument, because festivals boost the demand for local tourism. Not only has this festival facilitated the representation of a destination; in a country like India which is known for its diversified culture, fairs and festivals, economic development is very much possible by developing event tourism. Rather than going towards westernisation the event organisers started going back to the traditional methods for organising the events. In fact, in business events and MICE tourism the event organisers are also putting that artistic, traditional touch. From escorting to the end of the event, traditional themes have been selected and preferred. The pre-wedding shots and prominent fat marriages of Rajasthan state are going on world fame. The main reason behind this success is the adoption of tradition and culture of Rajasthan in a new luxurious way. Quinn (2010) said that the unique culture offered during the events are sometimes the main attraction for the tourists.

Literature review

Without literature review, no research can be complete. The review of literature is a backbone of any study. With the help of the literature review, the researchers are in the position to learn more about the subject and able to explore the point of their research in an in-depth way. Rapple (2011) defined literature reviews as being inordinately required in the majority of methodical fields. Reviewing the literature requires the ability to organise numerous responsibilities and assessing significant matter to synthesising information from a variety of sources, from critical assessment to summarising, evaluation and referencing skills (Budgen et al., 2006). The review of literature not only provides conceptual knowledge about the particular area but also crucial analysis of the study gaps. Thus, in the present chapter, to justify the research work the author has done an in-depth literature review of the keywords. Event tourism, creativity, innovation, events impact and the requirement of education tourism for supporting events have been studied and evaluated with the help of literature review. An attempt has been made to justify the case study method for this research study with the relevant literature review in the Methodology Approach section.

Creativity, innovation and event tourism

In such cut-throat competition it is necessary to be attentive, smart and rigorous with efforts to be different and unique. Especially when we discuss events, the need to be unique seems to be more in demand. This event category starts from old traditional cultural fairs and festivals to new, advanced events such as business events, knowledge events, sports events etc. This uniqueness comes from creativity. Creativity cannot come from machines; it is a skill, a passion and a motivation which individuals carry. According to Amabile (1997), a person must possess three factors to be creative – his knowledge, creative thinking skills and inherent enthusiasm to complete the assignment. Today we need to present old events creatively to attract tourists. Events are essential tourism products for any destination. Tourists want to experience events as tourism products work as an experience (Weiermair, 2006).

Creativity is not mere dreaming; it works on real grounds. To get results the person who is working in event tourism must evaluate every factor critically. As explained by Heinze (2007) the methodical creativity includes five types: i. making a fresh design that gives a new opportunity for cognitive structure; ii. discovery of a latest experimental experience that encourages new theorising; iii. investigate a new tactic by which possible problems can experimentally test; iv. development of a historical source that brings a fresh viewpoint and investigates the new area; and v. new amalgamation of previously disseminated ideas into common imaginary acts enable examination of varied events within a common cognitive frame.

Creativity brings innovations into the society. Innovation is measured as a success factor in every field. According to Drucker (1985), the creation of a new product or service is because of change as innovation is an opportunity that provides a base to create a different product or service. In event tourism innovation works as a foundation. Innovative services and products are needed in tourism markets (Weiermair, 2006, for Pechlaner et al., 2006). The countries which are making innovations in their tourism products are enjoying significant gains. Event tourism can emerge as a more attractive product if the destinations adapt innovations in the formulation, implementation and evaluation process of the events. First, from designing to execution, with the help of marketing and information technology, all need to be done innovatively. Secondly, the willingness is required in the community to adopt these innovations. People resist changes, and because of that, the destination is stuck in those old patterns. They don't see the marketing and information communication technologies as requirements for promoting their traditional fairs, festivals and events. Murphy (2005) said the more effortlessly the innovation can be attempted, the more directly it will be accepted. Information technology can be used to promote and provide extensive marketing of the old events and of course for the new events also. IT is a source of communicating (Ryssel and Ritter, 2004).

Not only for communication, information technology can be used for creating the value of the product or service as well as for problem-solving (Melville et al., 2006). The destinations such as Hadoti which are rich in many tourism products primarily in the traditional events, fairs and festivals resist somehow in adapting the new technologies for the promotion and spreading the information of their hidden art and culture. No trail of innovations or the help of information technology is undoubtedly a big reason behind the failure in promoting the events on the globe. Trialability is the extent to which it is feasible to endeavour using information technology innovation (Moore and Benbasat, 1991). Stressing the importance of information and communication technologies, Buhalis and Law (2008) defined that ICT is required in several innovations and investigating subjects.

Innovations in event tourism can stimulate many changes mainly related to economic growth. Innovation is measured as an essential resource for competitive advantage and economic development. Innovations are vital in redefining the market (Lawless and Anderson, 1996). Many countries are enjoying economic growth today because they have adopted innovation in their tourism products and services. Tourists are attracted to these countries because of their exclusive products, for example Dubai. That's the reason why innovation appeared as a tool of growth and prosperity in numerous countries (Fagerberg and Godinho, 2004).

Events and their impact

Events and event tourism are the part of the tourism industry. Today events are not only the source of entertainment or fulfilment of religious rituals; it is above and beyond that. National and international tourists are visiting destinations for participating in events. There are events related with the talk shows of the Saints, Mahatmas and Gurus, events associated with business meetings, events concerned with sports, events related with education – conferences, seminars, summits etc. and much more. When visitors came to attend and participate in these events, they feel attracted towards the event activities and turn into tourists to the destination, so events create revenue for the destination. As Getz (1997) described, events create immense tourism. Utilisation of tourism products in a geographical area primarily brings economic impacts (Stiernstrand, 1996). The importance of events is higher for the developing countries as to survive the cutthroat competition they need to make substantial gains to their economy. Events give employment, resources and attraction for tourism, so events are valuable for developing countries (Guerrier et al., 1998).

It is a myth that events like MICE, sports and new events can bring employment opportunities and revenues and that events need significant investment; only then they will deliver returns. No, it is not like this. The local events – fairs and festivals with low investment – can also create job opportunities, generate revenues and build an image of a destination as an event tourism destination. But the local people who are the performers of these festivals are not aware of this fact. Festivals are indulgenced as tourist products (Cudny, 2006). The image of a country can change through the festivals and cultural events (Ali and Wall, 1977). Big events leave a long-term outcome on the destination and development of the industry (Mossberg, 1997). Emphasis should be given by the government, private players and stakeholders of the tourism industry to categorise the tourists of festival tourism. Unless festival tourism and event tourism are not counted as separate segments the possibilities of growth are less. And this area will be treated as a secondary or add-on area packaged with the main tourism products. Tourism where the main objective is the involvement in events which are related to culture, films, local festivals, fun and sports, should come into festival tourism.

Education tourism as a learning experience for event tourism

Sudden factors sometimes bring surprises, but sometimes also bring shock. Most of the time the mistake made by the tourism and event industry, especially while organising a traditional cultural event or festival, is to bring the tourists to the place where the event is going on. Everyone is not same in adaptability – some tourists may feel comfortable and they may enjoy the new environment, but some may not. A successful event is an event where all the tourists regardless of their age, financial backgrounds, educational level etc. can enjoy the event. One way to find out the mindset of these potential tourists of festival tourism and event tourism can be education tourism, which gives pre-information about the place, event etc. through tutorial learning that brings the queries of the tourists in front of the organisers. Adopting education tourism can be an excellent method to know about the questions and curiosity level of the tourists. Moreover, it helps both the event organisers and the tourists. The ultimate purpose of any event is the satisfaction of the participants. Destinations compete with each other for excellence, individuals, funds and tourists to make the community wealthy and more livable (Haider et al., 1993). The government may focus on harmonisation, scheduling, parliamentary security, guideline, funding, impetus, endorsement and protection for tourism (Hall and Williams, 2008).

Content marketing for event tourism

Content marketing can play a vital role in promoting and branding event tourism. Although other than the industry experts, people are still not very clear with the concept of content marketing. There is confusion how and why this marketing is different and more important than other marketing strategies. Content marketing is a formation of significant, convincing, interesting and precious content in continuous manner according to various behavioural changes of customers. It is very much needed in marketing to keep present customers, attract new customers and make a brand image of the company. Although content marketing is not a tool of direct selling it is effective if the content is good enough to inspire the customers (Kinsta, 2018). Successful content marketing is that which has the significant content to solve the queries of the customers, and should be real and on time when customers need it most. Content marketing is a step-by-step method for earning profits while satisfying the customers through the help of digital content via electronic channels. Event tourism essentially needs the content marketing strategies for speedy recognition and growth. With few innovative efforts in the content on the websites and social media, a destination can create wonders for the number of tourists. Content marketing is based on the theory to educate the customers, not to sell the products to them. For the product and service industry, content marketing works in a different way. As tourism is a service industry it needs content more attractive and authentic. In India where the tourists many times face issues related to safety, content marketing seems more required. Figure 3.1 represents the different components of content marketing for manufacturing goods and Figure 3.2, for the service industry/tourism industry.

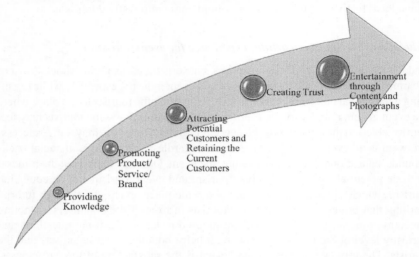

Figure 3.1 Content marketing through digital channels
(Source: the author)

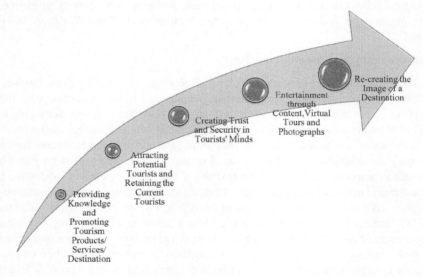

Figure 3.2 Content marketing through digital channels in tourism and hospitality industry
(Source: the author)

Fair and festivals of Hadoti region

There are many festivals in the Hadoti region, but no complete synopsis of all offered festivals exists, especially of the small local festivals. The area includes four districts, namely Kota, Bundi, Baran and Jhalawar. The attractive thing about this region is that all the communities have different festivals. The area offers a combination of big and small festivals. Guided and planned tours, exhibitions and shows are organised during these festivals, which also perform the role of humanising and dissemination of knowledge about the cultural, heritage and religious values in the area. The best-identified festival in Kota, in the Hadoti region, is the Dusshera Festival, which is also known as National Dusshera Festival. The other important and famous festivals and fairs of the region are Kajali Teej of Bundi, also known as the Bundi Utsav Karthik Fair, and the Chandrabhaga Fair. Festivals like the Dol Fair of Baran, Nahan Fair of Sangod (near Kota), and the Tribal Fair of Sitabariand Ramleela of Patunda (Baran) are of great importance regarding local community engagement (Sharma, 2015).

Methodological approach

Case study method

For the research, the case study method has been chosen. A case study is a methodical investigation into an event or a set of related events which aims to describe and explain the occurrence of concentration (Bromley, 1990). In a case, study facts come mainly from certification, archival records, discussions, direct explanation, contributor surveillance and human artefacts. Case studies are the ideal policy when 'how' and 'why' questions are present (Yin, 1984; 1994). Guba and Lincoln (1981) outlined the most realistic, constructive and evaluative knowledge on case study. The present case study is a combination of practical, investigative and evaluative factors. According to Tellis (1997), the case study is related to a possible structure. A case study is a depiction summary (McDonough and McDonough, 1997). According to Johnson (2006), a case study is an excellent method of research related to the community-based problem. The author has adopted a case study method in the present research as event tourism is not possible without community engagement. The author has taken interviews of the principal persons, who were involved as organisers and/or artists in the festivals, fairs and events of Hadoti region. The author has also taken interviews of academicians and students who are engaged in Heritage and Tourism studies. A case study method in research is vital to the topics related to education (Gulsecen and Kubat, 2006). Stake (1995) pointed out that in the process of a case study the focal point is on what is deliberate (the case) rather than how it is intentional (the technique). He also highlighted that the competence and type of case studies depend upon the reason of the examination. There are case studies which are based on a particular reason.

The case

The Hadoti region is blessed with many festivals and fairs. The present study is related to Dushhera Mela festival of Kota City and Nahan Festival of Baran. An attempt has been made to find out the answer and the viewpoint of the experts and students regarding the event tourism in Hadoti region. Event organisers (2), a folk dance expert (1), a politician (1), students (2) and the general public (4) are interviewed to find out the responses to the following questions: i. Do you think that Hadoti region has the potential for event tourism? ii. What is the level of innovations the region is adopting in the events? iii. What is needed to do for attracting tourist towards events and festivals of Hadoti region?

Analysis of the interview

Do you think that Hadoti region has the potential for event tourism?
The eight persons who interviewed are of the view that Hadoti region has excellent potential for event tourism. The organiser of Festival Nahan at Baran Mr. Chaturbhuj Sen said that the festival holds its importance in the area. Around 1 lakh people participate in the festival. Mr. Om Gunjal who was a Ward Parshad told that Dushhera Mela holds the potential to attract international tourists. According to the students and general public, Hadoti region was a perfect blend of everything from the traditional to modern; the place can organise many events.

What is the level of innovations the region is adopting in the events?
In the response of those mentioned previously, all are of the same views that innovations are required during the festivals. At the same time, we can't forget our cultural values and beliefs. Mr. Hari K. Singh who was a folk dance expert in Sharia Tribes Dance form of Baran, Shahabad and Kishganj and represented this dance form in Poland and many other places of India said that we need innovations in promoting our traditional festivals and events but we do need to focus on the motive behind organising these festivals and events. According to all the respondents' level of innovation is quite low in Event Tourism at Haodti.

What is needed to be done for attracting tourists towards events and festivals of Hadoti region?
According to Mr. Chaturbhuj Sen, for promoting the old festivals, we need to take support from private players. Students were of the view that many of the local people and students have only heard the name of the festivals but don't know details. So first we need to give knowledge to the students about the festivals and different types of events. Then only we can think to attract tourists to the region. On the other hand, Mr. Om Gunjal stressed upon the marketing of festivals, especially of Dushhera Festival. According to him, the region can attract not only domestic but international tourists if we spread the details online and promote the festival through different blogs, websites and virtual tours. The event tourism will not only open the ways of earning but also enhance the image of the Kota city and the region.

Strengths and weakness of event tourism in Hadoti

Strengths: From the analysis of interviews, the considerations from the Hadoti region regarding event tourism, the main strength of the region is that the region is an excellent combination of culture, heritage, and modernisation. Hadoti is a destination rich with natural resources. Immense water bodies give the opportunity to organise water sports events and big mountains open up a path for rock climbing and mountaineering. Many places got their identity because of sports events. The international Olympics of 1992 produced a lot of returns and magnetism for tourism (Park, 2002:197). National football league has also become a brand name for the city and improved the image of Holland (Gessel, 2000:112). The Kota City of Hadoti is very well known as an education and coaching hub of India. Four government universities are established here, as well as private universities and many private colleges are running courses in the region. Academicians are coming from all over the world here for conferences, seminars, workshops and lectures. Thus, it creates an opportunity for MICE Events. All four districts of Hadoti, namely Kota, Bundi, Baran and Jhalawar, have heritage properties which can be used for wedding events.

Weaknesses: Some identified weaknesses are: i. lack of awareness in the community regarding the old festivals as well as of new events; ii. unfavourable climatic conditions; iii. no formal courses on event, event management, marketing and event tourism; and iv. competition with other cities and states. The young generation is not willingly able to be involved in old festivals.

Benefits of local events, fairs and festivals

According to McDonnell et al. (1999), the leading industries that get benefits from events are travel and tour, restaurants, shopping centres, and accommodation. Undoubtedly organising the events provides opportunities to a destination to grow

Introduction of New Tourism Product

Required Low Investment

Facilitates Entrepreneurship

New Source of Employment

Boosting Other Industries (Hotel, Food Industry, Travel, and Transport)

Increase Demand of Souvenirs and Other Art and Craft Products from the Local Market

Retention of Youth in the Rural Areas

Creates Platform to showcase Talent to Local Artists

Conservation of Culture, Art, and Tradition

Develops Community Connect

Demolish Poor Image of a Place/Destination

Figure 3.3 Benefits of local events, fairs and festivals
(Source: the author)

in every means. Event tourism works as a new tourism product which is already available with the place and community. By using some strategic actions, any place can open doors for revenue and recreation. According to Goldblatt (2002), organising festivals in off seasons can be the best tool for the small city to attract tourists and to generate income.

Conclusion

The study concluded that Hadoti region holds immense potential for event tourism. The stakeholders need to make proper strategies to promote the events of the region on the national and international level. Innovations are required to adopt in implementation of events. The community needs to focus on new events also. While organising the old festivals the feeling to take forward the culture and to give protection to the traditional values should inculcate in youths. The new technologies should be used in promoting and marketing the event tourism. Content marketing connects can be adopted in event tourism to reach the masses.

References

Ali, I.M. and Wall, G. (1977, October/December). The impact of tourism in Trinidad and Tobago. *Annals of Tourism Research*, pp. 43–49.

Amabile, T.M. (1997). Motivating creativity in organizations: On doing what you love and loving what you do. *California Management Review*, **40**(1), pp. 39–58.

Bromley, D.B. (1990). Academic contributions to psychological counselling: I. A philosophy of science for the study of individual cases. *Counselling Psychology Quarterly*, **3**(3), pp. 299–307.

Budgen, D., Turner, M. and Khalil, M. (2006). Lessons from applying the systematic literature review process within the software engineering domain. *Journal of Systems and Software*, **80**(4), pp. 571–583.

Buhalis, D. and Law, R. (2008). Progress in information technology and tourism management: 20 years on and 10 years after the internet – The state of the e-tourism research. *Tourism Management*, **29**(4), pp. 609–623.

Cudny, W. (2006). Festiwal dialogu czterech kultur jako przykład strategicznego produktu turystycznego dla Łodzi. *Turystyka i Hotelarstwo*, **10**, pp. 117–128.

Drucker, P.F. (1985). *Innovation and entrepreneurship: Practices and principles*. London: Heinemann.

Fagerberg, J. and Godinho, M.M. (2004). Innovation and catching-up. In J. Fagerberg, D. Mowery, and R. Nelson (eds.), *The Oxford handbook of innovation*. Oxford: Oxford University Press, pp. 514–544.

Gessel, P.V. (2000). Events: Outstanding means for joint promotion. *Event Management*, **6**, pp. 111–116.

Getz, D. (1997). *Event management and event tourism*. New York: Cognizant Communications Corp.

Goldblatt, J.J. (2002). *Special events best practices in modern event management*. New York: John Wiley & Sons, Inc., pp. 1–25.

Guba, E.G. and Lincoln, Y.S. (1981). *Effective evaluation*. San Francisco: Jossey-Bass Publishers.

Guerrier, Y., Robertson, M. and Tyler, D. (1998). *Managing tourism in cities*. Chichester: John Wiley & Sons Ltd.

Gulsecen, S. and Kubat, A. (2006). Teaching ICT to teacher candidates using PBL: A qualitative and quantitative evaluation. *Educational Technology & Society*, 9(2), pp. 96–106.

Haider, D.H., Kotler, P. and Rein, I. (1993). *Marketing places: Attracting investment, industry, and tourism to cities, states, and nations*. New York: Maxwell Macmillan International.

Hall, C.M. and Williams, A.M. (2008). *Tourism and innovation*. London: Routledge.

Heinze, T. (2007). *Creativity capabilities and the promotion of highly innovative research in Europe and the United States*. Final Report, Reference Number: EU-NEST/CREA-511889. Retrieved from: www.crea.server.de (accessed: the 22nd March, 2018).

Johnson, M.P. (2006). Decision models for the location of community corrections centers. *Environment and Planning B-Planning & Design*, 33(3), pp. 393–412.

Kinsta. (2018). *Content marketing essentials 2013*. Retrieved from: www.mandloys.com/contentmarketing/ (accessed: the 22nd March, 2018).

Lawless, M. and Anderson, P. (1996). Generational technological change: Effect of innovation and local rivalry on performance. *Academy of Management Journal*, 39(5), pp. 1185–1217.

McDonnell, I., Allen, J. and O'Toole, W. (1999). *Festival and special event management*. Brisbane: John Wiley & Sons Australia Ltd.

McDonough, J. and McDonough, S. (1997). *Research methods for English language teachers*. London: Arnold.

Melville, N., Gurbaxani, V. and Kraemer, K. (2006). The productivity impact of information technology across competitive regimes: The role of industry concentration and dynamism. *Decision Support Systems*, 43, pp. 229–242.

Moore, G.C. and Benbasat, I. (1991). Development of an instrument to measure the perceptions of adopting an information technology innovation. *Information Systems Research*, 2(3), pp. 192–221.

Mossberg, L.L. (1997). The event market. *Annals of Tourism Research*, 24(3), pp. 748–751.

Murphy, E. (2005). Issues in the adoption of broadband-enabled learning. *British Journal of Educational Technology*, 36(3), pp. 525–536.

Park, K.S. (2002). A case study of post exposition site utilization in Korea. *Event Management*, 7, pp. 197–204.

Pechlaner, H., Fischer, E. and Hamman, E.M. (2006). Leadership and innovation processes-development of products and services based on core competencies. *Journal of Quality Assurance in Hospitality and Tourism*, 6(3), pp. 31–57.

Quinn, B. (2010). Arts festivals, urban tourism and cultural policy. *Journal of Policy Research in Tourism, Leisure & Events*, 2, pp. 264–279.

Rapple, C. (2011). *The role of the critical review article in alleviating information overload*. Retrieved from: http://www.annualreviews.org/userimages/ ContentEditor/1300384004941/Annual_Reviews_WhitePaper_Web_2011.pdf (accessed: the 22nd March, 2018).

Ryssel, R. and Ritter, T. (2004). The impact of information technology deployment on trust, commitment and value creation in business relationships. *Journal of Business & Industrial Marketing*, 193, pp. 197–207.

Sharma, A. (2015). Educational tourism: Strategy for sustainable tourism development with reference of Hadauti and Shekhawati regions of Rajasthan, India. *Journal of Knowledge Management, Economics and Information Technology*, 5(4), pp. 1–17.

Sharma, A. (in press). Festivals for sustainable tourism development: A case study of Hadoti Region, Rajasthan. In J. Mair (ed.) *Handbook of festivals*. Oxon: Routledge.

Stake, R.E. (1995). *The art of case study research*. Thousand Oaks: Sage Publications.

Stiernstrand, J. (1996). The Nordic model: A theoretical model for economic impact. *Analysis of Event Tourism Festival Management and Event Tourism*, **3**, pp. 165–174.

Tellis, W. (1997). *Introduction to case study*. Retrieved from: www.nova.edu/ssss/QR/QR3-2/tellis1.html (accessed: the 22nd March, 2018).

Weiermair, K. (2006). *Product improvement or innovation: What is the key to success in tourism? Innovation and growth in tourism*. Paris: OECD, pp. 53–69.

Yin, R.K. (1984). *Case study research: Design and methods*. Beverly Hills: Sage Publications.

Yin, R.K. (1994). *Case study research: Design and methods*. Newbury Park: Sage Publications.

4 Role of ethnic cultural events to build an authentic destination image

A case of 'Pohela Boishakh' in Bangladesh

*Saadia Shabnam, Haywantee Ramkissoon
and Afreen Choudhury*

Introduction

Event-based tourism developed around a cultural festival is considered as an essential cultural emblem for their socio-cultural, political and economic roles (Getz and Andersson, 2010). Festivals provide important opportunities for destination marketing organisations to promote themselves locally to their own people and internationally to target foreign tourists as the potential market (Mossberg and Getz, 2006; Getz and Page, 2016). Cultural celebrations include different festivals or events across the world e.g. carnivals, religious events, arts and entertainment. Different mega events such as the Olympics, FIFA World Cup, New Year celebrations of different countries, and the Tomatina Festival in Spain attract many tourists from across the world. These festivals and events differ in their scope to create an appeal for tourists. O'Sullivan and Jackson (2002) demonstrate that a small-scale 'home-grown' festival with local essence is essentially initiated by local people, mostly run by volunteers for the benefit of the local community. Some are aimed at attracting visitors, called 'tourist-tempter' festivals that can effectively stimulate local economic development. Festivals and events often promote the cultural heritage of a country and are considered not only as cultural tourism but also as urban and rural tourism. Researchers believe that festivals could be identified as a separate asset and treated as a separate type of tourism (Cudny, 2011).

One of the effective strategies for destinations seeking product differentiation has been organising events around the festival theme. The promotion of ethnic cultural festivals can be the opportunity for destination marketers to integrate events and festivals in their destination development strategies. The role of planned events to attract tourists to a destination is well recognised by scholars (Getz, 2008; Getz et al., 2006; Niekerk, 2017). For the greater marketing implication of the event tourism, it is essential to understand the stakeholder relations around the event to uncover the dynamics between and among these parties (Larson, 2002; Larson and Wikström, 2001).

Earlier conceptualisation of stakeholder interaction is built on the traditional systems view (Getz et al., 2006). There is limited focus in the literature on the unique pattern of resource dependency and lack of coordination among stakeholder parties in a developing country's socio-political setting (Lamberti et al., 2011). The current study addresses this gap in literature by developing and proposing a conceptual model of stakeholder network and relations in a developing country context. The exploratory case study builds on insights from organisers, event managers, and the local host institution to help identify the key stakeholders, and the nature of their relationships. Results of these interviews were interpreted to capture the unique characteristics of stakeholders and their relationships for a potential branding opportunity for the Bengali New Year festival, 'Pohela Boishakh'. The theoretical objective is to generate concepts defining the scope of stakeholders' roles and relationship dynamics that can be applied to develop a sustainable authentic event brand to attract tourists. Findings from participants' discourse draw both theoretical and practical management implications. The theoretical contribution is particularly with regards to the conceptual modelling of festival stakeholder roles in a developing country. As part of the festival, events can be viewed as a perfect tool for destination image marketing for their ability to animate local socio-cultural aspects.

Stakeholders' engagement

The sustainability of event tourism in a cultural festival context depends on the socio-political and physical support of its stakeholders. Event-based tourism is a 'mixed industry' in which non-profit institutions, private firms, and public agencies all co-exist (Getz and Andersson, 2010). Therefore, the dynamics of stakeholder relationships largely determines the success of an event, the scope and nature of inter-organisational relationships in the festival context, and how they affect the local organisation.

Festival tourism has many positive consequences such as generating income or enhancing the quality of life for the local inhabitants through developing tourism infrastructure (Cudny, 2013). The inflow of tourists, participants and resources create economic mobilisation and infrastructural development as well as provide job opportunities in the service sectors. Due to the increase in tourist attractions, large-scale festivals with strong cultural components are substantially increasing (Lee et al., 2004), attracting interest from many destination marketers. The latter increasingly seek to promote their local festivals and events, which demands significant efforts from various stakeholders involved e.g. the local community and other industries (Nunkoo and Ramkissoon, 2012). Visitors may assign meanings and develop an emotional bond with the festival or event (Ramkissoon and Mavondo, 2015; Ramkissoon et al., 2018), and further assist in destination marketers' efforts in developing a festival brand.

Stakeholder engagement is therefore very important in the promotion of festivals and events. Drawing from stakeholder theory, a stakeholder is defined as the people or any entity that directly or indirectly affects or is affected by the activities of an organisation (Andersson and Getz, 2008). According to Lyck et al. (2012), festivals in a specific perspective take its departure in a thematic categorisation of festivals. In terms of producing and marketing a festival, Larson (2002) recognised the following festival stakeholders: the festival organiser, the local trade and industry (suppliers of products and services), sponsors (companies using the festival as their marketing event), public authorities (e.g. ministry of cultural affairs, the local municipality and public security organisations), associations and clubs (members of performing clubs participating in festival events), the media industry (journalists representing television and radio stations, newspapers and magazines). In investing in the stakeholder relationship to grow, develop, maintain, or abandon (Batt and Purchase, 2004), it is essential to uncover the stakeholder relationship dynamics for festivals such as the new year celebration of 'Pohela Boishakh'.

Culture is ever-evolving and it is reasonable to assume authenticity as a concept related to identity and culture of the locals (Croes and Kubickova, 2013). In hospitality and tourism, authenticity is deemed as a driving force to stimulate individuals to travel to certain destinations (Kolar and Zabkar, 2010; Ramkissoon and Uysal, 2011, 2014). Travellers seek authentic experiences that are contrasting to their daily routines (Lu et al., 2015; Ramkissoon, 2015). Tourists search for exotic cultural experiences, often participate in ethnic events and festivals, visit heritage sites, watch traditional dances or ceremonies, and shop for local ethnic handicrafts and souvenirs (Yang et al., 2008; Yang, 2011). An authentic ethnic cultural festival thus can be adopted as a strategy for regional and economic development (McIntosh and Johnson, 2005).

It is also important how stakeholders construct the meaning of authenticity and how they want to represent the local heritage and pride to tourists. This process of construction and the resulting meaning of authenticity by the stakeholders are unique to each cultural destination (Croes and Kubickova, 2013), thereby the representation of authenticity converts the destination into a unique product to the tourists (Ramkissoon et al., 2011). Despite mounting research attention focusing on the importance of tourists' perception of the authenticity of festival experiences (Gilmore and Pine, 2007; Lu et al., 2015), there is still a research gap connecting tourists' authenticity perceptions of festivals and the image of the destination especially from an ethnic cultural perspective (Afifi et al., 2017). This chapter, therefore, collects evidence of the stakeholder relationship dynamics from a cultural discourse that has evolved around the context of developing ethnic festival tourism.

The case study: 'Pohela Boishakh'

'Pohela Boishakh' or the first day of Bengali New Year (Bengali: 'Bangla Nôbobôrsho'), is the traditional new year day of the Bengali people. According to the lunisolar Bengali calendar every year, April 14, the first day of the first month, Boishakh is celebrated as a national holiday in Bangladesh. In the Indian states of West Bengal, Tripura and elsewhere people of Bengali heritage irrespective of their religious faith, celebrate the same. It therefore almost always falls on or around April 14 every year on the Gregorian calendar.

The traditional greeting for Bengali New Year is 'Shubho Nabobarsho'. According to history, in 1985, a community cultural organisation, Charupith initiated

Mangal Shobhjatra. The festival is celebrated with processions, fairs and visits to family and friends. In subsequent years, it was then organised by Dhaka University, in Bangladesh. The procession showcasing the traditional themes and motifs carried by local participants wearing traditional dress spontaneously joining to celebrate the first day of Bengali New Year is inscribed by UNESCO in 2016 as a 'cultural heritage of humanity' (UNESCO, 2016).

The festival became a popular means of establishing cultural identity, pride and heritage among the people of this locality as they were resisting the then ruling power during the period of 1950s to 1960s (Kratoska et al., 2005). The celebrations start at dawn welcoming the new sunrise with a rendition of Rabindranath Tagore's song 'Esho he Baishakh' by the performers from the cultural organisation, 'Chhayanat' under the banyan tree at Ramna, a local park of historical significance.

This is a major event showcasing authentic Bengali ensembles, masks and floats with at least three themes, one highlighting evil, another courage, and thirdly, peace. From this time, each year the procession has different themes relevant to the country's culture and political state that gives the festival a dynamic status. Local community cultural organisations and musical bands also perform on this occasion. Local artisans bring their specialties to the fairs called 'Boishakhi Mela'. Other traditional events held to celebrate 'Pohela Boishakh' include bull racing in Munshiganj, wrestling in Chittagong, boat racing, cockfights and pigeon racing. It also highlights the pride of Bangladeshi people for their folk heritage. Amidst the recent worldwide upsurge of religious fundamentalism, the festival of 'Pohela Boishakh' can be the symbol of the contrasting appeal of socio-cultural freedom from the influence of religion, creed, caste, gender or age.

'Pohela Boishakh' new year day is celebrated in other areas of Indian subcontinent under various names. In parts of Southeast Asia such as Myanmar, Sri Lanka, and Cambodia, the same day is celebrated as the New Year for many Buddhist communities, which is likely a reflection of their shared culture. In the north and central India, the festival is called 'Vaisakhi' by Hindus and Sikhs, which too marks the solar new year. Other examples include 'Rongali Bihu' in Assam, 'Vishuva Sankranti' in Odisha, and the same festival named 'Puthandu' in Tamil Nadu. In Kerala it is named as 'Vishu', 'Sheetal' in Mithila, and 'Bikram Samwat / Naya Barsh' in Nepal. In Sri Lanka it is 'Aluth Avuruthu', 'Songkran' in Thailand and Laos, 'Chol Chnam Thmey' in Cambodia, and 'Thingyan' in Myanmar. It proves that there is wide regional acceptance of this festival among south and middle Asian countries. Destination marketers are provided with opportunities to successfully brand these festivals and attract both domestic and international visitors around this time.

Getz (1997) develops a model for managing and marketing events that reflect the organisation-centric view where organisations secure resources from their environment as their input, and produce events as their products. Here organisations are stand-alone players within an apolitical environment which negotiates with multiple parties to meet their business goals (Larson, 2002, 2009; Larson and Wikström, 2001). Based on the participants' discourse, this chapter puts forward an argument that the hallmark public events are co-produced by a network of interdependent organisations and their stakeholder groups. There are examples that the large-scale activities for festivals can drive regional development through a significant influence on the economy as well as enhance the socio-cultural and political stability of the community or the tourist destination (Arcodia and Whitford, 2006; Chen, 2014).

Methodology

A review of extant literature in festival tourism suggests the development of a context-specific framework, taking all stakeholders and resources into account. Considering the need to delve further on the stakeholder involvement, the current study employs Getz's model of stakeholders in the festival network (Getz et al., 2006) to explore the nature and dynamics of stakeholder relationship in the context of 'Pohela Boishakh' – the festival of Bengali new year celebration. The framework underpins the exploration of festival stakeholders, their interdependence in the dynamic network, mobility of resources and the existing structural and institutional support. Drawing from insights gathered from stakeholders participating in the New Year celebrations in Bangladesh, this case study provides a better understanding of the relationship and network among different stakeholders, and their role to build and sustain a festival brand in developing countries.

Open-ended questions were used to conduct personal interviews with local branding experts, event managers, academics and members of participating host institutions. Protocol of the questions and lines of inquiry closely followed the factors recognised in the model of festival stakeholder network (Getz et al., 2006). Interview questions focused on five major key themes: i. individual and community participation; ii. institutional role and support; iii. tourism capital as events and festivals; iv. identification of suppliers and organisers; and v. scope for an umbrella branding. Twelve face-to-face interviews, with thirty-five to fifty minutes duration each, were conducted with persons who have an active participation in the field of event management, selected primarily based on judgment and snowball sampling. Four research assistants took interviews in different locations in Dhaka city, the capital of Bangladesh and the host city for the largest Bengali new year festival. Interviews were recorded in local Bengali language and translated into English by the bilingual researcher as the standard procedure (Hossain et al., 2013). Respondents' discourses were analysed to elicit preliminary insights. News, press releases, and assessment reports of national and international agencies highlighting the participatory stakeholder roles were consulted to incorporate views from contemporary media.

Discussion of findings

While the findings from the study on a single country cannot be generalised, there is considerable value in employing in-depth interviews of representatives of the festival event under investigation. The current study sets the platform to explore the unique perspective of the developing countries, and stakeholders'

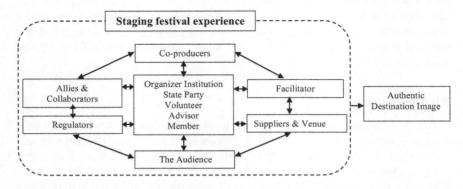

Figure 4.1 Conceptual framework of authentic festival experience

(Source: conceptualised based on Getz Model of Stakeholder Network in Festival [Getz et al., 2006])

views on the contemporary issues needed to be uncovered to establish an authentic ethnic festival tourism brand. The conceptual model (see Figure 4.1) draws from Getz et al. (2006)'s framework and a review of extant literature.

For the successful marketing, events in this festival would benefit if they were to be tourism-oriented (Getz and Andersson, 2010) and it might be debated that the greater marketing orientation will have an adverse impact on the festival's core cultural components. Such particular festival and its event components play important roles in the renewal of national identity, and tourism may not be regarded as a necessary component (Jiang et al., 2016; Ramkissoon, 2017). However, there is an opportunity for destination branding around the theme of the festival.

Stakeholder network in event tourism to build authentic destination image: An interpretive model

In the light of the current study results, researchers identify the components of the possible relationship dynamics in the stakeholder relationship congenial for staging the authentic local festival of 'Pohela Boishakh' to build a favourable destination image for the Bengal region (Figure 4.1). At a festival, the host plays a role to 'stage' the authenticity through various events and exhibitions that creates appeal to the global tourists to the destination. As shown in Figure 4.1, the stakeholder network creates a conducive platform for intense public participation showcasing the authentic cultural ensembles that can build the destination attractiveness in the region. The subsequently discussed results are organised into the model that serves as a visual summation of the preliminary results obtained from this current study.

'Staging' authenticity and role of stakeholders

Tourists participating in ethnic festivals expect an authentic experience. It is often difficult for tourists to distinguish between 'true authenticity' and 'staged authenticity' (MacCannell, 1973; Lu et al., 2015). In the context of an ethnic festival, events, participants and their attires, artefacts, settings of events, decorations, visits to the heritage sites and folk villages, cultural theme parks, and local cuisine can be considered as authentic when they conform to native traditions and reflect local heritage. The spokesperson from the Faculty of Fine Arts, University of Dhaka states that

> The Mangal Shobhajatra, the main attraction of Pohela Boishakhis orga- nized by students and teachers of Dhaka University's Faculty of Fine Arts in Bangladesh is open to the public to celebrate. The variability and viabil- ity of the elements and artefacts are ensured by bearers and practitioners as part of their creative endeavour to create a visible cultural identity. It earned a considerable growth of the celebration in the last 20 years. For greater protection and preservation of local heritage, appropriate safeguarding measures are also proposed in the decision of the intergovernmental com- mittee that includes formal and informal education, research and documen- tation, public lectures and museum exhibitions. Ministry of Cultural Affairs, experts and researchers, actively participate and give consent in the nomination of the festival artefacts as they represent the core cultural symbol for the nation.

It reveals that the success of creating favourable authenticity perceptions through staging events for any cultural festival largely relies on the role that stakeholders play. Authenticity can be a critical marketing tool for the creation of an ethnic festival brand like 'Pohela Boishakh'. Since the major success of the festival lies in the spontaneous public participation, who make all the events colourful, it should not be restricted for the sake of international tourism. As one participant argues:

> Success of our cultural festival lies in the spontaneous participation of our local people. People from all over the country, people from all professions feel that it is an event very close to their heart. So for the sake of the security due to attract the foreign tourists, if we restrict the chance of local people's par- ticipation, the festival will lose its color and its life.

It is also echoed in the literature that understanding the pervasiveness of mass participation in the festival encourage all relevant stakeholders to cooperate to a greater extent despite of benefit asymmetry (Lamberti et al., 2011). Therefore, community participation, in an ethnic festival is one of the important dimensions of event tourism in developing countries that shape the overall stakeholder relations.

Resource dependency

The inter-party relationship in the 'Pohela Boishakh' festival context takes a tra- ditional resource dependency view where the organiser has the high need and others have high control over the resources. There is the historical trend of buyer-supplier relations primarily based on trust as revealed from one of the participants:

> For numerous small entrepreneurs and other non-profit organizations, resource acquisition and financial viability are the real challenges. In such environments, most of the parties basically work based on trust and depends on the informal but effective networking.

Contrasting to Donaldson's (1996) basic premise of resource dependency theory, there is little formal collaboration between buyer and supplier of resources. As a major stakeholder of 'Pohela Boishakh' festival, the government provides financial support to implement festival activities at major events. The Ministry of Cultural Affairs, cultural experts and researchers actively participate in safeguarding measures including formal and informal education, documentation of activities performed and public participation, public lectures, fairs and exhibitions of heritage symbols. Due to the resource limitation and dependency on local ingredients and ensembles, the contingency for scarcity is almost non-existent. There is little evidence of a symbiotic relation among different resource users. Fluctuations and variability of resource supplies usually worked out through the informal liaison between stakeholder parties.

Creating a balance between tradition and innovation

A spokesperson from the Faculty of Fine Arts said:

> To my knowledge, Pohela Boishakh was based on the opening of a new ledger book (halkhata) for the year, which was done by both Hindu and Muslim traders. If we check the Hijri, Gregorian and Bangla calendars, we can see that Pohela Boishakh celebration started from the reign of Mughal Emperor Akbar. For a proper collection of taxes, Akbar introduced a new calendar, giving importance to agriculture and harvests. So, this was done for the agro-based society of Bengal. Most of the elements of our folk traditions are related to agriculture. The main aspect of the celebration is to bid goodbye to evil and welcome prosperity.

Age-old agrarian cultural heritage is reflected in the motifs and artefacts that are showcased in different events during the festival. The students and teachers constitute a cohesive community of bearers of the local cultural emblem. Inscription of the festival elements make the local cultural heritage more visible to the world and these elements transcend the message beyond local boundaries. At the same time, by varying the artefacts from year to year they also demonstrate their creativity and ensures the viability of the festival through increased acceptance by the new generation. However, more diversified events, heritage locations, traditional games and display of folk culture can be integrated to make the festival vibrant while preserving the ancient traditions. In one stakeholder's opinion:

> It is our own cultural festival which has its very own heritage. If we really think of turning the festival into a point of tourist attraction, then we should give it an international flavor. Things should be organized in a more formal fashion where all involved parties will have specific roles to perform. Moreover, more interesting features should be incorporated, more locations should be involved and at the same time security concern is also there.

Umbrella branding – nation and the festival

Festivals and events are often viewed as tools to promote the destination image and place marketing because of its temporal and spatial connections to construct social relations (Black, 2016; Massey, 1994). Festival or event tourism acts as a platform for showcasing the living expressions and traditions of a community that are transmitted through generations (UNESCO, 2016). In order to promote and encourage event tourism, it is important to build up a strategy to attract international tourists. According to Andersson and Getz (2008), non-profit and service organisations also try to sustain their core beliefs and identities, although in the festival sector, their mandates are likely to be self-defined and their membership or governance might be flexible when it comes to making changes.

The main role events play in tourism is portraying an image of the cultural heritage of a specific region. It can be described as a catalyst, image making and animator of a culture. Events should be planned to be the 'living' demonstration of local culture with a capacity of innovation within the constant social framework (Black, 2016). Events that are built around the core national identity would provide a consistent link between the past heritage and present purpose and creates appeal to the contemporary tourists. As expressed by an event manager:

> Without the intention of creating any debate, it can be said that it can be one way for Bangladesh to show its secular face to the world through highlighting our natural heritage.

Large-scale activities and features of events planned and developed around the core theme of the festival can create greater interest among tourists. Festivals and events are a part of their cultural heritage tour. So well planned events in the festival season of 'Pohela Boishakh' can extend the possibilities of economic development and contribute socially, economically and culturally to the country. This is reflected in stakeholders' views:

> It helps to build positive impacts of tourism by facilitating interaction between residents and tourists, getting a greater appreciation for local heritage, and that can eventually be a path for constructing the national image.

Issues and challenges in developing festival tourism

The United Nations educational and scientific and cultural organization (UNESCO) proclaimed 'The Mangal Shobhajatra' festival as 'Intangible Cultural Heritage of Humanity' at the 11th session of the Inter-Governmental Committee on Safeguarding Intangible Cultural Heritage held in the Ethiopian capital Addis Ababa (The Daily Star, 2017). "The Mangal Shobhajatra festival symbolises the pride the people of Bangladesh have in their folk heritage, as well as their strength and courage to fight against sinister forces and their vindication of truth and justice", UNESCO noted (UNESCO, 2016). It also stated in that occasion that "the New Year's procession represents solidarity and a shared value for democracy, uniting people irrespective of caste, creed, religion, gender or age. Knowledge and skills are transmitted by students and teachers within the community" (The Prothom Alo, 2016).

Festival stakeholders – types, roles and relationship dynamics

According to Pepperdine and Ewing (2001:77), "stakeholder involvement is an essential ingredient, for it allows the identification of locally relevant and meaningful indicators and, subsequently, the development of a locally adaptable management strategy". A typology of stakeholder parties and their specific roles have been developed (see Figure 4.1) as respondents identified stakeholders and their roles for the event 'Pohela Boishakh'. Identified parties are organisers, facilitators, collaborators, regulators, suppliers and venues along with the participants. Multiple stakeholders often hold multiple roles while engaged in a synergistic partnership and there is always a potential for conflicts of interest.

The event of 'Pohela Boishakh' is publicly owned and the major stakeholder is the Institute of Fine Arts of Dhaka University which is a not-for-profit institution. One of the organisers narrates:

> Since during the festival time, the city and festival events are regarded as belonging to the public, issues such as festival entrance fees, access for different target groups, and often the high demand for public services such as police and public health services, are certainly interesting aspects not only in branding but also in a political sense. These would be really important areas to focus if we target to turn it into a profitable tourism event.

Again, similar views from another stakeholder are:

> To make it attractive to the international tourists, it needs to be a planned package of events that involves developing new infrastructures, wide international media coverage, welcoming atmosphere with the flavor of local authenticity. At present how this event is observed, who is organizing the event, all these are not above the controversy. There are some political and security

issues. So things should be much more organized and planned if we really want to present our heritage to the world.

Reid and Arcodia (2002) state the importance of implementing a framework to assess stakeholders' roles and incorporate them into the planning process is important for effective festival management and helping in preventing the failure of events. Events in any cultural festival symbolise different paradigms of traditional and evolving cultural components. These also are places of discourse between minority and majority groupings that might otherwise be only experienced as the majority-dominated structure of culture (Richards and Ryan, 2004). These events also mirror the authentic ethnicity in contrast to the mimicry of the globalised culture. Therefore, the development of relationship dynamics can be well directed to build an authentic destination image.

Resource mobilisation

Studies in the domain of festival tourism and marketing often modelled festival events from the perspective of a common organisation-centric view where organisations secure resources from their own pool and become the direct beneficiary of the financial outcomes (Getz et al., 2006). But in case of a public festival, mobilisation of financial resources throughout the network of stakeholders involve multi-faceted transaction in the 'political market square' (Larson and Wikström, 2001) which is distinct from the festival management by organisations stand alone.

Non-profit organisers of the major event of 'Mongol Shovajatra' depend on the sponsors and charities for their major expenditure and there is no assurance for the fund management. Most other events like fair and cultural performances are arranged by different organisations in various locations, often for the local community. A planned network of resource mobilisation should be developed based on the events designed around the core cultural exhibits. Here arises the importance to understand the resource dependency theory from the context of multiple stakeholder perspectives of a public festival.

Developing community-led cultural tourism

At the destination level, the event tourism can act as a catalyst to create tourist attraction through place marketing. The process of developing and facilitating an event and managing them as a sustainable portfolio needs a marketing orientation. For a public event, attracting tourists as an additional segment generates the concern of professional event management.

Capacity building for managing cultural tourism should start with sensitising the community on responsible tourism, benefits and pitfalls thus they become aware of their own role in such event marketing, for example, the folk artists need to be skillful in showcasing their authentic cultural performances and lifestyle for tourists. Communities need to understand that the cultural tourism presents the local cultural capital to the world and protects the local heritage. Capacity building needs to address innovating activity packages for the visitors where tourists can actively participate in different events. There is a need for organised tours to various heritage sites, hotels and restaurants with local cuisines as well as with all the amenities for foreign tourists, arts and crafts workshops, jamming sessions with modern and traditional performances etc. to ensure the authentic tourism experience. Tourists enjoy not only the final product but also the process of production, training, composing, design, mask making, participating in the rally, taking part in traditional games etc.

Suitable festival activities

Staging authenticity requires a balanced event portfolio that incorporates diversified forms of 'planned events, business, festivals and culture, sport and entertainment' (Getz, 2013) essentially targeting global tourists. A well-balanced and sustainable event portfolio developed effectively around the core cultural values builds the festival brand and enhances the value of the umbrella brand for the destination. According to Niekerk (2017), a global appeal, the scale and symbolic status of the event creates destination development opportunities. For destination planners, it is also important to consider that events and festivals have their own lifecycle trajectories (Holmes and Ali-Knight, 2017) that will have an influence on the sustainability of the destination. At this point, the local destination planners have the opportunity of huge public participation and the historical root of the event of 'Pohela Boishakh' which promises a comparatively longer festival lifecycle. The tourism destination may need to develop their event portfolio in such a way that it reinforces the local Bengali cultural components as brand elements and attracts tourists. As a sponsor and event manager of an advertising agency narrated:

> "We have many cultural symbols that are very rich representing the thousand years" folk tradition of Bengal area. Baul and Bhatiali songs, musical instruments like Ektara, Dugdugi and local games like Kabadi all symbolize the way people interact, build social bonds among themselves. When I travelled abroad with musical bands, I experienced their wide acceptance in other cultures. Nowadays, many musicians are creating fusions based on our own songs. So, they can have an appeal to the international tourist if they are properly highlighted.

It is worth noting that in 2008, 'Baul songs' (UNESCO, 2008), in 2013, traditional art of 'Jamdani' weaving (UNESCO, 2013) and in 2017, traditional art of 'Shital Pati' weaving (UNESCO, 2017) got the recognition as the Intangible Cultural Heritage of Humanity by UNESCO (UNESCO, 2016), empasising that local culture if well represented can be an authentic reflection of the local heritage; it remains important to create brand elements to present a charming cultural ensemble.

According to Getz (2013), in the pubic festival, events should be designed as demand-driven, managed through a bottom-up approach ensuring mass participation in the destination to make it well-integrated and sustainable. So the suitability of events and activities would benefit from a careful situation and demand analysis of the tourists visiting the region.

Professional marketing orientation

Marketing orientation of festivals differs based on the scope and resource availability of the events and festivals (Mayfield and Crompton, 1995). These are largely dependent on the stakeholders' relations and networking. 'Pohela Boishakh', as older events that are attended by the locals, tend to have less of a marketing orientation. Researchers identify marketing orientation as a key success factor for festivals and events (Lade and Jackson, 2004). A participant, a major corporate sponsor, Robi, a Telecom company, expressed

> When we are developing our individual corporate event for our client targeting this event, that is obviously key to our marketing strategy, it's to develop customer relationship. But if you look at the original festival, it is based on the tradition and it would be pretty difficult to make it professionally disciplined due to participation of the general public.

Implications and future research

The future effort for theory development should integrate the anthropology, geography and economics of authentic events carrying the flavour of local festivals. As more and more regions use festivals to promote tourism to develop the regional economy (Felsenstein and Fleischer, 2003), the Bengali new year festival 'Pohela Boishakh' can be a centre point for the development of tourism in the region. Such ethnic festivals have become a popular tourism trend in gaining the attention of tourists to travel for authentic ethnic festivals. The reason they have grown rapidly in terms of quantity and scale (Burr, 1997) is tourists' increasing attraction toward the authentic regional culture. Countries, especially those which are developing and at the stage of transition, embrace festivals as a critical tourism strategy (Getz, 2008). Understanding the stakeholders and their relationship dynamics in the backdrop of unique historical and socio-political background is the key to success for developing 'Pohela Boishakh' as a festival brand. From an inconspicuous event of a local character, this festival has potential to grow into one of the major cultural heritage events in the Bengal region. The stakeholder framework of this study can be the starting point in the development and implementation of a comprehensive marketing plan for many adjacent tourist destinations in the region. Suitable festival activities can be designed based on planning win-win strategies for stakeholders where the stakeholder framework can reveal specific roles, responsibilities and interests of different stakeholder parties.

Conclusion

The large extent of public participation and the highly variable level of power, legitimacy and resource dependency among stakeholders make it especially challenging for destination marketers to leverage from the local festival of 'Pohela Boishakh'. It is likely that a tourism orientation increases marketing efforts and sophistication of such a mass scale festival (Mehmetoglu and Ellingsen, 2005). For greater marketing success and global appeal, festival and event management would benefit from a more organised institutional structure in their resource environment. This must go beyond present strategies employed to obtain and utilise resources. It could involve a unique support network that will work as a safety net to sustain in any crisis.

References

Afifi, E., Mavondo, F., Ramkissoon, H. and Aleti, T. (2017). The role of advertising stereotypes in destination image formation and behavioural intentions of tourists to consume indigenous tourism attractions. In *Time for big ideas? Re-thinking the field for tomorrow*. Dunedin, New Zealand: CAUTHE2017.

Andersson, T.D. and Getz, D. (2008). Stakeholder management strategies of festivals. *Journal of Convention & Event Tourism*, **9**(3), pp. 199–220.

Arcodia, C. and Whitford, M. (2006). Festival attendance and the development of social capital. *Journal of Convention & Event Tourism*, **8**(2), pp. 1–18.

Batt, P.J. and Purchase, S. (2004). Managing collaboration within networks and relationships. *Industrial Marketing Management*, **33**(3), pp. 169–174.

Black, N. (2016). Festival connections: How consistent and innovative connections enable small-scale rural festivals to contribute to socially sustainable communities. *International Journal of Event and Festival Management*, **7**(3), pp. 172–187.

Burr, S.W. (1997). Love thy neighbor and prosper community festivals and events. *Parks and Recreation*, **32**(9), pp. 106–118.

Chen, C.A. (2014). Suitable festival activities for Taiwan's tourism and nation branding with the application of the PR AHP Program. *Asia Pacific Journal of Tourism Research*, **19**(12), pp. 1381–1398.

Croes, R. and Kubickova, M. (2013). From potential to ability to compete: Towards a performance-based tourism competitiveness index. *Journal of Destination Marketing & Management*, **2**(3), pp. 146–154.

Cudny, W. (2011). Film festivals in Łódź as a main component of urban cultural tourism. In D. Szymańska and J. Biegańska (eds.) *Bulletin of geography: Socio – Economic series, no. 15*. Toruń: Nicolaus Copernicus University, pp. 131–141.

Cudny, W. (2013). Festival tourism: The concept, key functions and dysfunctions in the context of tourism geography studies. *Geografický časopis*, **65**(2), pp. 105–118.

The Daily Star. (2017). *Re-framing the debate*. Retrieved from: www.thedailystar.net/news-detail-135436 (accessed: the 15th May, 2018).

Donaldson, L. (1996). The normal science of structural contingency theory. In S. Clegg, C. Hardy and W. Nord (eds.) *Handbook of organization studies*. London: Sage Publications, pp. 57–77.

Felsenstein, D. and Fleischer, A. (2003). Local festivals and tourism promotion: The role of public assistance and visitor expenditure. *Journal of Travel Research*, **41**(4), pp. 385–392.

Getz, D. (1997). Trends and issues in sport event tourism. *Tourism Recreation Research*, **22**(2), pp. 61–62.

Getz, D. (2008). Event tourism: Definition, evolution, and research. *Tourism Management*, **29**(3), pp. 403–428.

Getz, D. (2013). *Event tourism: Concepts, international case studies, and research*. New York: Cognizant Communication Corp.

Getz, D. and Andersson, T. (2010). Festival stakeholders: Exploring relationships and dependency through a four-country comparison. *Journal of Hospitality & Tourism Research*, **34**(4), pp. 531–556.

Getz, D., Andersson, T. and Larson, M. (2006). Festival stakeholder roles: Concepts and case studies. *Event Management*, **10**(2–3), pp. 103–122.

Getz, D. and Page, S.J. (2016). Progress and prospects for event tourism research. *Tourism Management*, **52**, pp. 593–631.

Gilmore, J.H. and Pine, B.J. (2007). *Authenticity: What consumers really want*. Boston: Harvard Business Press.

Holmes, K. and Ali-Knight, J. (2017). The event and festival life cycle: Developing a new model for a new context. *International Journal of Contemporary Hospitality Management*, **29**(3), pp. 986–1004.

Hossain, M.E., Quaddus, M. and Shanka, T. (2013). A field study of factors and variables regarding tour destination loyalty of Cox's Bazar in Bangladesh. *Tourism Analysis*, **18**(4), pp. 429–442.

Jiang, Y., Ramkissoon, H. and Mavondo, F. (2016). Destination marketing and visitor experiences: The development of a conceptual framework. *Journal of Hospitality Marketing & Management*, **25**(6), pp. 653–675.

Kolar, T. and Zabkar, V. (2010). A consumer-based model of authenticity: An oxymoron or the foundation of cultural heritage marketing? *Tourism Management*, **31**(5), pp. 652–664.

Kratoska, P.H., Raben, R. and Nordholt, H.S. (eds.). (2005). *Locating Southeast Asia: Geographies of knowledge and politics of space*. Singapore: Singapore University Press.

Lade, C. and Jackson, J. (2004). Key success factors in regional festivals: Some Australian experiences. *Event Management*, **9**(1–1), pp. 1–11.

Lamberti, L., Noci, G., Guo, J. and Zhu, S. (2011). Mega-events as drivers of community participation in developing countries: The case of Shanghai World Expo. *Tourism Management*, **32**(6), pp. 1474–1483.

Larson, M. (2002). A political approach to relationship marketing: Case study of the Storsjöyran Festival. *International Journal of Tourism Research*, **4**(2), pp. 119–143.

Larson, M. (2009). Festival innovation: Complex and dynamic network interaction. *Scandinavian Journal of Hospitality and Tourism*, **9**(2–3), pp. 288–307.

Larson, M. and Wikström, E. (2001). Organizing events: Managing conflict and consensus in a political market square. *Event Management*, **7**(1), pp. 51–65.

Lee, C.K., Lee, Y.K. and Wicks, B.E. (2004). Segmentation of festival motivation by nationality and satisfaction. *Tourism Management*, **25**(1), pp. 61–70.

Lu, L., Chi, C.G. and Liu, Y. (2015). Authenticity, involvement, and image: Evaluating tourist experiences at historic districts. *Tourism Management*, **50**, pp. 85–96.

Lyck, L., Long, P. and Grige, A.X. (eds.). (2012). *Tourism, festivals and cultural events in times of crisis*. Copenhagen: Copenhagen Business School.

MacCannell, D. (1973). Staged authenticity: Arrangements of social space in tourist settings. *American Journal of Sociology*, **79**(3), pp. 589–603.

Massey, D. (1994). *Space, place and gender*. Cambridge: Polity Press.

Mayfield, T.L. and Crompton, J.L. (1995). Development of an instrument for identifying community reasons for staging a festival. *Journal of Travel Research*, **33**(3), pp. 37–44.

McIntosh, A.J. and Johnson, H. (2005). Understanding the nature of the Marae experience: Views from hosts and visitors at the Nga Hau E Wha National Marae, Christchurch, New Zealand. In C. Ryan and M. Aicken (eds.) *Indigenous tourism: The commodification and management of culture*. Oxford: Elsevier, pp. 35–50.

Mehmetoglu, M. and Ellingsen, K.A. (2005). Do small-scale festivals adopt "market orientation" as a management philosophy? *Event Management*, **9**(3), pp. 119–132.

Mossberg, L. and Getz, D. (2006). Stakeholder influences on the ownership and management of festival brands. *Scandinavian Journal of Hospitality and Tourism*, **6**(4), pp. 308–326.

Niekerk, M.V. (2017). Contemporary issues in events, festivals and destination management. *International Journal of Contemporary Hospitality Management*, **29**(3), pp. 842–847.

Nunkoo, R. and Ramkissoon, H. (2012). Power, trust, social exchange and community support. *Annals of Tourism Research*, **39**(2), pp. 997–1023.

O'Sullivan, D. and Jackson, M.J. (2002). Festival tourism: A contributor to sustainable local economic development? *Journal of Sustainable Tourism*, **10**(4), pp. 325–342.

Pepperdine, S. and Ewing, S. (2001). Integrating social sustainability considerations in natural resource management. In G. Lawrence, V. Higgins and S. Lockie (eds.) *Environment, society and natural resource management: Theoretical perspectives from Australasia and the Americas*. London: Edward Elgar, pp. 67–80.

The Prothom Alo. (2016). *Pohela Boishakh's rally gets UNESCO's recognition*. Retrieved from: http://en.prothomalo.com/bangladesh/news/131111/Pohela-Boishakh%E2%80%99s-rally-gets-UNESCO%E2%80%99s-recognition (accessed: the 15th May, 2018).

Ramkissoon, H. (2015). Authenticity, satisfaction, and place attachment: A conceptual framework for cultural tourism in African island economies. *Development Southern Africa*, **32**(3), pp. 292–302.

Ramkissoon, H. (2016). Place satisfaction, place attachment and quality of life: Development of a conceptual framework for island destinations. In P. Modica and M. Uysal (eds.) *Sustainable island tourism: Seasonality, competitiveness and quality of life*. Wallingford: CAB International, pp. 106–116.

Ramkissoon, H. (2017). Hospitality consumers' decision-making. In D. Gursoy (ed.) *Routledge handbook of hospitality marketing*. Oxon: Routledge.

Ramkissoon, H. and Mavondo, F.T. (2015). The satisfaction – Place attachment relationship: Potential mediators and moderators. *Journal of Business Research*, **68**(12), pp. 2593–2602.

Ramkissoon, H., Mavondo, F.T. and Uysal, M. (2018). Social involvement and park citizenship as moderators for quality-of-life in a national park. *Journal of Sustainable Tourism*, **26**(3), pp. 341–361.

Ramkissoon, H. and Uysal, M. (2011). A cross-cultural comparison of tourists' cultural behavioural intentions. *e-Review of Tourism Research*, **9**(5), pp. 190–220.

Ramkissoon, H. and Uysal, M. (2014). Authenticity as a value co-creator of tourism experiences. In N.K. Prebensen, J.S. Chen and M. Uysal (eds.) *Creating experience value in tourism*. Wallingford: CABI, pp. 113–124.

Ramkissoon, H., Uysal, M. and Brown, K. (2011). Relationship between destination image and behavioral intentions of tourists to consume cultural attractions. *Journal of Hospitality Marketing & Management*, **20**(5), pp. 575–595.

Reid, S. and Arcodia, C. (2002). Understanding the role of the stakeholder in event management. *Sport & Tourism*, **7**(3), pp. 20–22.

Richards, P. and Ryan, C. (2004). The Aotearoa traditional Maori performing arts festival 1972–2000. A case study of cultural event maturation. *Journal of Tourism and Cultural Change*, **2**(2), pp. 94–117.

UNESCO. (2008). *Intangible cultural heritage: Baul songs*. Retrieved from: https://ich. unesco.org/en/RL/baul-songs-00107 (accessed: the 09th May, 2018).

UNESCO. (2013). *Intangible cultural heritage: Traditional art of Jamdani weaving.* Retrieved from: https://ich.unesco.org/en/RL/traditional-art-of-jamdani-weaving-00879 (accessed: the 09th May, 2018).

UNESCO. (2016). *Intangible cultural heritage: Mangal Shobhajatra on Pahela Baishakh.* Retrieved from: https://ich.unesco.org/en/RL/mangal-shobhajatra-on-pahela-baishakh-01091 (accessed: the 09th May, 2018).

UNESCO. (2017). *Intangible cultural heritage: Traditional art of Shital Pati weaving of Sylhet*. Retrieved from: https://ich.unesco.org/en/RL/traditional-art-of-shital-pati-weaving-of-sylhet-01112 (accessed: the 09th May, 2018).

Yang, L. (2011). Ethnic tourism and cultural representation. *Annals of Tourism Research*, **38**(2), pp. 561–585.

Yang, L., Wall, G. and Smith, S.L. (2008). Ethnic tourism development: Chinese Government Perspectives. *Annals of Tourism Research*, **35**(3), pp. 751–771.

5 Malana heritage village

The gateway for great tourism events

Shikha Sharma

Introduction

India is a diverse land. It has treasure of mesmerising places and rich cultural heritage. Each culture has its uniqueness and diversity in Indian context. This is the best aspect of Indian heritage and it shows unity in diversity. In this diversity of cultures there is a heritage village in the Himalayas known as the 'Athens of the Himalayas'. It is the oldest democracy of the world and often referred to as the Lost World. This is the heritage village of Malana. Even today, in this time of technology and globalisation this village is untouched by the the outside. It is a place which manages its own affairs even today. Malana is shadowed by the majestic peaks of 'Chandrakhani' and 'Deotibba'. It stands amidst the Himalayas fiercely and silently guarding its own culture. This chapter outlines religious, social, economic and environmental aspects followed by importance analysis of festivals in this part of the world.

The culture and tourism events of Malana

The culture of Malana is unique and world renowned. The Malanis (the inhabitants of Malana) consider themselves pure and they do not allow outsiders to touch the walls or belongings of the natives. Malanese are considered as the descendants of Alexander and their rituals involve purity and traditions. Natives of Malana have their own religious beliefs. Apart from their undying faith in 'Shiva', they believe in their 'Devta', the 'Jamlu Rishi'. It is said that the sage from the 'Puranas' once inhabited the land and laid the foundation of the democracy, which still works as a fully functional parliamentary system. The people of Malana have deep faith in their judicial system. The judicial system of Malana contrasts itself from the Indian judicial system. In case of any conflict and its resolution they cut the right foreleg of each lamb one and a half inch deep, stuff it with poison and sew it back with the help of needle and thread. The person whose lamb dies first is implied to lose the judgement. It is believed that the decision is taken by their Devta.

The social structure of Malana is unique in many senses. The society is not open for change and considers all others to be inferior. The 'Jamblu Devta' governs the Malana society. The village administration is democratic. The society worships the devil and the festivals are quite strange and unique from rest part of India.

The festivals of Malana are a way to celebrate life. They showcase the liveliness of the natives and their instinct to celebrate life and culture. The Malan's festivals are unique and thrilling. The valley celebrates two major festivals, Fagli and Shaun are the major festivals. The Fagli festival is celebrated in February and Shaun is celebrated in August.

A torchlight procession in Malana village evokes an imagery of exoticism of the Orient. One can be hoodwinked in relating this fiery congregation with the infamous Ku Klux Klan. Take a second look and a group of villagers is seen rejoicing the 'Fagdi Mela', one of their two biggest festivals. In Fagli festival a mask dance is performed, as the festival is celebrated with dance and strange rituals. This 'Mask Dance festival' is an occasion when everybody takes a bath and wear a devil mask on his/her face. A group of people wearing nothing but cannabis leaves and demon-like masks dance around the houses spreading cow dung, which provides insulation from the cold as well. Another interesting aspect of the festival is the procession for Emperor Akbar.

The local men and women, dressed in the traditional attire consisting of 'Chola Kalgi' (round cap) and tight pyjamas, take to dancing around a fire. The drums and flute are played to propitiate the local fire god. The glimpse of men dancing while holding fire-torched sticks is an incredible sight. An ancient ritual is followed in Malana and Tosh. The entire village comes out at night with their fire-torched pole to appease the local fire god. On this night they sacrifice a goat to Banasura Rakshasha. The animal sacrifice is a purification custom which is common in this area. The meat of the animal feeds the entire community.

Malana is not Shangri-la, with its brutal winters, closed social norms, and difficult interactions with the outside world. One can believe that nothing good can come from this hamlet except a high quality cannabis, but looking back at their festive spirit, there is something which attract the tourist to these people after all.

As the name suggests, Phagli fair falls during the month of Phalgun (i.e. the second half of February and first half of March). Phagli is celebrated in most of the villages of Kullu valley but it holds a very important place amongst the people of village Malana. It depicts the victory of good over evil and shows the struggle between God and the devil for supremacy. Ultimately, God emerges victorious. A person is disguised as a demon by putting a mask on his face and tying some grass around his body. God is represented by a 'gur' (God's spokesman). They perform special dances called 'Deo Khel' (acted upon by the gur) and 'Raksh Khel' (performed by the person who is impersonating the demon). The demon was known as 'Tundi Raksh' who used to trouble the people living between Malana and Archhandi villages. He was finally killed by Manu Rishi and Shandalya Rishi (sages).

To commemorate this event, the fair is held in Malana, Jana, Soil and Halan (villages) and in all the temples of Jamlu. Yellow barley grass is grown by the people before the festival. This grass is grown under shade in their houses and then worn by the villagers in the form of garlands. Some people simply wear it on their caps during the fair.

Malanis admire their culture, customs and religious beliefs. They generally do not like to change though some traces of modernisation are visible. People in

Malana consider all non-Malani to be inferior and consequently untouchable. Visitors to Malana town must pay particular attention to stick to the prescribed paths and not to touch any of the walls, houses or people there. If this does occur, visitors are expected to pay a forfeit sum, which will cover the sacrificial slaughter of a lamb in order purify the object that has been made impure. Malani people may touch impure people or houses as long as they follow the prescribed purification ritual before they enter their house or before they eat. Malanis may never accept food cooked by a non-Malani person, unless they are out of the valley (in which case their Devta cannot see them). Malanis may offer visitors food but all utensils will have to undergo a strict purification ritual before they can be used again.

Malana's crème has a notorious legacy in international stoner culture. It has won the Best Hashish title twice, in 1994 and 1996, at *High Times* magazine's Cannabis Cup. Marijuanaphiles the world over have since made this region a popular weed-tourist destination, branded in travel and ganja-hunting literature as the exotic and alluring 'Malana and the Magic Valley'. It was inevitable that the farmers would start to realise the global potential of their plants – and that the cops would take any and all measures to prevent these rural agriculturalists from increasing production. The most effective tool in authorities' arsenal is satellite technology, but the farmers have found a workaround.

The 'Phagli festival' is celebrated every year in Himachal Pradesh with much fanfare. Visitors throng the villages of Himachal Pradesh to partake in the festivities. The festival provides the perfect escape from the humdrum of daily life. Locals find a relief from the monotonous existence and partake in the festivities to celebrate life, colour and happiness. Himachal Pradesh, which is rightly called an Abode of Clouds, forms the perfect backdrop for this marvellous festival. This land of exquisite beauty forms a fantastic setting for the Phagli fair as well. The festival of Phagli boasts of not just a fantastic location but also a foray into the lives of local villagers. It provides a wonderful ambience as well as a unique macroscopic view of the Indian traditions and culture. Locals as well as tourists gather every year to celebrate this unique festival and usher in the month of Phalgun – spring. The reasons behind this festival are numerous. The most commonly understood reason is obviously to celebrate spring, but there are other mythical and historical reasons behind this festival. The Phagli festival celebrates the essential victory of good over evil, the supremacy of divine powers over demons. It also commemorates the killing of a demon by the local god, who the local villagers prayed to for their safety.

The same way as the finest and most gorgeous things in the world are simply to be perceived and not to be seen and heard, quite the same way, the passion of spring is only to be felt and enjoyed thus. The Phagli Fair, with its unique intensity, its vibrant colours and warm hospitality is just like spring – magical and indescribable.

Month of celebration of festival

Every year, in the month of Phalgun, in the beautiful state of Himachal Pradesh, the Phagli Festival is celebrated with much fanfare. In fact, the name of the festival – Phagli – is derived from the name of this month of Phalgun. The Hindu month of Phalgun falls in the months of February–March according to the Roman calendar. This is the time of spring in the Indian subcontinent and the Phagli Festival is organised to celebrate the oncoming of the beautiful season of spring.

Each year, the Phagli Festival is organised with widespread merriment and great elaboration. Cheerful locals from the nearby villages drop by to take part in the extensive festivities. Men and women adorn their brightest costumes and visit the fair organised to commemorate the spring season, and carousing children enjoy the festival to its fullest.

The month of Phalgun which signals the end of winter and the commencement of spring is symbolic of growth. The Phagli Festival forms the perfect backdrop to celebrate the season of spring, which, for the most part, is synonymous with new life and fresh beginnings. Obviously then, it makes sense to celebrate these new beginnings with gaiety and extensive festivities, which the Phagli festival does with much panache.

Description of Phagli fair in Himachal Pradesh

The Phagli fair is one of the most important festivals of North India, especially for the locals of the state of Himachal Pradesh, which forms the perfect backdrop for this festival. Organised in Malana in Himachal Pradesh, this festival is a unique celebration of good over evil. During the festival, wearing yellow barley grass on one's clothing is customary and greeting fellow revellers involved offering this grass. The specialty of yellow barley is that it is grown entirely in shade.

One of the numerous legends associated with the festival is the story of the demon Tundi Rakshas. According to this legend, Tundi Rakshas was troubling the people of the villages Mala and Archhandi. The villagers prayed to Shandalya Rishi, who, in turn, called on the local god – Jamlu Devta – who finally killed the demon. During the Phagli fair, all the villagers from the nearby villages of Jana, Malana, Halan and Soil, get together and worship Jamlu Devta to commemorate this event. Irrespective of class or caste, everyone gathers together during the festival and there is an exchange of ideas along with entertainment and trade which is the staple in any fair.

During the festival, one can also buy local specialties; handmade cutlery items and utensils are a major hit with the visitors of the fair. Local photographs and art made in the traditional styles, along with pottery items and joy rides are a staple of the fair.

Importance of the event

It is one of the most historic and culturally most important events in Malana. It provides cultural ethos to the place. The festivals are a way to depict life, and what else can better depict the life of people of Malana than this festival. It is the main cultural event in their life. The importance of this festive event can be highlighted in the following ways:

This festival relieves Malanis from monotony of life: The normal day-to-day life of the locals is very monotonous. The women are busy with household work and men in fields. Women also accompany them in field for cultivation and harvesting. When this festival arrives it helps them to relieve from daily routes and engage in festive season and celebrations.

The festivals create an environment of cultural harmony – believe it or not culture is inseparable from life. For these people culture *is* the life. It is for their culture, tradition and heritage they do not intermingle with outside world. Fagli is a way to create an essence of cultural harmony and create an environment of a lifetime experience for the tourists.

The festivals teach the lesson to forget enmity and embrace one another in a bond of love. This can be easily seen on the day the festival is celebrated. The entire community gathers and unites together to forget enmity and embrace one another with open arms.

Moral, ethical, social values of life mix up with entertainment through this festival. Fagli highlights morality, ethical norms, and social value along with the dances and processions which is the major source of entertainment for the entire community.

Such events help to be closer to religion and culture. Fagli is a way of connecting the old generation to the new ones. It is a way to make the new generation aware about the religious and cultural aspects related to the fair and why it is so important for the locals. By understanding the social structure and the community background one can easily relate to the religion and culture.

Such events also help to promote peace and harmony. They help in developing harmonious relationship not only between the Malanis but also between the tourists and Malanese. Though they do not consider them to be one of them, it helps tourists to be one amongst them.

Fagli is a dynamic way of carrying the message of the past generations to the present ones and from the present to the future ones. The message is to spread the culture and tradition in the actual essence it has. Communal harmony is also boosted with such kind of events within a community. The entire community feels connected and together on such occasions. It shows how much they value their culture and traditions. Different aspects of the religion are also showcased in this way. The mythological aspect is highlighted in prime place and then come the various folklores, folk dances and folk songs which originate from such stories and inspirational stories from the mythologies. So it also helps in preserving our culture and heritage and provides an opportunity to gather for the betterment of the entire community. Such types of events are also stress relievers. They act as relieving from the day-to-day strains of life and mingling and meeting new and old members of the community.

Fagli spreads colour in the valley. It is colourful time in the valley, and Fagli adds colour to the culture of Malana. It is once-in-a-year opportunity for gathering of family and friends. The festival is not only a time to celebrate for humans but also cattle are involved in it. Special offerings are made to cattle by the head of the family after early morning prayers after taking a bath and worshipping the god. The poor are also fed in it.

It is a great way for cultural exchange. Many international tourists visit this place especially during this time of the year to view the colours of Malana in their topmost bliss. Social relationship and communication understandings also develop in such kind of events. Fagli creates an atmosphere of happiness all-around: A major advantage of celebrating a festival is that it helps to instil happiness amongst the people. The people visit one another or gather around at a particular place; it is also the best time for them to talk over and chill out in a relaxed environment. This is why Fagli serves as a welcome break from the mundane routine of performing household chores and field works to adding colours to the life.

Fagli also helps promote tourism. Festivals are celebrated to promote tourism, the traditional handicrafts, and the potential of the state as well as the unity in diversity of its people. So Fagli fulfils all these aspects in a better way.

Fagli teaches us to take care of the poor. At festival times a very important charity activity is feeding the poor and giving them alms. It serves as a wonderful gesture especially from the rich people to give back to the society. In a nutshell, the occasion increases the feeling of brotherhood amongst the neighbours as they meet and have a good time.

It is advantageous for local business. It is during festival times that tourists buy and spend a lot, whether it is on accommodation, food or hashish. It also helps to decorate the homes. It is during a festival that the shopkeepers have a gala time and they wait especially for these occasions to make a sound profit.

Fagli is the bond of love. The world is full of enmity and prejudices among the people as they try to compete with each other both in terms of wealth and fame. During the festival, they can meet and forge a bond of companionship and love. God has taught people to love and not indulge in blind hatred, therefore it is vital for them to assimilate the teachings and implement them in real life during the festival. It would go a long way in removing animosities from the prejudiced minds and make the world a better place.

The importance of Fagli in the life of Malanis is that it is a symbol of bringing harmony and peace in the society. It is the biggest tool of unity. Leaving all personal grievances behind, people from different corners of the society unite in a festive mood and only think about overall wellbeing. This is the time when societies forget about personal benefits and only concentrate on the purpose of celebration. The importance of festivals in life is that they help us to be in touch with our roots. Each of these festivals is based on some mythological story, or a specific reason to rejoice in the moment. Festivals in life bring happiness, fun and joy. To celebrate the special spiritual moment, people living in far countries assemble and unite with their families.

Any festival is not a ritual. They are not any social customs. They are ways to remember the sacrifices, good things our ancestors have done for us and offer our holy prayer to God. Festivals like Fagli represent the victory of good over evil. The importance of festivals in life is that they are the reason for localities being able to enjoy the colours of life. It bears the message of good will. Festivals can be social, religious and nationally important. Festivals are celebrated with enthusiasm. Social festivals are for social harmony. Religious festivals are of mythological origin. Celebrations of national festivals aim at national unity.

The other importance of Fagli in life is that it helps us forget our loss and temporarily get over the bitterness. The huge social gathering is really helpful for the refreshment of the soul and the mind. It helps to leave the unpleasant memories behind and make a fresh start. It makes local people proud of their unique customs and traditions and thus of their own democratic setup. The importance of festivals in life can't be underrated given the reason that they help us unite, be positive and get involved with each other. With a better understanding of the importance of Fagli in the lives of these people, only then can one try to understand the spiritual significance of the celebrations.

Fagli also helps in creating harmony with nature. The gods are worshipped and nature is allured. This also speeds up the economic development of the area. Today Malana is world known destination – on one hand due to its hashish and other due to the festival it celebrates in the month of February every year. International and national tourists from different parts of the world and country try to make it on the day which embarks the opening of this festival.

Conclusion

The fairs of the valley portray rich cultural heritage of the valley. These fairs carry enormous religious worth and preserve a rich heritage native's belief in divine powers. During these fairs, the spirit of Kullu is visible on the faces of happy people. These simple rural folks take delight in songs, dances, laughter and celebration. The people are in a happy and festive mood. They visit their relatives to greet them. On the day of fair, the guests are heartily welcomed and the hosts feel great honour in serving them with food and drinks. For local people, it is time to relax and enjoy with their friends and relatives. Phalgun month (mid-February and mid-March) marks the beginning of fairs and festivals in the valley. The fair of Phagli is held between mid-February to mid- March. The fair depicts the victory of sages Manu and Shandalya over the demon Tundi Raksh. From this day onwards, there are various fairs taking place at almost every village. Nowadays, these fairs also have economic importance besides religious significance. During these fairs, people buy and sell various articles of basic necessity. Even as the years have passed, people still celebrate these fairs with full enthusiasm and exuberance as it used to be in the good old days. These fairs will still remain an important aspect in the life of these people. Any fair always helps one to connect to God and do good deeds. India as a whole is rich in culture and diversity. It is known for various kinds of fairs and festivals held every year and throughout the year. The richness of culture makes India and Malana an unforgettable place to be and enjoy the cultural essence in each and every man and woman.

6 Role of information and communication technology in marketing and promoting tourism events of Rajasthan

Shruti Arora and Anukrati Sharma

Introduction

If a company wants to stay alive in a competitive market with constant development and change, and an economy in crisis, suppliers of tourism products and services need to know and predict changes in the motivations that determine tourists to buy a holiday package. A motive is an internal factor that arouses, directs and integrates a person's behaviour. The fields of event management and event tourism have grown dramatically since last few years. Events are an important motivator for increasing tourism, and they are also present in making destination development plans and tourism development strategies (Getz, 2008). People not only travel for leisure purpose to different places but also for a business purpose like workshops, conferences or specially to participate in an event they find interesting and knowledgeable and these people contribute directly or indirectly to the growth of tourist destination and event industry as a whole. As tourism is one of the greatest growing industries today, contained by the tourism industry events are getting more and more significant (Erfurt and Johnsen, 2003).

Events which are meaningfully targeted at the international tourism market may be explained as 'mega' by their size, attendance, target market, financial involvement, political effects, the extent of media coverage and impact on the economic and social fabric of the host community (Hall, 1992). Event tourism is systematic planning, development and marketing of festivals and special events as tourist attractions, image-makers, catalysts for infrastructure and economic growth, and animators of built attraction. Tourism management deals with tourism enlargement based on analysing the behaviour and inspiration of all kinds of tourists. And event management deals with event marketing, design and managing of an event. Moreover, it tries to understand the event experiences and to manage them. Hence, event tourism is the core of the two sectors. In other words, event tourism aims at full exploitation of the capabilities of events to achieve tourism development of host communities (Getz, 1997). Marketing of events forms an integral part of the event management, which deals with various aspects of organisation and event management. (Trost et al., 2012).

Rajasthan, one of the most popular national as well as international traveller destinations, witnesses a huge inflow of domestic and foreign tourists every year

(Sharma, 2013). The sunny weather of Jodhpur, the beautiful dunes of the Thar Desert, the amazing camel rides of Jaisalmer, the mouth-watering delicacies of Bikaner, the Pushkar animal fair – all are some of the attractive offerings Rajasthan has for its visitors. There are innumerable tourist places to visit in Rajasthan. Every place has something to offer to its guests. All the events organised in the state display the state's legacy, colourful artefacts, delicious food, traditional Rajasthani attire, folk songs, folk dance and various interesting competitions.

As opposite to resort holidays, cultural and heritage attractions are getting higher popularity, and tourists are more interested in getting an authentic experience (Getz, 2008). Tourists get an opportunity to witness different colours of the state through its events. This makes the tourists crowd into Rajasthan during the time of various events. The strong war in today's business environment means that tourism businesses have to work tough to maintain and develop their competitiveness. The success of a business depends on its ability to obtain and utilise updated information to assist its management and marketing processes. Hence, information technology (IT) helps the organisation to handle information with passion, and influences business competitiveness through assisting decision makers to make appropriate investments and decisions. IT also helps to meet the demands for timely and accurate information by customers and plan further for their visits. Therefore, the advancement and expansion in technology that has occurred on a global scale, studying the role of Information and Communication technology (ICT) on tourism events are relevant and also to learn the various events that are being promoted through ICT.

Review of literature

Arora (2017) enlightens on the fact that events are playing an increasingly important role in the marketing and communications mix. Although organising an event is a difficult task for events of any kind, the organisers seek to attract fans and create an awareness of the event especially through Web marketing or making use of social media.

Tichaawa (2017) figures out that to increase their competitive position in the market, the tourism industry should incorporate ICT system strategically in their business practice to increase their performance, serve their target markets, improve their effectiveness, maximise their profitability, improve their services, and uphold their long-term profitability. Sairam et al. (2016) present an android mobile phone application to make it easier for a layman to plan an event in a hassle-free manner as event management is the application of project management to the creation and development of large or small-scale events such as festivals, conferences, concerts or conventions, This application will assist in planning a successful and fun event. This proves that there is a rapid growth technology.

Tom Twist (2016) said that it's seen by many that technology, namely social media, has created a global village, connecting everybody to everyone, everywhere. Some argue that this has made us less sociable, inhibiting face-to-face and physical interaction. However, the concept that globalisation and technology allow us to overcome the limitations of physical distance through our fingertips presents countless opportunities for the travel and tourism industry to flourish. Let's not forget that travel is essentially about connecting – places, people, experiences and memories. Websites, booking platforms, apps and using social media all provide the opportunity to engage and connect with customers on a variety of levels to allow an enhanced travel experience.

Ollo and Aramendia (2015) explain the use of ICT that seems an innovation in the companies for launching new products or services to the market, as well as improving or introducing new processes. Likewise, e-business increases the level of productivity, market share, and process innovation. The influence of ICTs on competitiveness, productivity, market share, and improvement are very unlike depending on the sub-sector. While in the accommodation and gastronomy sub-sectors ICTs have a great impact, in the travel agency sub-sectors they seem to promote an increase in market share and innovation, but it affects competition and productivity negatively.

It is essential that the current ICT should be reorganised and upgraded and flaw-less integration both internally and externally should be done to improve the tourism business operations. The incorporation of ICT in tourism would benefit both craftsman and customers bringing together other stakeholders on a common platform. The selection of the right information communications technology tool is very important to match the customer requirements with service dimensions. ICT's integration provides a power tool that brings advantages in promoting and intensifying the tourism industry (Bethapudi, 2015).

Research done by Egresi and Kara (2014) highlights the motives of tourists to attend the events. Accordingly, there is the subsistence of event motivations that are commonly valid. With some minor changes reflecting the nature of the festival or event or reflecting totally different geographical characteristics of the event place, this balance of motivations might then be simply transferred from one location to another, and it's valid for both large-scale and small-scale events in developed and developing countries. To magnetise potential tourists, exquisite communication strategies are needed, and in this digitalised world, it is necessary for the tourism industry to focus on ICTs and especially the Internet as tools of international communication. As well as bringing a better quality of service to the tourism industry, the Internet has pulled down prices, made information widely available, and allowed sellers and buyers to connect more easily and make transactions (Meriague, 2014).

Stephen and Hariharan (2014) explain events as an important marketing communication tool. Events can help in reinforcing the brand image by creating a long-lasting impression in the mind of the customers and through events image building, brand repositioning, add-on features, and displays can be accomplished. Jackson (2013) explains in his book that communication is important to how events endorse themselves to key audiences, but at the same time events can also be used by others for communicating some messages. While promoting an event online, there needed to be clarity on the meaning of the Internet and identified eight different modalities, like websites, e-mail, e-newsletters, micro blogs, social networking sites, intranets, extranets and weblogs.

Quinnan (2013) concludes that social media has changed the online marketing world forever. Event organisers continue to use these social sites as marketplaces for networking and expansion of their company. Whether the event company uses Twitter, Instagram or Facebook etc. they must have better understanding of how to utilise and benefit from these social media avenues and try to develop a strategy that is catered toward the target audience accordingly. Social media marketing campaigns need to be addressed from a psychological angle that permits marketers to see how consumers respond to the event as a product and the marketers themselves, as people. This new media was highlighted by Bartoletti (2013) as social media like Facebook, Twitter, Instagram etc.

In continuation, integrated new media marketing as given by Bartoletti (2013) is as follows:

Media	Purpose	Example
Facebook	dialogue development	asking questions, requesting feedback
Twitter	short text updates	publishing scoreboard, event-related news
Instagram	image upload	posting pictures of events or functions
Youtube	video supporter for other media platforms	uploading videos

Figure 6.1 Integrated new media marketing
(Source: Bartoletti, 2013)

Etiosa (2012) observed that event tourism is a sector that has all the potential of developing any tourism destination, or host community/city. It is like a tool used in placing a destination at a level where other nationalities and nationals want to imagine with. A host community can have an impact on hosting the events socio-culturally, environmentally, cost-effectively and politically. Additionally, there has to be a lot of teamwork among the organisers, associations and interest groups concerned within the hosting of events in the community so that there could be more commitment, keenness and focus towards the goals and objectives of these events and therefore the aspirations of the people for which the events are meant.

According to the authors of this chapter, IT is regularly reshaping the basic structure of tourism industry and society. Therefore it is advantageous for tourism managers to be aware of the recent changes in IT and their relationship with customer service to promote events and attract more tourists. Also IT development is more sophisticated, so the policymakers may find increasing difficulty in selecting, analysing, implementing, and operating new IT systems. The help of technology and using social media as a platform for marketing and promoting the events gives tourists more information about the local traditions, food and lifestyle of a particular place and also a reflection of the culture of the state that creates curiosity to visit a particular event and destination. Therefore, event marketing needs proper attention so as to inform the public at the right time, in a correct manner with proper advertising. More tourists indirectly help in revenue generation.

Methodology

The presented chapter aims at understanding past and current research so that a few guidelines for future studies can be given, and therefore understand the tourism events with their marketing and promotion. To fulfil this motive, it was decided to examine as many articles as possible to discover several areas. The study is done by secondary data like the research papers, articles, news, and blogs that were published by major tourism and hospitality, information technology, events and various marketing journals, newspapers and magazines between 2012 and 2017 and on which content analysis is done. During the examination, the researcher read the abstract with the full paper to determine the conclusion of the study. The objective of the study is to explore the role of IT with its applications to promote tourism products, to know how IT acts as a platform for events, to learn various motivational factors for attending an event and how ICT helps in marketing and promoting the events.

Impact on tourism events through information technology

Accompanying the technological uprising, there are many new opportunities and challenges for the tourism industry. In other words, information technology has become fundamental and lifeblood to the ability of the industry to operate successfully and competitively.

A tourist before going for a pleasure or vacation trip searches the Internet to gather necessary information and also to know about the experience of various other people who have already visited a particular place from various social networking sites like Facebook, Instagram etc. The Internet is now firmly established as a marketing tool and serves as an integral part of the marketing mix.

The tourism department of various states with the assistance of social media experts is launching various promotional campaigns on the social media circuit. The campaign initially focuses on imparting information to see places in popular tourist cities which will be uploaded to premier social media sites as Facebook, Twitter, Instagram and Google plus etc. All hotels and restaurants of the city along with uploading their details and pictures will promote these destinations. In some specific ways, information technology can impact tourism as presented in Figure 6.2

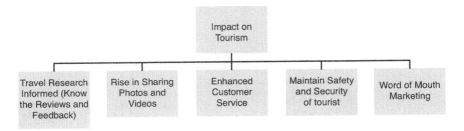

Figure 6.2 Here are few ways that information technology has impacted on tourism
(Source: the authors)

For example, to know the impact of ICT on tourism, according to Eventbrite (2018), Pinterest is a uniquely visual platform with 175 million monthly active users, 81 per cent of whom are women. Most popular among well-educated women of all ages and higher income levels, it is a good platform to encourage craft fairs, fashion events or food festivals etc and attract tourists. As the tourism sector must know, a woman plays an influential role in making vacation decisions. Also among 250 million monthly strong users (40 per cent of which use the platform daily), LinkedIn is exclusive among the top social networks as a proficient networking platform. It is a great fit for expected attendees of seminars, conferences, training, or educational events. And sometimes people plan a business trip with a family trip. And with above 2 billion monthly active users, Facebook is the most popular social network across ages, genders and occupation and income levels. Anyone can invite everyone to their events.

General aspects of tourist motivation – factors and classifications

There are numerous classifications of motivational factors given by many persons. In, 'Consumer Behaviour in Tourism' by Swarbrooke and Horner (2004), two classifications are projected. The first divides tourist motivations into two categories: motivations that guide a person to decide to travel and motivations that lead a person to select a particular holiday, in a certain destination, at a certain period. The second classification is more complex and is accepted by many researchers. According to it, the motivational factors are:

i   Psychological (relaxation, exercise and health);
ii   Emotional (nostalgia, romance, adventure, fantasy, spiritual needs);
iii Personal (visits to relatives and friends, new friends);
iv   Personal development (raising the level of knowledge, learning a new skill);
v   Status (fashion, exclusivity, getting a good offer);
vi   Culture (sightseeing, the experience of other cultures).

According to Crompton and McKay (1997), motivations of tourism signify an active progression of internal factors such as needs/wants that create an emotional and mental state of tension within individuals. Each traveller is different and has different factors that motivate them, but the most important factors that determine the motivation to travel for an individual are (Figure 6.3):

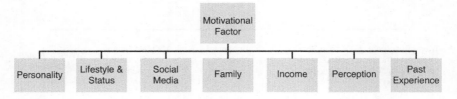

Figure 6.3 Factors determining an individual's motivation to travel
(Source: the authors)

In most situations, more than one factor is responsible while making the decision. Sometimes even deciding a tourist destination also depends on the age segments. Teenagers, young people, parents, and elders have different reasons to undertake a journey. So, after knowing the travelers' motivations, marketers can easily establish customer wants and design the tourist offer and promote them accordingly (Mahika, 2011).

Over time, an increasing number of destinations have opened up and invested in tourism growth, evolving modern tourism into a key driver for socio-economic progress, through the formation of jobs and enterprises, infrastructure development, and the export income earned. Tourism has become one of the major international trade categories, 'Incredible India'. India has a massive potential for tourism and has been marketing its tourism potential aggressively year after year. Now the event organisers are developing historical and cultural themes during an event to attract visitors and creating a cultural image in the host cities (Becker, 2014).

IT has played an important role in the tourism industry over the last decade. Technology has helped reduce costs and improve operational efficiency, services and customer experience (Law et al., 2009). Both customers and businesses can benefit from improved communication, reservations and guest service systems. The few examples that IT continues to improve the tourism industry are as follows.

The Internet and marketing

The Internet has a powerful impact on tourism. This includes looking at pictures of the events organised for tourists and reviews from past guests. It is imperative for a business to effectively utilise online advertising, social media, and blogs to convenience their customers, especially when there is much competition. While travelling also, tourists are having more authentic experiences and are looking for ways to experience cities like locals do; they increasingly want to live like a local for the duration of their trip with the help of technology (Bock, 2015).

Mobile telecommunication

Mobiles and smartphones have replaced large desktop computers. This is helpful, because travellers allow customers in getting full updated knowledge about the events organised in that particular area and also the actual timings. The various tourism events that are promoted with the help of information technology to attract tourism at various places like in Rajasthan are shown in Figure 6.4.

These various events are organised at different times for the tourist. Many people interested accordingly attend these events for their fun, entertainment, learning cultural knowledge and also to take parts in these events. Over the past few years, Rajasthan has hosted various events ranging from dance or music festivals to ballooning events and literature gala. Therefore, the tourists get a closer view of the countryside and the people, and witness a great admirable experience or different colours of the state through its events.

Figure 6.4 Various tourism events promoted through ICT
(Source: modified from Rajasthan Tourism, 2018)

In fact, for tourists interested in an adventure, parasailing and ballooning are two annual events that are organised in Jaipur, Jodhpur, Jaisalmer and Pushkar to attract a large number of tourists. The atmosphere of Rajasthan is more peaceful and suitable for organising events, business and conferences due to forts and palaces that have a trendy and graceful appearance. The most popular cities that have a good arrangement for MICE activities and are close to centres of tourist attractions are Jaipur, Udaipur and Jodhpur.

Conclusion and recommendations

This chapter aimed to examine the development and expansion of technology that has turned the whole world into a global village. For this purpose, research done by different people has been studied and concluded that with the help of information and communication technology while travelling also, tourists are progressively able to get more knowledge about a particular event, as tourists want to live, stay and enjoy more like a local citizen during the period of their trip. Tourists are all over the world. The global village we live in today means everyone can get information about everything – all they need is a good quality broadband connection! It is mandatory to make full use of information and communication technology, to inform timely with a proper message to the tourist about a particular event; this also helps in building an image about a particular destination.

Rajasthan is well known on the world map for its tourism products and hospitality (Sharma, 2013). Jaipur, Udaipur, and Jodhpur, being known as tourist destinations and having various forts and heritage properties, organises a huge number of events. If all these tourism events are planned carefully, they offer abundant entertainment to the tourist as they bring together a varied range of individuals that also helps to make the destination a landmark, which may be for fun, fashion, shopping, entertainment or a bag full of all these.

One thing that technology does well is connect things. Developments in technology have led to big changes in the way that customers use it to enhance their full travel experience. Event organisers can take full advantage for promoting their tourism events while making a better use of technology i.e. promoting tourism events through creating the best content using highly accessible techniques to facilitate communications, influence and interaction with peers and with public audiences, typically via the Internet or mobile communications networks. The event organisers can adopt guerrilla marketing strategies which involve the use of unorthodox and sometimes unusual methods whereby marketers try to get attention for their events in front of a built-in audience. A new concept – eye tracking technique – should be adopted by the event organisers which is a sophisticated device that tracks and records where people look and how they move their gaze. Event apps are an innovative tool that makes things easier, quicker and more interactive about the event. If the event is promoted through the means of information technology, then content marketing strategies can be adopted; one can also create a blog for suggestions and feedback. Safety and security measures for tourists, especially for females and children, should be taken into consideration by the event organisers throughout the event (Arora, 2017).

Hence, one must embrace newly developed and effective information technology solutions to run travel operations smoothly and efficiently. At the same time, the prime focus should be on providing excellent customer service. For all these, the only answer is to embrace best and updated information technology to give customer-focused travel solutions and aim at providing a one-stop solution for all travel-related services through information technology. Further study can be done on the role of government in marketing and promoting the tourism events in Rajasthan and comparison of various tourism events in other states of India. Research can be conducted on the role of events in destination marketing.

References

Arora, S. (2017). *Growth &development of event management sector in Rajasthan: An evaluation.* Unpublished PhD thesis. University of Kota, Rajasthan.

Bartoletti, M. (2013). *The importance of social media in their contribution to the marketing of sport events*. Unpublished Bachelor of Business Administration in Tourism and Hospitality Management thesis. Modul Vienna University, Vienna.

Becker, P. (2014). *The different types of tourists and their motives when visiting Alaska during the Iditarod*. Unpublished Master thesis in Tourism Studies. The University of Tromso, Tromso.

Bethapudi, A. (2015). Role of ICT in promoting a rural tourism product. *Journal of Tourism and Hospitality*, **4**(3), pp. 1–3.

Bock, K. (2015). The changing nature of city tourism and its possible implications for the future of cities. *European Journal of Future Research*, **3**(1), pp. 1–8. Retrieved from: https://link.springer.com/content/pdf/10.1007%2Fs40309-015-0078-5.pdf (accessed: the 20th April, 2018).

Crompton, J.L. and Mckay, S.L. (1997). Motives of visitors attending festivals and events. *Annals of Tourism Research*, **24**(2), pp. 425–439.

Egresi, I. and Kara, F. (2014). Motives of tourists attending small-scale events: The case of three local festivals and events in İstanbul, Turkey. *GeoJournal of Tourism and Geosites*, **14**(2), pp. 93–110.

Erfurt, R.A. and Johnsen, J. (2003). Influence of an event on a destination's image—The case of the annual meeting of the World Economic Forum (WEF) in Davos/Switzerland. *Tourism Review*, **58**(4), pp. 21–27.

Etiosa, O. (2012). *The impacts of event tourism on host communities. Case: The City of Pietarsaari*. Retrieved from: www.theseus.fi/bitstream/handle/10024/43714/omoregie_etiosa.pdf?sequence=1 (accessed: the 20th April, 2018).

Eventbrite. (2018). *The top 6 networks for social media event marketing*. Retrieved from: www.eventbrite.com/blog/social-media-event-marketing-ds00/(accessed: the 20th April, 2018).

Getz, D. (1997). *Event management and event tourism*. New York: Cognizant Corporations Corp, p. 16.

Getz, D. (2008). Event tourism: Definition, evolution and research. *Tourism Management*, **29**(3), pp. 403–428.

Hall, C. (1992). *Hallmark tourism events: Impacts, management and planning*. London: Belhaven Press.

Jackson, N. (2013). *Promoting and marketing events: Theory and practice*. Oxon: Routledge.

Law, R., Leung, R. and Buhalis, D. (2009). Information technology applications in hospitality and tourism: A review of publications from 2005 to 2007. *Journal of Travel and Tourism Marketing*, **26**(5–6), pp. 599–623.

Mahika, E. (2011). Current trends in tourist motivation. *Cactus Tourism Journal*, **2**(2), pp. 15–24.

Meriague, O. (2014). *The role of ICT in the tourism industry*. Retrieved from: www.moroccoworldnews.com/2014/01/121365/the-role-of-ict-in-the-tourism-industry/ (accessed: the 20th April, 2018).

Ollo, A. and Aramendia, M. (2015). *ICT impact on tourism industry*. Retrieved from: www.researchgate.net/publication/268563002_ICT_impact_on_tourism_industry (accessed: the 20th April, 2018).

Quinnan, K. (2013). *A guide to event promotion: Internet marketing for a live musical event in Las Vegas*. Retrieved from: https://digitalscholarship.unlv.edu/cgi/viewcontent.cgi?referer=www.google.co.uk/&httpsredir=1&article=3046&context=thesesdissertations (accessed: the 20th April, 2018).

Rajasthan Tourism. (2018). *About us*. Retrieved from: http://tourism.rajasthan.gov.in/ (accessed: the 20th April, 2018).

Sairam, S., Suresh, S., Hegde, S. and Shaikh, B. (2016). Event management an Android application. *International Journal of Innovative Research in Science, Engineering and Technology*, **5**(3), pp. 63–84.

Sharma, A. (2013). A SWOT analysis of Rajasthan tourism. *SAJMR Spectrum: A Journal of Multidisciplinary Research*, **2**(6), pp. 17–28.

Stephen, A. and Hariharan. (2014). *A book on event management*. New Delhi: Himalaya Publishing House, pp. 27–28.

Swarbrooke, J. and Horner, S. (2004). *Consumer behavior in tourism*. Oxford: Butterworth Heinemann.

Tichaawa, T. (2017). The impact of Information Communication Technologies (ICTs) on tourism businesses in East London, South Africa. *Acta Universitatis Danubius*, **13**(13), pp. 18–29.

Trost, K., Klaric, S. and Dropulic, M. (2012). Events as a framework for tourist destination branding: Case studies of two cultural events in Croatia. *TURIZAM*, **16**(2), pp. 65–77.

Twist, T. (2016). *The impact of technology on the travel and tourism sector*. Retrieved from: www.linkedin.com/pulse/impact-technology-travel-tourism-sector-tom-twist (accessed: the 20th April, 2018).

7 Social media impact on tourism events

A case study in Jordan

Ahmad R. Albattat, Salam Tadros,
Karen Miranda-Fernandez

Introduction

Social media platforms are a dominant digital communication channel through which customers are kept informed, learn about new things, share information on and interact with brands they consider, purchase and evaluate (Chappuis et al., 2011; Qualman, 2013). In 2014, more than 2.7 billion people globally are online which is equivalent to approximately 40 per cent of the world's population (ICT, 2014). Therefore, social media is gaining prominence as an element of destination marketing organisation (DMO) and marketing strategy. It provides DMOs with a tool to reach a global audience with limited resources.

Social media are changing the way society consumes and contributes to the creation of information. Technology now allows individuals to easily contribute their thoughts, opinions and creations to the Internet. This has radically altered the way in which information is created and disseminated (Buhalis and Law, 2008; Gretzel et al., 2000; Senecal and Nantel, 2004; Xiang and Gretzel, 2010). Consumers are increasingly using social media sites to search for information and turning away from traditional media, such as television, radio and magazines (Mangold and Faulds, 2009). The advent of social media has transformed traditional one-way communication into multi-dimensional, two-way, peer-to-peer communication (Berthon et al., 2008).

According to Safko and Brake (2009:6) social media refers to "Activities, practices, and behaviours among communities of people who gather online to share information, knowledge, and opinions using conversational media". Conversational media are Web-based applications that make it possible to create and easily transmit content in the form of words, pictures, videos and audios. Social media also refers to 'participatory', 'conversational', and 'fluid' online communities (Qualman, 2013; Tuten, 2008) focused on user-generated content (Buhalis and Law, 2008; Buss and Strauss, 2009; Ruzic and Bilos, 2010; Xiang and Gretzel, 2010). It is considered an Internet-based application that conveys consumer-generated content (Blackshaw and Nazzaro, 2006). The applications refer to consumers' activities related to the Internet such as 'posting', 'tagging', 'digging', or 'blogging'. Consumer-generated content is considered "a mixture of fact and opinion, impression and sentiment, founded and unfounded tidbits, experiences, and even rumor" (Blackshaw and Nazzaro, 2006:4). It is created, disseminated and used by consumers and aimed at educating each other about products, brands, services and issues (Blackshaw and Nazzaro, 2006). One study revealed that the chief motivations of consumers for posting content on social media were found to consist of a hunger for fame, the urge to have fun, and a desire to share experiences with friends (Bughin, 2007).

Thevenot (2007) shows that as social media rises in popularity, users gain more power as the authority of marketers and institutions declines. In relation to tourism, marketers and institutions no longer have ultimate control over the image of their destination or product. Web 2.0 facilitates the integration of the following five functional properties: information representation, collaboration, communication, interactivity and transactions (Gretzel et al., 2000). Current campaigns and initiatives suggest that a limited number of tourism organisations are beginning to study social media and develop strategies to use it to their advantage. Tourism organisations that do not adopt social media will lack a competitive advantage (Wang et al., 2002). However, what could be more harmful than not understanding or adopting social media practices in a poor manner (Wang et al., 2002)? Hence, a clear understanding of why and how social media function is vital to tourism destination marketing.

Leung et al. (2013) produced a review of the literature related to social media use in the fields of tourism and hospitality. They found that research centred on the consumer generally involved the travelers' use of social media during the travel planning process. Research focused on the suppliers commonly involved promotion, business management and market research. Furthermore, despite an observed increase in attention the scholarly community has paid to social media, a trend that has undoubtedly continued, several studies noted that the industry has been slow to use social media effectively and capitalise on the opportunities it offers. The advent of the Internet and social media have impacted the methods of marketing communication, for example, Facebook, Twitter and YouTube (Evans, 2010). It has become a powerful source of 'word of mouth' communication; because social media provides sites for consumers to share their experiences and opinions with others, it can have a positive influence on consumers if there are satisfied customers or a negative influence on others if there are unsatisfied customers (Trusov et al., 2009). In addition, social media influences the purchase decision-making process.

Social media has already been recognised as a new form of word-of-mouth (WOM) communication which is highly influential on consumers' decision-making process (Hills and Cairncross, 2011). In fact, for high involvement products, 50 per cent of purchases originate from WOM sharing. Digital knowledge-sharing and gathering on multiple social channels encompasses the customer's 'digital journey' where the brand experience is social and emotional, as well as transactional. Common social channels include Facebook, Twitter, Wikipedia, Pinterest and TripAdvisor, as well as a myriad of mobile applications (apps) for smartphones. These channels and others have altered the marketing landscape from a traditional one-to-many broadcast of messages to an inclusive many-to-many conversation accelerating WOM influence on purchasing decisions. The new media, such as the Internet, social media and mobile phones, are increasingly replacing traditional mass media (Bruhn et al., 2012). For example, in the tourism and hospitality industry, online hotel reviews are one of the most important forms of electronic word of mouth (eWOM). In total, 81 per cent of consumers find online user reviews to be an important information source when choosing between hotels, while 49 per cent add that they would not book a hotel without reviews (Boykin, 2015). Online reviews are seen as highly credible, with 88 per cent of travellers trusting them as much as personal recommendations from friends or family members (Anderson, 2010).

While the availability of social media is now widespread and companies in many industries are integrating social media into their communication strategies, little marketing research has been done to reveal the effects of social media interaction on consumer attitudes and behaviours and its underlying processes. Most of the existing research only deals with the characteristics of social media and how the differences from traditional media are challenging marketing strategies (Kietzmann et al., 2011). Customers now expect companies to have a social media presence, which adds brand credibility. Savvy companies position themselves in their customer's environments, and allocate marketing budgets to the digital economy. A recent social media marketing survey found that 92 per cent of brand managers felt social media was indispensable to their firm's marketing goals.

Tourism and culture

According to Robinson and Novelli (2005) tourism is defined as "Travel for pleasure; also the theory and practice of touring, the business of attracting, accommodating and entertaining tourists, and the business of operating tours. Tourism may be international, or within the traveler country". The World Tourism Organization defines tourism more generally, in terms which go "beyond the common perception of tourism as being limited to holiday activity only", as people "traveling to and staying in places outside their usual environment for not more than one consecutive year for leisure, business and other purposes" (UNWTO, 1995). Tourism can be domestic or international; international tourism has both incoming and outgoing implications on a country's balance of payments. Today, tourism is a major source of income for many countries, and affects the economy of both the source and host countries, in some cases being of vital importance

A review of the past literature on tourist motivation indicates that the analysis of motivations based on the two dimensions of push and pull factors have been generally accepted (Yuan and McDonald, 1990; Uysal and Hagan, 1993). The concept behind the push and pull dimension is that people travel because they are pushed by their own internal forces and pulled by the external forces of destination attributes. Most of the push factors which are origin-related are intangible or intrinsic desires of the individual travellers. Pull factors, on the contrary, are those that emerge as a result of the attractiveness of a destination as it is perceived by the travellers. They include tangible resources and travelers' perception and expectation such as novelty, benefit expectation and marketed image of the destination (Baloglu and Uysal, 1996).

According to UNWTO estimates, cultural tourism has been one of the market segments which have shown the highest rate of growth, representing one fifth of the tourism market. The prospects for the next two decades, given that certain source markets will be evolving, look very promising.

Culture is manifested through religion, festivals, costumes, cuisine, arts and crafts, architecture, music, dance, folklore and literature. It is also manifested in monuments and sites – built attractions which are testimonies to a people's history. The traveller who purposely travels to experience various cultures and to view monuments and sites as well as to attend festivals and religious events is what might be called the cultural tourist.

Culture is the lifeblood of tourism. People travel, not just to relax and recreate but also to satisfy their need for diversity and their curiosity on how other people live in environments different from their own. Other people's lifestyles are expressed through their religion, festivals, costumes, cuisine, arts and crafts, architecture, music and dance, folklore, and literature. These cultural manifestations differentiate one group of people from another. They make life colourful and interesting. People also travel for the specific purpose of visiting the great monuments and sites of the world such as the Angkor Wat in Cambodia; the Taj Mahal in India; the Great Wall of China or the Borobudur and the Prambanan in Indonesia. Thus, culture is manifested in both the living and dynamic aspects of a people's everyday life as well as in built heritage as monuments and sites. There are tourists who also travel for the specific purpose of attending religious and nonreligious festivals, art and museum exhibits, musical events (opera, concerts etc.) and theatrical presentations. Some tour operators in Europe refer to these trips are 'art holidays' or 'educational holidays'. All the previously mentioned activities describe what one may call 'cultural tourism'.

Silberberg (1995) defines cultural tourism, of which cultural heritage tourism is part, as visits by persons from outside the host community motivated wholly or in part by interest in historical, artistic, scientific or lifestyle/heritage offerings of a community, region, group or institution. Among the many attractions located on a tourism destination, cultural and historical attractions take a relevant position. Yeoman et al. (2004), Ritchie and Zins (1978), Tahana and Oppermann (1998), Zeppel and Hall (1992) believe that cultural tourism, in fact, is an increasing tourism segment, characterised by people wishing to visit places to know more about their history, lifestyle, natural resources, wine and food traditions, local identity and languages. According to the World Tourism Organization (UNWTO, 2013), global cultural holidays in 2009 were 375 million and in 2004 amounted to 40 per cent of the total international flows. The cultural attractions of a place help to distinguish the destination in the competitive market and allow tourists to live unique experiences (Munar and Ooi, 2012). Experiences, in fact, are emerging as distinct sources of value also in the field of cultural tourism, and this concept is becoming increasingly popular in the literature on cultural tourism (Cetin and Bilgihan, 2016; Radder and Han, 2015).

In cultural tourism, Jurowski (2009) found that the visit of art galleries affects the sense of learning and education of tourists, and that visiting cultural and historic sites is more related to the aesthetic experience, with a total involvement of visitors. Radder and Han (2015) found that cultural tourism experiences are strictly related to education and entertainment. According to Cetin and Bilgihan (2016), a survey on cultural tourists in Istanbul revealed that five main dimensions can affect cultural experiences at destination; these are: social interaction, local authenticity, local culture, service facilities and challenge. Social interaction is especially related to the friendliness and kindness of residents and to the positive relationships created with other tourists. Local authenticity refers both to the originality and the uniqueness of local resources, and to the ability of local resources to positively affect the mental state of tourists. Local culture regards everything that is part of the local culture of a destination and is composed by heritage, art, history, cultural events and architecture. These resources are considered an important part of the experience by tourists and have the potential to educate tourists while entertaining them (Cohen, 1979). Service facilities dimension is associated with the infrastructures and facilities able to create a positive environment for tourists, giving a sense of cleanliness, safety and familiarity. Finally, challenge is related to the sense of discovery and novelty due to the visit of resources that are different from those visited in the place of origin.

Despite the fact that tourism and cultural attractions are recognised to be the core components of a destination and their evaluation is very difficult for potential tourists, there are still only a few studies on the analysis of online reviews related to these attractions. Online reviews, in fact, help to know the strengths and weaknesses perceived by tourists and, consequently, allow improving service quality (Fang et al., 2016). Also owing to online reviews, it is also possible to monitor the reputation and image of the attraction, and to compare the competitive positioning of the attraction with other attractions at destination (Albarq, 2014; Zhu and Zhang, 2010). Finally, the knowledge of tourists' perceptions allows to define more detailed strategies: the quality perceived by tourists about a cultural attraction has a strong influence on their level of satisfaction and, consequently, on the decision to return to visit the attraction and the entire destination, and on the intentions to spread a positive WOM and eWOM (Buhalis, 1998; Litvin et al., 2008; Poon, 1993; Sotiriadis and van Zyl, 2013). Despite the importance of online reviews as tools to understand tourists' perceptions on cultural attractions, the studies on the relationships between tourists' experiences and cultural attractions through online reviews are still at a very early stage (Munar and Ooi, 2012).

Role of social media in tourism

The role of social media in tourism has been increasingly noted and researched as an emerging topic. Social media plays an increasingly important role in many aspects of tourism, especially in information searching and decision-making behaviours (Fotis et al., 2012) and tourism promotion (VTIC, 2012). Many countries regard social media as an important tool to promote their tourism industries, for example: Australia is encouraging the Australian tourism industry to positively embrace social media in promoting their business. Australian operators are being offered the chance to promote their tourism business or region using Tourism Australia's record breaking fan base by listing themselves in a 'things to do' section on its Facebook page (Zeng and Gerritsen, 2014). Meanwhile, Australian National Online Strategy Committee developed the 'Tourism e-kit' tutorials package, in which 'Social Media for Tourism' is the important component.

Marketing is no longer about the stuff that you make, but about the stories you tell; marketing message matters especially when using social media as a marketing tool. According to Sigala et al. (2012), the use of social media as part of the travel information search activity is becoming the norm. In the business perspective, social media are perceived as effective tools and fruitful platforms for deepening customer engagement and enhancing customer–business interactions. Since the hospitality industry is a very customer-centric industry, it prides itself by reaching out to its guests and providing a personalised experience. In traditional marketing, human lives are saturated by print media, radio and television and to which high cost and one-way communication is the downside. Social media encourages customer engagement, and it being on Web 2.0 promotes two-way traffic. It allows for a faster response and a lower cost investment than is typically achieved with traditional marketing. Through social media, consumers share experiences with and suggest ideas to others while developing new relationships within their communities. For this reason, many hospitality firms consider social media a powerful tool to enhance consumer loyalty and satisfaction. It comes as no surprise that the lodging industry is paying attention to the use of social media when it comes to marketing and engagement of guests. A survey showed that more than 90 per cent of hospitality businesses were using social media for business purposes (First Merchant Services and Coyle Hospitality Group, 2012).

According to Ayeh et al. (2013), tourists use social media to learn more about a destination, and to become increasingly aware and independent in making travel decisions. A fundamental part of social media in the Web 2.0 is represented by the dissemination of content generated by users (user-generated contents, UGC). This content is often represented by opinions and comments on products and services bought, or on experiences lived by the users. This content determines a spread of eWOM. In the tourism field, the most important forms of eWOM are the online reviews written on social networks and on travel communities by real and potential tourists. Online reviews are able to influence entire phases of the travel planning process, including pre-, during- and post-trips (Gretzel et al., 2000; Leung et al., 2013; Litvin et al., 2008). Tourists, in fact, are increasingly using online review websites to obtain advice and make decisions to plan their travel, obtain information during the visit, share their experience and leave comments about the destination (Cox et al., 2009; Fotis et al., 2012; Zeng and Gerritsen, 2014). This important role of social media has revolutionised not only the decision-making process of tourists but also the communication of tourism service providers with them, and consequently the marketing of tourism destinations.

Marketing mix

Marketing simplistically means putting the right product in the right place, at the right price, at the right time. Though this sounds like an easy enough proposition, a lot of hard work and research need to go into setting up this simple definition. And if even one element is off the mark, a promising product or service can fail completely and end up costing the company substantially. The use of a marketing mix is an excellent way to help ensure that putting the right product in the right place will happen. The marketing mix is a crucial tool to help understand what the product or service can offer and how to plan for a successful product offering. The marketing mix is most commonly executed through the Four Ps of marketing: price, product, promotion and place.

The concept of marketing mix originated in the 1950s; it was first published in the marketing literature in the 1960s (Borden, 1964). The most popular model of marketing mix, McCarthy in the 1970s (Anderson and Taylor, 1995), revolved around the Four Ps to determine a mix that satisfies consumer wants and needs and provides the firms with a competitive position in the market leading to long-term growth and profit. Academics and marketing practitioners point out that services differ from products; they are intangible, heterogeneous, perishable and insepa-rable from the service provider. Therefore, additional Ps have evolved to help create a comprehensive framework for marketing services known as the Eight Ps in a service business as: product, price, place, promotion, people, process, physical evidence and productivity (Grönroos, 1997).

Events

The events sector of the tourism industry is young, dynamic, growing and maturing at rapid rate. From its origin in North America and Europe, it is now a truly global sector of the tourism industry. The benefits of event management and event tourism are increasingly being realised by many developing countries. Events can be traced back to early history, when communities would gather for religious worship and celebration. Of course, these were not considered events at the time. As society started to create towns and social systems, event venues became an intrinsic dimension of the town planning process. Roman critics often included arenas and amphitheatres for shows and events, forums or marketplaces for trading and com-munity events, and shrines and churches for religious celebration were also evi-dent. As these facilities became embedded in social structures, they became a key part of town planning, and in Europe and Asia at least, they are an essential aspect of the layout and structure of modern towns and cities. The evolution of medieval town planning would create places for markets, religious activity and trade fairs – hence the term 'marketplace'. The location of these marketplaces in the city cen-tres would assist in providing events with an element of centrality to daily lives, a theme that continues to this day.

In the 18th and 19th centuries, the Industrial Revolution produced a wider range of products and equipment. The commensurate growth in the world trade led to the development of trade fairs and exhibitions. Enhanced transportation permitted people to travel further, facilitating growth of the hotel sector. Hotels soon built ballrooms and other facilities suitable for events. Event venues added a new dimension in the 1970s with the introduction of a new generation of large-scale, multi-purpose venues. The evolution of the events sector reflects the social, political, economic, environmental and technological growth of society. For these same reasons, the events sector will also change in the future (Robinson et al., 2010). To handle the confusion, Arcodia and Barker (2003) have categorised events into three main groups which are business events, cultural events and sporting events. Business events include conferences and trade fairs, while cultural events include festivals and exhibitions. The sporting games are the last group and include the Olympic Games, soccer world cups, car races and many other sporting events. These groupings seem to be appropriate as they encompass all sorts of events and allow the researcher to give the audience a more specific, categorised overview of events. A primary concern of an event entrepreneur or host organisation is whether an event is within budget and, hopefully, results in a surplus or profit. This is a simple matter of whether the income from sponsorship, merchandise and ticket sales exceeds the costs of conducting and marketing the event. However, from the perspectives of the host communities and governments, a wider range of economic impacts is often of equal or greater significance.

One of the most important impacts is the tourism revenue generated by an event. In addition to their spending at the event, external visitors are likely to send money on travel, accommodation, goods and services in the host city or region. This expenditure can have a considerable impact as it circulates through the local economy. Effective tourism promotion can result in visitors to the event extending their length of stay and visiting other regional tourism destinations and attractions. In addition to the tourism generated during the event, events may attract media coverage and exposure that enhance the profile of the host town or city, resulting in improved long-term tourism image and visitation (Allen et al., 2008).

Festivals

Towns, villages and cities are increasingly keen to share their culture, environment and spending opportunities with visitors by the promotion of festivals. The income that can be generated by festivals is clear but the true value of visitor spend is more complex to calculate with accuracy. Festivals have the potential to provide opportunities for sustainable local economic development (O'Sullivan and Jackson, 2002). Felsenstein and Fleischer (2003) believe that DMOs promote local cultural festivals as tourism attractions for they are felt to possess attributes that make them appealing to visitors. Like other cultural tourism products (Copley and Robson, 1996), these festivals can provide an opportunity to showcase the destination's rich intangible heritage, local traditions, ethnic backgrounds and cultural landscapes. Community festivals, in particular, celebrate both group and place identity (de Bres and Davis, 2001), leading Getz (1989:125) to observe that "their special appeal stems from the innate uniqueness of each event and their ambience which elevates them above ordinary life". As such, these events are thought to provide an opportunity for international tourists to experience authentic cultural ambience, meet local residents, and partake in something authentically indigenous (Getz, 1989).

Getz (1991) believed that festivals also need to satisfy a second aspect of sustainable tourism; they must be tourism attractions in their own right that appeal to non-local visitors. If they fail to appeal to tourists, then they cannot be called tourist attractions. Local leisure or recreational attractions may be the more appropriate term. In theory, some people assert that festivals can extend peak season or create new seasons (Derrett, 2004). Gunn (1998) as cited in Benckendorff and Pearce (2003) indicates that attractions serve two key functions in any destination. The most important is to act as a demand generator that induces visitation or causes tourists to extend their stays. Alternatively, they can have utility if they provide high quality experiences that enhance satisfaction levels.

Festival organisers often question the economic values of events (Gursoy et al., 2004), with many viewing the festival not as a money-making tourist attraction but as an enjoyable community-based event (de Bres and Davis, 2001). Festivals tend to be eclectic, narrowly focused on neighbourhoods or minority communities, very local in nature, and often celebrate highly personal events, albeit in a public forum. Festivals generally are viewed by their organisers and host communities as being social or cultural celebrations. More and more, they are also being viewed as tourist attractions which have a considerable economic impact on the surrounding region. Undoubtedly, the ability of festivals to become successful tourist attractions depends in part on their goals and the way in which they are managed (Frisby and Getz, 1989).

Pearce's (1991:46) definition of a tourist attraction is as "a named site with a specific human or natural feature which is the focus of visitor and management attention". Indeed, they are similar to other attractions in their impact on visitation. Tourism attraction systems theory illustrates that the more powerful the attraction, the greater its ability to draw visitors to, or retain them in a destination (McIntosh and Goeldner, 1990). Lesser attractions, on the other hand, may provide ancillary activities, but will do little to attract tourists. Attractions can, therefore, form an intrinsic part of a trip and be a major motivator for selecting a destination, or they can be optional, discretionary activities engaged in while at a destination.

The use of local festivals as an instrument for tourism development has gained worldwide momentum in recent years. While in some instances time-honored existing local cultural or religious events have been revived or repackaged as tourism events, in other cases new festivals have been invented and promoted for the singular purpose of drawing new visitors to a city or region. The most obvious reasons for the popularity of the local festival as a tourism promotion tool are: i. festivals increase the demand for local tourism (Smith and Jenner, 1998); and ii. successful festivals can help recreate the image of a place or contribute toward the exposure of a location trying to get on the tourism map (Kotler et al., 1993). Finally, the strategic placement of a festival in the local tourism calendar can help extend the tourism season (Getz, 2005). Some organisers may see festivals as recreational pursuits that should be managed on a somewhat loose and informal basis. However, many may resist the trend toward professionalism because they fear that community involvement and control may diminish if a 'business-like' approach develops. There may also be a concern that the event will become a 'tourist trap' in which authenticity diminishes or disappears and problems of over-crowding and commercialism take over (Getz and Frisby, 1988).

Some tourism festivals in Jordan

Jerash festival of culture and arts

The Jerash Festival, started 31 years ago, is an annual celebration of local, Arabic and international culture during the summer. It is held annually under the royal patronage to connect the past with the future on the huge Roman theatres, the same as the great silk road civilisations. It is held in the old Greco-Roman town of Jerash, known in old times as Gerasa, and located 46 km north of Amman. Since 1981, the city has hosted an annual Festival of Culture and Arts, which features an eclectic array of performances, including plays, poetry readings, opera and musical concerts from around the world, folklore dances by local and international groups, ballet, concerts, popular singers and sales of traditional handicrafts, all in the brilliantly floodlit dramatic surroundings of the Jerash ruins, from China, Russia, Japan, Indonesia, India, Pakistan, Spain, United Kingdom, United States, and most of the Arabic countries. It transforms the ancient city into one of the world's liveliest and most spectacular cultural events. The 31st Jerash Festival for Culture and Arts in 2016 attracted over 100,000 visitors and the attendance rates were 'much higher' than the last year.

Fuheis festival of culture and arts

Fuheis is a town in the Jordanian governorate of Balqa, just 20 kilometres north-west of Amman. The town has 20,000 residents, and is majority Christian. It lies in Wadi Shueib (Valley of Jethro), between Salt and Amman. The city welcomes annually every summer bands and artists from different parts of the world such as Syria, Palestine and Lebanon to perform in concerts and poetry evenings. Several visual artists from Jordan and Palestine exhibit their work at the festival. Visitors from Palestine, Lebanon and the Arab Gulf are expected to attend the festival as well as Jordanian expatriates spending the summer in the Kingdom. Fuheis festival has a cultural message that proves that Jordan and its neighbouring countries can celebrate art and hold on to our heritage.

The festival, started in August 1998, consists of valuable participating events, stars, cultural, intellectual, political and other events. The festival carries the theme of 'Jordan's history and civilization'. The cultural programme of the festival hosts a group of Jordanian, Arab and international artists. The festival is focused on attracting the families, is distinctive and doesn't seek for any financial gain. The reduced ticket price, which is not more than twenty Jordanian Dinars, equivalent to seven US dollars, is valid for admission to all the festival activities, including singing, theatre, music and lyrical heritage.

Al-Fuhais Newspaper has published a press release entitled 'Atalah Al-Fuheis' as a documentary for the festival. In 2005 the introduction of 'Alqanater Theater' was a value added to the festival and distributed free tickets to the people of the region as a kind of motivation to support the festival as the festival takes place in their region and feel the benefit from the festival. In 2008 the festival organised in consistence of the selection of Salt city of Jordanian culture, which helped the management of the festival to get the necessary financial support and fund for the festival and attract famous artists from Arab countries. The festival later worked on supporting the Jordanian artists and giving them the opportunities for creativity. It also worked on supporting the special needs people, enabling them to attend and participate in the events. The festival is sponsored by the royal family and contributes to the development of tourism.

Music festivals by artists from the west

Andrea Bocelli, the world's most beloved tenor with a career that spans over 20 years, is expected to be performing his first concert in Jordan. Few singers have touched as many hearts as having Andrea Bocelli – an Italian classical crossover tenor, recording artist, and singer-songwriter. The tenor has sung to sold-out audiences all over the world, and his admirers have included popes, presidents and royals as well as some of the greatest stars of classical and popular music. "Thanks to music, the doors of the world have opened up to me in so many ways. I like to describe myself as a cultural activist because music has the power to bridge the gap between nations and cultures and art – music brings the world together" (Friends of Jordan Festivals, 2017). In addition to Dima Bawab, the concert will also feature Carlo Bernini, music conductor; Elisa Balbo, soprano; Ilaria della Bidia, guest artist and Carisma, guitar duo.

The renowned Greek composer and pianist Yanni performed September 2016 to close a festival at the Amman Citadel, Jordan. A series of concerts is planned at the Citadel as part of the Jordan Festival 2016, featuring Lebanese singer and oud player Marcel Khalife and Turkish dance troupe Fire of Anatolia. The festival designed for everybody of all ages and all interests. All this is going to happen at Amman Citadel, so the view is going to be lovely and we hope it will draw awareness to the heritage of Amman. Jordanian organisers were proud to host international artists and to celebrate their history and heritage at the same time. The festival worked closely with the Jordan Tourism Board and the Ministry of Tourism to ensure that the performers enjoy their stay in the Kingdom. Although dance performances have not drawn large audiences in the past, the Fire of Anatolia was chosen because of its 'beautiful' performances. They have performed thousands of shows all over the world; they have received worldwide recognition, and the festival brings this to the Jordanian audience and gives them the opportunity to attend such shows. One of the main challenges was bringing artists whose style is new to Jordanian audiences, and developing local appreciation for performances like folk dancing.

Challenges for tourism festivals in Jordan

The festival should get more funds from the government and private sector; funding should be required for the festival's importance locally and internationally. A solution must be found for the sitting area and control the doors as well as the problem of traffic jams during the festival days. Failure to find a permanent site for the festival away from the residential and religious areas where the festival is held makes it inconvenient, as well as the lack of adequate parking for the visitors to the festival. The management of the festival should be full-time work. Unfortunately, the management of the festival is voluntary and their original work is affecting their festival management. In 2002 the festival stopped for financial reasons, but with a very limited balance, the festival back to the life in 2003, with early preparations to include the elite stars of singing and heritage of Jordan and the Arab artists.

Conclusion

The tourism industry is the one of the largest contributing sectors to Jordan's economy. In a dynamic globalised environment countries are keen to build a competitive image by dispersing their culture, values and environment with tourists and nationals through many means one of which is festivals. Social media has been significantly influential on the choice of the destination. Therefore, creating and developing dedicated websites and the extensive use of social media to promote the country, its events and festivals has been correlated with the increased number of tourists visiting a country. Any destination should address essential issues to ensure constant flow of business such as infrastructure, accessibility, information technology, e-commerce safety and security, and guiding services. Community is also an inseparable component and adds value to any country because tourists enrich their experiences through their interaction with local communities. Tourists need detailed information to make informed choices about the destinations they are visiting and to choose the activities they want to participate in. When national and international events are involved, countries need to address many barriers and reduce their direct and indirect negative impacts. For example: More funding from the public and private sectors should be directed towards event and festival organisation and promotion. In addition, controlling the festival site, proximity, sitting areas and parking have proved critical to the success and sustainability of events and festivals. To ensure success in festival promotion, it is recommended that along with having a dedicated fund for promoting festivals, it is necessary to have a website, and to expand the online outreach to social media platforms is critical. Social networking sites such as Twitter and Facebook are essential for maintaining a competitive edge. Promoting festivals without having active social media accounts risks missing out on numerous marketing opportunities.

References

Albarq, A.N. (2014). Industrial purchase among Saudi managers: Does country of origin matter? *International Journal of Marketing Studies*, **6**(1), p. 116.

Allen, J., O'Toole, W., Harris, R. and McDonell, I. (2008). *Festival and special event management*. Chichester: John Wiley & Sons.

Anderson, J. (2010). *Event management simplified*. 1663 Liberty Drive, Bloomington, IN 47403: Author House.

Anderson, L.M. and Taylor, R.L. (1995). McCarthy's 4PS: Timeworn or time-tested? *Journal of Marketing Theory and Practice*, **3**(3), pp. 1–9.

Arcodia, C.V. and Barker, T. (2003). The employability prospects of graduates in event management: Using data from job advertisements. In R.W. Braithwaite (ed.) *CAUTHE 2003: Riding the wave of tourism and hospitality research*. Coffs Harbour: CAUTHE, pp. 1–16.

Ayeh, J.K., Au, N. and Law, R. (2013). Predicting the intention to use consumer-generated media for travel planning. *Tourism Management*, **35**, pp. 132–143.

Baloglu, S. and Uysal, M. (1996). Market segments of push and pull motivations: A canonical correlation approach. *International Journal of Contemporary Hospitality Management*, **3**(8), pp. 32–38.

Benckendorff, P.J. and Pearce, P.L. (2003). Australian tourism attractions: The links between organisational characteristics and planning. *Journal of Travel Research*, **42**(1), pp. 24–35.

Berthon, P., Pitt, L. and Campbell, C. (2008). Ad lib: When customers create the ad. *California Management Review*, **50**(4), pp. 6–30.

Blackshaw, P. and Nazzaro, M. (2006). *Consumer-Generated Media (CGM): Word-of-Mouth in the age of the web-fortified consumer*. New York: Nielsen Buzz Metrics, p. 4.

Borden, N.H. (1964). The concept of the marketing mix. *Journal of Advertising Research*, **4**(2), pp. 2–7.

Boykin, J. (2015). *Start monitoring your online reviews now: No excuse for ignoring online reputation*. Retrieved from: www.internetmarketingninjas.com./blog/marketing/start-monitoring-your-online-reviews-now-no-excuse-for-ignoring-onlinereputation-jimandann/ (accessed: the 07th January, 2018).

Bruhn, M., Schoenmueller, V. and Schäfer, D.B. (2012). Are social media replacing traditional media in terms of brand equity creation? *Management Research Review*, **35**(9), pp. 770–790.

Bughin, J.R. (2007, August). How companies can make the most of user-generated content. *McKinsey Quarterly*, pp. 1–4.

Buhalis, D. (1998). Strategic use of information technologies in the tourism industry. *Tourism Management*, **19**(5), pp. 409–421.

Buhalis, D. and Law, R. (2008). Progress in information technology and tourism management: 20 years on and 10 years after the Internet – The state of eTourism research. *Tourism Management*, **29**(4), pp. 609–623.

Buss, A. and Strauss, N. (2009). *Online communities handbook: Building your business and brand on the web*. Berkeley: New Riders.

Cetin, G. and Bilgihan, A. (2016). Components of cultural tourists' experiences in destinations. *Current Issues in Tourism*, **19**(2), pp. 137–154.

Chappuis, B., Gaffey, B. and Parvizi, P. (2011, July). Are your customers becoming digital junkies? *McKinsey Quarterly*, pp. 1–4.

Cohen, E. (1979). A phenomenology of tourist experiences. *Sociology*, **13**(2), pp. 179–201.

Copley, P. and Robson, I. (1996). Tourism, arts marketing and the modernist paradox. In M. Robinson, N. Evans and P. Callaghan (eds.) *Tourism and culture: Image, identity and marketing*. Sunderland: The Centre for Travel and Tourism/British Education Publishers, pp. 15–34.

Cox, C., Burgess, S., Sellitto, C. and Buultjens, J. (2009). The role of user-generated content in tourists' travel planning behavior. *Journal of Hospitality Marketing & Management*, **18**(8), pp. 743–764.

De Bres, K. and Davis, J. (2001). Celebrating group and place identity: A case study of a new regional festival. *Tourism Geographies*, **3**(3), pp. 326–337.

Derrett, R. (2004). Festivals, events and the destination. In I. Yeoman, M. Robertson, J. Ali-Knight, S. Drummond and U. McMahon-Beattie (eds.) *Festival and events management: An international arts and culture perspective*. Oxford: Butterworth-Heinemann, pp. 32–50.

Evans, D. (2010). *Social media marketing: The next generation of business engagement*. Chichester: John Wiley & Sons.

Fang, B., Ye, Q., Kucukusta, D. and Law, R. (2016). Analysis of the perceived value of online tourism reviews: Influence of readability and reviewer characteristics. *Tourism Management*, **52**, pp. 498–506.

Felsenstein, D. and Fleischer, A. (2003). Local festivals and tourism promotion: The role of public assistance and visitor expenditure. *Journal of Travel Research*, **41**, pp. 385–392.

First Merchant Services, L.L.C. and Coyle Hospitality Group. (2012). *Social media in the hospitality industry: 2012 trend report*. Retrieved from: www.coylehospitality.com/wp-content/uploads/2012/ 09/2012-Social-Media-Trends-in-the-Hospitality-Industry-Report.pdf (accessed: the 18th October, 2012).

Fotis, J., Buhalis, D. and Rossides, N. (2012). *Social media use and impact during the holiday travel planning process*. Berlin: Springer-Verlag.

Frisby, W. and Getz, D. (1989). Festival management: A case study perspective. *Journal of Travel Research*, **28**(1), pp. 7–11.

Friends of Jordan Festivals. (2017). *Andrea Bocelli*. Retrieved from: http://www.friends ofjordanfestivals.com/?portfolio=andrea-bocellli (accessed: the 12th December, 2017).

Getz, D. (1989). Special events: Defining the product. *Tourism Management*, **10**(2), pp. 125–137.

Getz, D. (1991). *Festivals, special events, and tourism*. New York: Van Nostrand Reinhold.

Getz, D. (2005). *Event management and event tourism*. Putnam Valley: Cognizant Communication Corp.

Getz, D. and Frisby, W. (1988). Evaluating management effectiveness in community-run festivals. *Journal of Travel Research*, **27**(1), pp. 22–27.

Gretzel, U., Yuan, Y.L. and Fesenmaier, D.R. (2000). Preparing for the new economy: Advertising strategies and change in destination marketing organizations. *Journal of Travel Research*, **39**(2), pp. 146–156.

Grönroos, C. (1997). Keynote paper from marketing mix to relationship marketing-towards a paradigm shift in marketing. *Management Decision*, **35**(4), pp. 322–339.

Gunn, C. (1988). *Vacationscape: Designing tourist regions*. 2d ed. New York: Van Nostrand Reinhold.

Gursoy, D., Kim, K. and Uysal, M. (2004). Perceived impacts of festivals and special events by organizers: An extension and validation. *Tourism Management*, **25**(2), pp. 171–181.

Information and Communication Technology. (2014) Measuring the Information Society Report. International Telecommunication Unit. Place Des Nations, CH-1211, Geneva, Switzerland, ISBN: 978-92-61-15291-8.

Jurowski, C. (2009). *An examination of the four realms of tourism experience theory*. Retrieved from: https://scholarworks.umass.edu/refereed/Sessions/Wednesday/23/ (accessed: the 07th January, 2017).

Kietzmann, J.H., Hermkens, K., McCarthy, I.P. and Silvestre, B.S. (2011). Social media? Get serious! Understanding the functional building blocks of social media. *Business Horizons*, **54**(3), pp. 241–251.

Kotler, P., Haider, D.H. and Rein, I. (1993). *Marketing places*. New York: Free Press.

Leung, D., Law, R., Van Hoof, H. and Buhalis, D. (2013). Social media in tourism and hospitality: A literature review. *Journal of Travel & Tourism Marketing*, **30**(1–2), pp. 3–22.

Litvin, S.W., Goldsmith, R.E. and Pan, B. (2008). Electronic word-of-mouth in hospitality and tourism management. *Tourism Management*, **29**(3), pp. 458–468.

Mangold, W.G. and Faulds, D.J. (2009). Social media: The new hybrid element of the promotion mix. *Business Horizons*, **52**(4), pp. 357–365.

McIntosh, R.W. and Goeldner, C.R. (1990). *Instructor's manual and test bank to accompany tourism: Principles, practices, philosophies*. Wiley

Munar, A. M., & Ooi, C-S. (2012). The Truth of the Crowds: Social Media and the Heritage Experience. In L. Smith, E. Waterton and S. Watson (eds.), *The Cultural Moment in Tourism*. Abingdon: Routledge, pp. 255–273.

O'Sullivan, D. and Jackson, M.J. (2002). Festival tourism: A contributor to sustainable local economic development? *Journal of Sustainable Tourism*, **10**(4), pp. 325–342.

Pearce, P.L. (1991). Analysing tourist attractions. *Journal of Tourism Studies*, **2**(1), pp. 46–55.

Poon, A. (1993). *Tourism, technology and competitive strategies*. London: CAB International.

Qualman, E. (2013). *Socialnomics: How social media transforms the way we live and do business*. Chichester: John Wiley & Sons.

Radder, L. and Han, X. (2015). An examination of the museum experience based on Pine and Gilmore's experience economy realms. *Journal of Applied Business Research*, **31**(2), pp. 455–470.

Ritchie, J.B. and Zins, M. (1978). Culture as determinant of the attractiveness of a tourism region. *Annals of Tourism Research*, **5**(2), pp. 252–267.

Robinson, M. and Novelli, M. (2005). Niche tourism: An introduction. In M. Novelli (ed.) *Niche tourism: Contemporary issues, trends and cases*. Oxford: Butterworth-Heinemann, pp. 1–14.

Robinson, P., Wale, D. and Dickson, G. (2010). *Event management*. Wallingford: CAB International.

Rupert Hills, J. and Cairncross, G. (2011). Small accommodation providers and UGC web sites: Perceptions and practices. *International Journal of Contemporary Hospitality Management*, **23**(1), pp. 26–43.

Ruzic, D. and Bilos, A. (2010). Social media in Destination Marketing Organization (DMOs). *Tourism & Hospitality Industry, New Trends in Tourism and Hospitality Management Conference*, **20**, pp. 178–190.

Safko, L. and Brake, D.K. (2009). *The social media bible: Tactics, tools, and strategies for business success*. Hoboken: John Wiley & Sons, ISBN: 0470912685, 9780470912683.

Senecal, S. and Nantel, J. (2004). The influence of online product recommendations on consumers' online choices. *Journal of Retailing*, **80**(2), pp. 159–169.

Sigala, M., Christou, E. and Gretzel, U. (2012). *Social media in travel, tourism and hospitality: Theory, practice and cases*. Farnham: Ashgate Publishing, Ltd.

Silberberg, T. (1995). Cultural tourism and business opportunities for museums and heritage sites. *Tourism Management*, **16**(5), pp. 361–365.

Smith, C. and Jenner, P. (1998). The impact of festivals and special events on tourism: Occasional studies. In *Travel and Tourism Analyst, 4*. London: Economist Publications.

Sotiriadis, M.D. and Van Zyl, C. (2013). Electronic word-of-mouth and online reviews in tourism services: The use of twitter by tourists. *Electronic Commerce Research*, **13**(1), pp. 103–124.

Tahana, N. and Oppermann, M. (1998). Maori cultural performances and tourism. *Tourism Recreation Research*, **23**(1), pp. 23–30.

Thevenot, L. (2007). Governing life by standards: A view from engagements. *Social Studies of Science*, **39**(5), pp. 793–813.

Trusov, M., Bucklin, R.E. and Pauwels, K.H. (2009). Effects of word-of-mouth versus traditional marketing: Findings from an Internet social networking site. *Journal of Marketing*, **73**, pp. 90–102.

Tuten, T.L. (2008). *Advertising 2.0: Social media marketing in a web 2.0 world*. London: Greenwood Publishing Group.

UNWTO. (1995). *Summary of statistics*. Madrid: UNWTO.

UNWTO. (2013). *World tourism barometer-11*. Madrid: UNWTO.

Uysal, M. and Hagan, L.A.R. (1993). Motivation of pleasure travel and tourism. *Encyclopedia of Hospitality and Tourism*, **21**, pp. 798–810.

VTIC. (2012). *The definitive proof of social media's worth to tourism*. Retrieved from: www.victorianchamber.com.au/policy-and-advocacy/news/blog/2012/07/05/definitive-proof-social-media%E2%80%99s-worth-tourism (accessed: the 07th January, 2017).

Wang, Y., Quaehee, Y. and Fesenmaier, D. (2002). Defining the virtual tourism community: Implications for tourism marketing. *Tourism Management*, **23**, pp. 407–417.

Xiang, Z. and Gretzel, U. (2010). Role of social media in online travel information search. *Tourism Management*, **31**(2), pp. 179–188.

Yeoman, I., Robertson, M., Ali-Knight, J. and McMahon-Beattie, U. (2004). *Festival and events management: An international arts and culture perspective*. New York: Elsevier.

Yuan, S. and McDonald, C. (1990). Motivational determinates of international pleasure time. *Journal of Travel Research*, **29**(1), pp. 42–44.

Zeng, B. and Gerritsen, R. (2014). What do we know about social media in tourism? A review. *Tourism Management Perspectives*, **10**, pp. 27–36.

Zeppel, H. and Hall, C.M. (1992). Arts and heritage tourism. In B. Weiler and C.M. Hall (eds.) *Special interest tourism*. London: Belhaven, pp. 47–68.

Zhu, F. and Zhang, X. (2010). Impact of online consumer reviews on sales: The moderating role of product and consumer characteristics. *Journal of Marketing*, **74**(2), pp. 133–148.

8 Effectiveness of social media sharing on tourism event choice

Bekir Bora Dedeoğlu and Kemal Gürkan Küçükergin

Introduction

Destinations significantly compete with each other in terms of attracting tourists (Kester and Croce, 2011). Especially the destinations with similar geographical features might face competition problems while offering similar product and services. Despite the fact that natural attractions are unique to the region (Hurt et al., 2012), the services offered by the destinations show remarkable similarities. Natural attractions are the elements that should not be touched too much, and it results in losing the competitive advantage gained as a result of product diversification. Therefore, destinations need to discover different attractions in addition to the natural ones. At this point, activities come into play. Defined as "an occurrence at a given place and time; a special set of circumstances; a noteworthy occurrence" (Getz, 2007:18), event is an attraction which has its own unique features (Getz, 2008). Getz (2007) indicates that events can be divided into two groups as planned and unplanned events. However, planned events are the ones examined in the studies because they are organised and easier to manage. Getz (2007) points out that the planned events can be categorised as cultural celebrations, political and state, arts and entertainment, business and trade, educational and scientific, sport competition, recreational and private events. In addition to this classification, the events can be classified as mega, big, regional and local events considering their extent, and as festival, sport and MICE events considering their content (Allen et al., 2012). Also, Getz classified the types of planned events as hallmark, premier or prestige, mega, media, cause-related, corporate, publicity stunt, special, spectator and interactive and participant events considering their functions. Nevertheless, an event could have multiple goals because of including many different functions at the same time. For instance, large-scaled events such as World Championship, European Football Championship, and World Olympics which are organised by specific organisations in a specific region and for a specific time period can be put under the categories of hallmark, mega and prestige events, and they are also classified as sport events (Getz, 2007; Jago and Shaw, 1998). Also, relatively small-scaled events organised each year by the same country or local authorities such as International Antalya Film Festival in Antalya, Rio Festival in Rio and Cannes Film Festival in Cannes have the hallmark and mega event functions while they can be placed under the cultural celebrations category, as well (Getz, 2007). Regardless of their types and functions, the events acting as an attractive element in the destination they are organised provides remarkable competitive advantage and they support the branding process of the destination (Getz, 2008). As a matter of fact, events are the brands in addition to being products offered to consumers (Kurtzman, 1994; Nelson and Vogler, 2002). Therefore, they should be considered and managed as a product or brand by the local managers or destination management organisations.

It was stressed in various studies that activities play an important role in the tourists' destination choices. It can be indicated that those studies focused on perceptions and attitudes which occur following the experience of the event. Particularly it was focused on how the emotional situation that the events created on the individuals would affect consumers' future destination visits (Kaplanidou, 2006; Kaplanidou and Vogt, 2007) when considered together with the relevant quality and value perceptions obtained from those events (Moon et al., 2013). However, it is not certain to what extent the tourists' perceptions of events that they have experienced would be effective in their event and destination choices. Moreover, the attractiveness and awareness regarding the events should be created and increased at first. As a matter of fact, Liang et al. (2008) indicate that events are a very important attraction element in order to raise the destination brand awareness which plays a remarkably significant role in destination choices. Therefore, it is necessary to focus on how an event would prompt the potential tourists' desire to experience it. Besides the motivations that encourage participation in the event such as cultural exploration, socialisation, entertainment, event attraction, novelty, uniqueness, escape and excitement (Formica and Uysal, 1996, 1998; Uysal et al., 1993; Crompton and Mckay, 1997), individuals with the motivation of gaining status within the society (Küçükergin and Dedeoğlu, 2014) can feel motivated to join in the event to tell others that they are in the place where the event is held (Getz, 2008). In other words, the event is such a touristic product that it provides potential tourists with the opportunity to integrate with different cultures and have different experiences, and it acts as a prestige source, as well. Especially the events organised in a country like Turkey which embodies many different cultures because serving as a bridge between Asian and European cultures can provide the tourists with opportunity of experiencing the unique and different experiences at the same time (Aktaş and Ekin, 2007; Sandole, 2009). Therefore, the term 'prestige' should be examined in a meticulous way. As a matter of fact, the perception of high prestige could prompt the purchasing motive for the individuals because of their specific expectations on product and services (e.g. social status, high quality, self-esteem) (Vigneron and Johnson, 1999). More clearly, consumers might prefer the product and services (brand, destination, event etc.) that they consider highly prestigious compared to the others considered as less prestigious. In this regard, tourists could intend to join prestigious events and share their experiences with others in order to gain social status. Therefore, the prestige levels of the events that are not preferred by the tourists should be increased. At this point, it should be focused on how and through which channels the prestige levels of the product and services (events) not being experienced by tourists could be increased.

The perception of prestige could be related to both high status (Baek et al., 2010) and social identity (Sirgy, 1982) of the product and services provided to the consumers. The consumers can purchase prestigious products with the motives of being recognised by the society and gaining social status (Leibenstein, 1950). This situation can be explained through the examination of consumer behaviours within the framework of snobbism, conformity and hedonism terms (Correia et al., 2016). On the one hand, consumers would like to show snobbish behaviours with the motive of going through different and unique experiences; on the other hand, they might want to behave in accordance with the social norms recognised by the society (conformity). In addition, individuals might prefer purchasing the products bearing the basic features of conspicuous consumption such as aesthetic beauty and excitement in order to satisfy their hedonic needs (hedonism). What needs to be considered at this point is how those wishes come into existence. So that the individuals can have such kinds of wishes, they should have a specific amount of information and awareness related to the product (service, brand, event etc.). When the awareness referring to the power of an object (product, service, brand etc.) in the mind of an individual (Aaker, 1996) increases, it might also increase the individual's perception of prestige regarding the product (Boo et al., 2009). Therefore, it is required to focus on awareness-raising components of the events. Nowadays, traditional media tools are effective in creating awareness of product and services. Despite that, social media mediums can be preferred more because of the different contributions they provide to the organisations. Particularly the content generated by consumers have a remarkably significant impact on others' choices. For this reason, organisations need to pay attention to the content generated by consumers in order to increase the awareness of their products and services (Tuten, 2008; Tussyadiah and Fesenmaier, 2009).

In the current literature, it is observed that a sufficient number of studies emphasising the importance of the event prestige for the event choices has not yet been carried out. Particularly it is not clear what kinds of factors would direct the potential tourists' perceptions of event prestige. In this scope, the importance of the perceptions of event prestige on destination choices and the impact of event awareness and social media sharing expected to contribute to prestige perception were attempted to be explained theoretically in the present study. In this regard, it is targeted to eliminate a significant shortcoming in the event literature. Thus, awareness of the mentioned factors can be raised for the local, regional and national authorities organising the events.

Conceptual framework

Social media sharing

The use and the importance of the Internet have gradually become more important, and it can be indicated that the share of social media within the Internet use rate is quite high. Especially considering the statistics on the Internet use, the efficiency of social media could be expected to increase. As a matter of fact, the majority of

Internet activities around the world is carried out via search engines and social media mediums (Alexa, 2014). When examining the searches done on Google, it is seen that social media websites such as Facebook and YouTube are at top ranks (Google Trend, 2014). As shown in various researches, Internet users spend lots of time on social media (Global Digital Statistics, 2014).

Because of providing important advantages, social media is an important tool for both consumers and organisations. Providing the consumers with the opportunity to share their experiences, which is not possible in the traditional media tools, the dominance of a more democratic environment and the chance to see the content generated by others are among the benefits of the currently used social media mediums (Drury, 2008; Lietsala and Sirkkunen, 2008). Due to providing such benefits to the consumers, it can be indicated that the use of social media mediums is increasing, and therefore, becoming more important. Social media mediums could provide benefit to the organisation as a lower-cost advertisement tool compared to traditional media, as well as ensuring the easy communication with the present and potential consumers (Barnes, 2010; Zimmerman and Ng, 2010). The fact that more and more consumers use social media mediums rather than traditional mediums has become one of the important subjects for the organisations. As a matter of fact, such kinds of contents are effective in directing the consumers towards a brand or getting certain amount of information about a brand. Therefore, organisations should understand the power of social media sharing in terms of directing the consumers. Otherwise, they might subject to lose competitive advantage against their rivals.

Social media sharing can be used interchangeably with the term 'user-generated content'. However, the point misunderstood in literature is that the terms 'user-generated content' and 'customer-generated content' are used interchangeably (Heinonen, 2011). However, it should not be ignored that user-generated content is generated by both organisations (firms) and consumers (Xiang and Gretzel, 2010) because these two content-generation types direct the attitudes and behaviours of consumers at different extents (Bruhn et al., 2012). More clearly, the content generated in the social media by consumers is considered sincerer and reliable compared to those generated by the organisations (Herrero et al., 2015). Nevertheless, firm-generated content should not be ignored, either. Potential consumers might want to check the accuracy of the information they get from the sharing generated by consumers through the sharing of organisations, and that of the information they get from the sharing generated by organisations through the sharing of users. Therefore, any of the contents generated by organisations and consumers should not be ignored.

Since organisations make their moves on their own social media mediums mainly with the marketing motive (e.g. providing information on the products, promotions, replying back to customer complaints), the consumers taking into consideration the sharing by the organisation would like to get direct information. Nevertheless, consumer-generated contents are shared with the influence of different motives (e.g. entertainment, socialisation, prestige boosting (Lee and Ma, 2012; Park et al., 2009; Stoeckl et al., 2007)) as well as the motive of sharing information. However, they might prompt the motives that would satisfy the hedonic needs besides the potential consumers' need for information-seeking. Similarly, it was found in a study carried out by Bruhn et al. (2012) that the firm-generated content had a positive impact on the brand awareness and the user-generated content (or consumer-generated content) positively affected the hedonic brand image. This finding reveals that the consumer-generated contents should be examined in a more comprehensive way. As a matter of fact, consumer-generated content can be created on different platforms, in different ways and with different motives. Similarly, Shao (2009) indicated that the contents can be generated by consumers in three ways as consuming, participating and producing behaviours. Consuming behaviour covers such actions as watching, reading and seeing the content, and individuals do not make any contribution to the content whereas participating behaviour indicates the interactions between the user and the other users, and the user and content. Lastly, producing behaviour refers to the actions including content generation as well as sharing text, images, audio and video (Shao, 2009).

On the other hand, consumers can generate participant and non-participant sharing regardless of the motives prompting them. Dedeoğlu (2016) indicated that individuals can generate sharing in two different types as participant and non-participant sharing, and therefore, the importance attached by potential consumers to those sharing types would differ, as well. According to Dedeoğlu (2016), participant sharing refers to the sharing that an individual posts on social media through particular mediums associated with the organisation, or just in order to reach a specific goal directly related to the organisation (e.g. providing information, evaluation), while non-participant sharing refers to sharing posted by an individual just because of his/her own motives (desire to be liked and approved by the society, socialisation, spending time, expressing him/herself) on his/her own or others' personal web-pages (blogs, social networks etc.) without participating in any activity (organisation's own web-site, forum, Facebook account, or assessment websites) of the organisation or seeking any goal associated with the organisation. Since participant sharing is generated on the platforms where the organisation is included, it further satisfies the information-seeking need of the individuals whereas the non-participant sharing could indirectly result in that consumers would experience an involvement about the product and services or their involvement level would increase without realising since that sharing is done by individuals themselves or their friends in the platforms where the organisations are not involved in. Despite the fact that the content generated by consumers were not examined under the categories of participant and non-participant sharing by Gretzel and Yoo (2008) in their study, the study findings showed why the contents could be perceived as important by the tourists. In the study of Gretzel and Yoo (2008:42), the perceptions of tourists regarding the sharing of other tourists were examined, and it was found that tourists firstly defined those contents as "a good way to learn about a travel destination, product or service". It was also seen that 85.3 per cent of the tourists defined the sharing as "they make it easier to imagine what a place will be like" and 76.8 per cent defined them as "they make me feel excited about travelling". In this regard, it should be understood what kind of sharing (participant or non-participant) satisfies the individual's need for informa- tion or makes them excited and lead to become interested in the product or ser- vices. Therefore, customer-generated content should be examined in a more elaborated way.

Event awareness

Besides contributing to marketing activities in a destination, events play an impor- tant role in destination marketing, as well (Chalip and Costa, 2005; Hede and Jago, 2005). In addition, as emphasised by Getz (2008), events should be considered as a unique brand since they have unique features (Nelson and Vogler, 2002). Thus, events which had a successful branding process would contribute to the branding process of the destination. At this point, awareness which is an important element for branding activities should be examined within the scope of events. As a matter of fact, awareness is not only a basic element of the branding but also is the first step in the branding process (Gartner, 2014; Pike and Page, 2014). Moreover, individuals with high brand awareness are more likely to show positive behaviours about the brand (Zajonc, 1980). Therefore, organisations should meticulously pay attention to the brand awareness to ensure a successful branding.

In addition to ensuring consumers' recalling or recognition of a brand which represents a specific product category (Aaker, 1991), it can be defined as "reflected by consumers' ability to identify the brand under different conditions" (Keller, 1993:3). Brand awareness also refers to the power of the brand in the mind of target audience (Pike et al., 2010). In this case, event awareness can be described as an element which ensures that potential tourists get information about the event at a certain level, and, the event can be differentiated from others. Aaker stressed that brand awareness is composed of different levels ranging from 'unaware of brand' to 'top of mind' (Aaker, 1991). In the awareness pyramid he developed, Aaker (1991) indicated that the lowest awareness level is brand recognition, and this level is based on testing with aided recall. The next level in the awareness pyramid is brand recall. The brand recall refers to the brand's capability to be defined by the consumer without mentioning the name of the brand in a specific product category. More clearly, potential consumers are not led with the help of the already existing brand names; therefore, it has been conceptualised as unaided recall unlike the recognition. Compared to the recognition, it is more difficult to manage the unaided recall; however, individuals might remember the statements created through aided recall more easily rather than unaided recall. And, top of mind awareness having a special position in the awareness pyramid refers to the name that is desired and comes into mind at first through unaided recall (Aaker, 1991). On the other hand, Keller (1993) examined brand awareness within the scope of brand information and divided it into two categories as brand recognition and brand recall. Brand recall is the ability to create memories with the brand whereas brand recognition indicates the ability of the consumer. In other words, brand recognition requires the ability of consumers to correctly differentiate the brand they have seen or heard before (Keller, 1993). Brand recognition is the lowest level of brand awareness, and it could be more important during the decision process related to purchasing activity (Pappu et al., 2005) since it becomes important when a consumer chooses a brand during the purchasing process (Huang and Cai, 2015). Particularly examining its importance for the tourists who have not had any experience with the brand, it can be indicated that the impact of brand recognition reaches a more important level. As a matter of fact, brand recognition is a level where the potential consumers get information about the brand (event) via specific mediums (through seeing or hearing) although they do not experience it, and this level is an element enabling them to correctly differentiate the brand. Therefore, the awareness levels regarding the events and under which conditions those levels would change should be meticulously examined.

Aaker (1991:69) emphasised that different and memorable messages, a brand-specific motto and an appropriate symbol should be used and being a sponsor for the events should be taken into consideration in order to create and raise awareness. Similarly, Keller (2012) indicated that some of the elements such as name, symbol, logo or slogan, advertisement and promotion, sponsorship, public relations and poster advertising could increase the awareness and familiarity of the consumers with the brand. These activities have started to be organised through different mediums in a more efficient way and without the influence of the organisation. As stated before, the increase in social media use, and accordingly, the increase in the number of sharing related to their experiences with the product have enabled other consumers having information, opinions and feelings about the product and services.

Tourists could pay special attention to the contents (rating and review) generated in the context of tourism for different reasons. Gretzel and Yoo (2008) mentioned that some of those reasons could be as follows: "They are a good way to learn about a travel destination, product or service; they help me evaluate alternatives; they make it easier to imagine what a place will be like; they make me feel excited about travelling". In this regard, as long as tourists pay attention, for different reasons, to the content generated by others, they might want to get information about the content of the sharing (product, service, brand, events, destination). More clearly, thanks to the sharing generated by other tourists, potential tourists might want to seek more information, and thus, their awareness levels regarding the subject (product, service, brand, events and destination) are expected to increase. In addition to importance attached to sharing with the information-seeking purpose, individuals can also attach importance to sharing within the scope of social identity or social learning theories. According to social learning theory, individuals might mimic the behaviours of others in order to get the desired outputs (Bandura, 1977). In line with this theory, if the outcomes of the other consumers' behaviours that the individuals observe are in line with their expectation (e.g. gaining prestige) might repeat the behaviours of those consumers to get the same outcomes (Webb and Zimmer-Gembeck, 2014). On the other hand, it should be taken into consideration that social media mediums are utilised in order to increase the concept of identity, which is one of the important components of the social identity theory

(Valkenburg et al., 2006). Considered from this perspective, it has similarities with the social identity theory. More clearly, in the event that individuals would perceive the content generated in social media mediums important, they might wish to take actions to be recognised by the community members and become a part of the community. For this reason, they might tend to show uniformity behaviours and attribute importance to the event because of the social pressure by the community (Tajfel and Turner, 1979; Deaux, 2000). In the light of these theories, potential tourists giving importance to the social media sharing on the brand with the expectation of being recognised by the society are likely to become more interested in the brand, and accordingly, their awareness related to brand is likely to increase, as well (Dedeoğlu, 2016). As a result, potential tourists could give importance to the sharing generated by others with the intention of getting information about the brand or being recognised by the society. Therefore, awareness levels of tourists regarding the brand (event) mentioned in the sharing can be expected to increase in both cases (Jin et al., 2013).

On the other hand, reverse-supply process is seen in touristic products and services. For this reason, consumers might purchase the product and services without being able to experience them. This situation puts the importance of the brands' awareness levels more into the forefront. As a matter of fact, Boo et al. (2009) also indicated that brand awareness plays a key role in branding activities within the scope of hospitality and tourism. It could result from the possibility that brand awareness acts as a pioneer image of the brand for the consumers (Gartner, 1994). In other words, consumers' brand awareness levels could be considered as their image perceptions regarding their first impressions about the brand. And these perceptions direct the individuals' attitudes towards the brand. In this regard, especially because the reverse-supply process is observed in the tourism industry, social media plays a significant role for the brand awareness, and the brand awareness plays the same role for the destination branding.

Event choice and event prestige

Prestige is a concept related to good reputation of individuals within the society. This reputation is determined through the individuals' social statuses, and from the consumer behaviour perspective, the social statuses emerge as a result of the prestige-worthy behaviours (Campbell, 2005; Correia et al., 2016). At this point, what needs to be taken into notice is the concept of brand prestige. Brand prestige indicates the relatively high-status-product positioning of a brand compared to the other brands within the similar category (Steenkamp et al., 2003).

Prestigious brands differ from the non-prestigious brand because of affecting the consumers' motives related to improving their social standings and self-expressions (O'Cass and Frost, 2002). More clearly, since the prestigious products are closely related to individuals' self-concept and social image perceptions, besides being luxurious products that cannot be purchased often and easily, individuals consider that high-prestigious products will bring social status, wealth or power to themselves (Alden et al., 1999). However, prestige is not only based on luxury consumption. Vigneron and Johnson (1999) categorised prestige brands into upmarket brands, premium brands, and luxury brands based on brand prestige level. Within this categorisation, luxury consumption indicates the last stage of a prestigious brand. On the other hand, because prestigious brands represent a high quality of life, consumers could prefer more prestigious brands in order to increase the quality of their lives (Hwang and Hyun, 2012). Besides, individuals wishing to use prestigious products might want to get the conspicuous, unique, social, hedonic and quality value perceptions (Baek et al., 2010; Vigneron and Johnson, 1999).

Consumers' wish for getting one, a few or all of those value perceptions might direct the consumer to use prestigious products. What needs to be taken into consideration at this point is how the individual would consider a product prestigious. Although Hwang and Hyun (2012) and Hwang and Han (2014) indicated that brand experience is of vital importance for the perceptions of brand prestige, the impact of reference groups on the prestige perceptions should not be ignored (Baek et al., 2010). As a matter of fact, before experiencing it, a brand should be liked and demanded by the public in order to be perceived as prestigious. Therefore, the brand-related opinions of the reference groups that the individuals are in interaction with should be taken into consideration because the community around the individuals is composed of reference groups. At this point, it is more likely and effective that the consumers' perceptions of brand prestige are directed by the opinions and ideas of reference groups rather than the experiences.

It would not be mistaken to say that the most effective reference groups are composed of the references in social media. In many studies, it is indicated that the content generated in social media mediums has a remarkable power of directing consumer behaviours (Khammash and Griffiths, 2011; See-To and Ho, 2014). Nevertheless, as stated before, social media sharing is effective for discovering and getting know the product rather than having a direct impact on the product choice. Therefore, social media sharing plays a role in arousing the potential tourists' interest in the events (Chalip and Costa, 2005) and increasing their awareness of the brand. At this point, the concept of awareness should be taken into notice because it can be possible for individuals to become aware of a product only if they attribute importance to it. And this importance, as indicated before, could be related to the presumption that individuals attach importance to the social media sharing with the motives of getting information about the product or being recognised by the society.

In this regard, potential tourists are expected to attach importance to the sharing of others for different reasons. Later, they obtain information about the event in accordance with the level of importance they attach to the product, and a relevant set of impressions could occur in their minds. As long as the impressions related to the event are high, the prestige perception will be high, as well. More clearly, potential tourists will consider the individuals generating the content as a reference group and will have a certain level of awareness of the event thanks to the sharing done by the reference groups. As their awareness levels increase, the event will be perceived as prestigious. As a result, potential tourists perceiving the event as

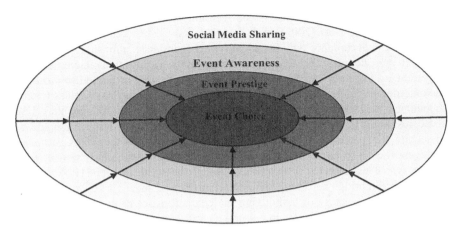

Figure 8.1 Steps of event choice
(Source: the authors, 2014)

prestigious would prefer, amongst the other events, the one mentioned in the social media sharing. In brief, as shown in Figure 8.1, social media sharing will increase the individuals' awareness levels on the event, and then the awareness level will increase the prestige perception related to the event, and finally the event will be chosen by the individuals.

Conclusion

Events make remarkable contributions to the regions where they are held. Therefore, event management units, particularly DMOs, should understand how the events can be turned into attractive and preferable organisations. Despite the fact that it is known that past experiences of the events have a significant impact on consumers' future event or destination choices, a sufficient number of studies have not yet been carried out on how to make a non-experienced event preferred by consumers. At this point, it was attempted in the present study to theoretically explain how the non-experienced events can become attractive events with the help of the content generated in social media mediums. In this regard, the reasons underlying the causative relationships among social media sharing, event awareness, event prestige and event choice were explained.

With the help of the present study, it was attempted to raise the awareness of DMOs, local authorities and event management units on the role that social media mediums play as a primary element in the event choices. Moreover, it was indicated that the social media sharing could form the perceptions and attitudes of potential tourists who have not yet experienced the event. At this point, it was found that prestige perceptions regarding the events could play an important role in terms of choosing the non-experienced events. In this regard, both DMOs and event management organisations should understand how to make the events perceived more prestigious, and take steps accordingly.

As indicated by Getz (2007), each event has unique features and the functions could differ in accordance with the event type. For instance, a music festival could provide a more convenient environment in terms of the socialisation motives whereas experiencing Formula I or FIFA World Cup could be further related to prestige-seeking motive. Similarly, Lee et al. (2004) emphasised that the motivations related to joining in the international events could be different; therefore, different marketing strategies should be developed. At this point, event planners and designers should, at first, know the specific purposes underlying the organisations of the events. Although the events act as an attractive factor for the destinations, particularly the needs of tourists which are expected to be satisfied through the event should be known.

Serving as a bridge between Continental Europe and Asia, Turkey has a special cultural pattern because of embodying the characteristics of these two different cultures. Thanks to its richness in cultural characteristics, it is a potential country that can prompt the motivations of having different experiences, uniqueness, excitement, learning and discovery, which have an important place among the event motivations. In addition, it should not be ignored that the majority of the international visits (76.9 per cent) are organised for the close geographical places (UNWTO, 2016). For this reason, it can be indicated that Turkey is at a preferable position because of its historical and cultural richness and having a geographical location close to European and Asian countries.

Nevertheless, one of the most significant deficiencies in Turkey is the low number of prestigious events. Although various cultural, art, food and drink, sport and business-themed events and festivals are organised in Turkey (Giritlioğlu et al., 2015), recognition of those events in international areas or by foreign tourists is very low. One of the main reasons is that sufficient number of studies has not been carried out on the events (Yürük et al., 2017). Failing to convey the social, cultural and economic benefits of the events for the DMOs and local authorities could have resulted in the low number of promotion activities in the field. For this reason, the recognition and prestige levels of the events with which the foreign tourists are relatively familiar should be increased. In this regard, both DMOs and event management organisations (EMOs) should ensure that experienced tourists, especially foreigners, joining in the event do generate content in the social media, and they should take encouraging actions accordingly. As long as the experienced tourists generate the content in a participant and non-participant way, as indicated by Dedeoğlu (2016), that content, depending on the type, will affect the information and interest levels with regard to the events in a different way. For instance, the sharing generated in the official social media account of the event (e.g. Instagram, twitter) will mainly be based on information-seeking. On the other hand, the sharing on the events generated by the experienced tourists on their own social media accounts will affect the others' interest levels rather than information levels (Dedeoğlu, 2016). In this way, information and interest levels of the potential tourists will be increased thanks to those contents, and it will be possible to prompt those tourists' motivation of experiencing the events.

Furthermore, as indicated by Zhou et al. (2017), Chinese medium-sized cities should have a strong touristic and cultural background in order to increase the competitive advantage they have. On the other hand, Turkey includes various small and medium-sized cities with unique characteristics. Besides its rooted historical and cultural assets, its natural beauties establish a good basis for many events. However, at this point, it can be indicated that some serious investment-based shortcomings do exist in Turkey. Those shortcomings can be seen in the research findings of Giritlioğlu et al. (2015). In the study carried out by Giritlioğlu et al. (2015), it was indicated that 111 different festivals were organised in Mediterranean Region embodying the most important touristic cities in Turkey; however, this figure represents only 8.8 per cent of the festivals in total. On the other hand, the regional, local, national and international recognition levels of those festivals were not mentioned in the study. In addition, the fact that the events in Turkey have not yet been examined sufficiently in the researches so far is another important handicap. And it is seen in those few studies that the reviews from the local participants were examined (e.g. Caber et al., 2016; Yürük et al., 2017). The lack of data makes it more difficult for DMOs and local authorities to estimate the efficiency and attractiveness of the events. Therefore, more empirical studies at the international level should be carried out on the events organised in Turkey.

References

Aaker, D.A. (1991). *Managing brand equity: Capitalizing on the value of a brand name.* New York: The Free Press.

Aaker, D.A. (1996). Measuring brand equity across products and markets. *California Management Review*, **38**(3), p. 103.

Aktaş, A. and Ekin, Y. (2007). Case study 5: The importance and the role of faith (religious) tourism in the alternative tourism resources in Turkey. In R. Raj and N. Morpeth (eds.) *Religious tourism and pilgrimage festivals management: An international perspective.* Wallingford: CABI Publishing, pp. 170–183.

Alden, D.L., Steenkamp, J.B.E. and Batra, R. (1999). Brand positioning through advertising in Asia, North America, and Europe: The role of global consumer culture. *The Journal of Marketing*, **63**, pp. 75–87.

Alexa. (2014). *Topsites.* Retrieved from: www.alexa.com/topsites son erişim (accessed: the 28th September, 2014).

Allen, J., O'toole, W., Harris, R. and McDonnell, I. (2012). *Festival and special event management.* Chichester: John Wiley & Sons.

Baek, T.H., Kim, J. and Yu, J.H. (2010). The differential roles of brand credibility and brand prestige in consumer brand choice. *Psychology and Marketing*, **27**(7), pp. 662–678.

Bandura, A. (1977). *Social learning theory.* Englewood Cliffs: Prentice-Hall.

Barnes, N.G. (2010). How do the most successful companies use social media. *Marketing Research*, **22**(1), pp. 8–13.

Boo, S., Busser, J. and Baloglu, S. (2009). A model of customer-based brand equity and its application to multiple destinations. *Tourism Management*, **30**(2), pp. 219–231.

Bruhn, M., Schoenmueller, V. and Schäfer, D.B. (2012). Are social media replacing traditional media in terms of brand equity creation? *Management Research Review*, **35**(9), pp. 770–790.

Caber, M., Güven, A. and Öztürk, A. (2016, July). Exploring how to match local products fair participation motivations of the visitors and businesses. *Journal of Convention and Event Tourism*, **17**(3), pp. 220–233.

Campbell, J.L. (2005). Where do we stand? Common mechanisms in organizations and social movements research. In G.F. Davis, D. McAdam, W.R. Scott and M.N. Zald (eds.) *Social movements and organization theory*. New York: Cambridge University Press, pp. 41–68.

Chalip, L. and Costa, C.A. (2005). Sport event tourism and the destination brand: Towards a general theory. *Sport in Society*, **8**(2), pp. 218–237.

Correia, A., Kozak, M. and Reis, H. (2016). Conspicuous consumption of the elite: Social and self-congruity in tourism choices. *Journal of Travel Research*, **55**(6), pp. 738–750.

Crompton, J.L. and McKay, S.L. (1997). Motives of visitors attending festival events. *Annals of Tourism Research*, **24**(2), pp. 425–439.

Deaux, K. (2000). Models, meaning and motivations. In D. Capozza and Brown, R. (eds.) *Social identity processes: Trends in theory and research*. London: Sage Publishing, pp. 1–14.

Dedeoğlu, B.B. (2016). *The relationship between social media, involvement and destination brand equity*. Unpublished dissertation. Institute of Social Sciences, Akdeniz University, Antalya, Turkey.

Drury, G. (2008). Opinion piece: Social media: Should marketers engage and how can it be done effectively? *Journal of Direct, Data and Digital Marketing Practice*, **9**(3), pp. 274–277.

Formica, S. and Uysal, M. (1996). A market segmentation of festival visitors: Umbria Jazz festival in Italy. *Festival Management and Event Tourism*, **3**(4), pp. 175–182.

Formica, S. and Uysal, M. (1998). Market segmentation of an international cultural-historical event in Italy. *Journal of Travel Research*, **36**(4), pp. 16–24.

Gartner, W.C. (1994). Image formation process. *Journal of Travel and Tourism Marketing*, **2**(2–3), pp. 191–216.

Gartner, W.C. (2014). Brand equity in a tourism destination. *Place Branding and Public Diplomacy*, **10**(2), pp. 108–116.

Getz, D. (2007). *Event studies: Theory, research and policy for planned events*. Oxford: Butterworth-Heinemann.

Getz, D. (2008). Event tourism: Definition, evolution, and research. *Tourism Management*, **29**(3), pp. 403–428.

Giritlioğlu, İ., Olcay, A. and Özekici, Y.K. (2015). *Bir turizm çeşitliliği olarak festival etkinliklerinin sınıflandırılması: Türkiye üzerine bir değerlendirme. Sosyal Bilimler Araştırmaları Dergisi* (in Turkey). Retrieved from: http://dergipark.gov.tr/download/article-file/273497 (accessed: the 22nd September, 2014).

Global Digital Statistics. (2014). *Home*. Retrieved from: https://bit.ly/2HiEkgU (accessed: the 22nd September, 2014).

Google Trend. (2014). *Home*. Retrieved from: www.google.com.tr/trends/explore#date=1%2F2014%2012mandcmpt=q (accessed: the 22nd September, 2014).

Gretzel, U. and Yoo, K.H. (2008). Use and impact of online travel reviews. In P. O'Connor, W. Höpken and U. Gretzel (eds.) *Information and communication technologies in tourism*. Vienna: Springer-Verlag Wien, pp. 35–46.

Hede, A.-M. and Jago, L.K. (2005). Perceptions of the host destination as a result of attendance at a special event: A post-consumption analysis. *International Journal of Event Management Research*, **1**(1), pp. 1–11.

Heinonen, K. (2011). Consumer activity in social media: Managerial approaches to consumers' social media behavior. *Journal of Consumer Behaviour*, **10**(6), pp. 356–364.

Herrero, Á., San Martín, H. and Hernández, J.M. (2015). How online search behavior is influenced by user-generated content on review websites and hotel interactive websites. *International Journal of Contemporary Hospitality Management*, **27**(7), pp. 1573–1597.

Huang, Z.J. and Cai, L.A. (2015). Modeling consumer-based brand equity for multinational hotel brands – When hosts become guests. *Tourism Management*, **46**, pp. 431–443.

Hurt, D.A., Delvecki, A., Payne, A. and Gress, G. (2012). Oklahoma tourism along route 66: Pioneers, perseverance, community, and freedom. *Material Culture*, **44**(1), pp. 31–49.

Hwang, J. and Han, H. (2014). Examining strategies for maximizing and utilizing brand prestige in the luxury cruise industry. *Tourism Management*, **40**, pp. 244–259.

Hwang, J. and Hyun, S.S. (2012). The antecedents and consequences of brand prestige in luxury restaurants. *Asia Pacific Journal of Tourism Research*, **17**(6), pp. 656–683.

Jago, L.K. and Shaw, R.N. (1998). Special events: A conceptual and definitional framework. *Festival Management and Event Tourism*, **5**(1–1), pp. 21–32.

Jin, N., Lee, H. and Lee, S. (2013). Event quality, perceived value, destination image, and behavioral intention of sports events: The case of the IAAF World Championship, Daegu, 2011. *Asia Pacific Journal of Tourism Research*, **18**(8), pp. 849–864.

Kaplanidou, K. (2006). Affective event and destination image: Their influence on Olympic travelers' behavioral intentions. *Event Management*, **10**(2–3), pp. 159–173.

Kaplanidou, K. and Vogt, C. (2007). The interrelationship between sport event and destination image and sport tourists' behaviours. *Journal of Sport and Tourism*, **12**(3–4), pp. 183–206.

Keller, K.L. (1993). Conceptualizing, measuring, and managing customer-based brand equity. *Journal of Marketing*, **57**(1), pp. 1–22.

Keller, K.L. (2012). *Strategic brand management: Building, measuring, and managing brand equity*. Upper Saddle River: Pearson Prentice Hall.

Kester, J. and Croce, V. (2011). *Tourism development in advanced and emerging economies: What does the travel and tourism competitiveness index tell us?* Retrieved from: www2.unwto.org/agora/tourism-development-advanced-and-emerging-economies-what-does-travel-tourism-competitiveness-i (accessed: the 22nd September, 2014).

Khammash, M. and Griffiths, G.H. (2011). 'Arrivederci CIAO. com, Buongiorno Bing. com' – Electronic Word-of-Mouth (eWOM), antecedences and consequences. *International Journal of Information Management*, **31**(1), pp. 82–87.

Küçükergin, K.G. and Dedeoğlu, B.B. (2014). The importance of employee hospitality and perceived price in the hotel industry. *Anatolia*, **25**(2), pp. 254–267.

Kurtzman, J. and Zauhar, J. (1994). Activity interdependence factors within sports tourism manifestations. *Journal of Sport Tourism*, **2**(1), pp. 22–28.

Lee, C.K., Lee, Y.K. and Wicks, B.E. (2004). Segmentation of festival motivation by nationality and satisfaction. *Tourism Management*, **25**(1), pp. 61–70.

Lee, C.S. and Ma, L. (2012). News sharing in social media: The effect of gratifications and prior experience. *Computers in Human Behavior*, **28**(2), pp. 331–339.

Leibenstein, H. (1950). Bandwagon, snob, and veblen effects in the theory of consumers' demand. *The Quarterly Journal of Economics*, **64**(2), pp. 183–207.

Liang, Y., Illum, S.F. and Cole, S.T. (2008). Benefits received and behavioural intentions of festival visitors in relation to distance travelled and their origins. *International Journal of Event Management Research*, **4**(1), pp. 12–23.

Lietsala, K. and Sirkkunen, E. (2008). *Social media: Introduction to the tools and processes of participatory economy*. Retrieved from: https://tampub.uta.fi/bitstream/han dle/10024/65560/978-951-44-7320-3.pdf?sequence=1&isAllowed=y (accessed: the 07th January, 2018).

Moon, K.S., Ko, Y.J., Connaughton, D.P. and Lee, J.H. (2013). A mediating role of destination image in the relationship between event quality, perceived value, and behavioral intention. *Journal of Sport and Tourism*, 18(1), pp. 49–66.

Nelson, S. and Vogler, J. (2002). Corporate brand and packaging design. *Design Management Review*, 13(4), pp. 32–37.

O'Cass, A. and Frost, H. (2002). Status brands: Examining the effects of non-product-related brand associations on status and conspicuous consumption. *Journal of Product and Brand Management*, 11(2), pp. 67–88.

Pappu, R., Quester, P.G. and Cooksey, R.W. (2005). Consumer-based brand equity: Improving the measurement-empirical evidence. *Journal of Product and Brand Management*, 14(3), pp. 143–154.

Park, N., Kee, K.F. and Valenzuela, S. (2009). Being immersed in social networking environment: Facebook groups, uses and gratifications, and social outcomes. *Cyber Psychology and Behavior*, 12(6), pp. 729–733.

Pike, S. and Page, S.J. (2014). Destination Marketing Organizations and destination marketing: A narrative analysis of the literature. *Tourism Management*, 41, pp. 202–227.

Pike, S., Bianchi, C., Kerr, G. and Patti, C. (2010). Consumer-based brand equity for Australia as a long-haul tourism destination in an emerging market. *International Marketing Review*, 27(4), pp. 434–449.

Sandole, D.J. (2009). Turkey's unique role in nipping in the bud the "clash of civilizations". *International Politics*, 46(5), pp. 636–655.

See-To, E.W. and Ho, K.K. (2014). Value co-creation and purchase intention in social network sites: The role of electronic word-of-mouth and trust – A theoretical analysis. *Computers in Human Behavior*, 31, pp. 182–189.

Shao, G. (2009). Understanding the appeal of user-generated media: A uses and gratification perspective. *Internet Research*, 19(1), pp. 7–25.

Sirgy, M.J. (1982). Self-concept in consumer behavior: A critical review. *Journal of Consumer Research*, 9(3), pp. 287–300.

Steenkamp, J.B.E., Batra, R. and Alden, D.L. (2003). How perceived brand globalness creates brand value. *Journal of International Business Studies*, 34(1), pp. 53–65.

Stoeckl, R., Rohrmeier, P. and Hess, T. (2007). *Motivations to produce user generated content: Differences between webloggers and videobloggers*. Retrieved from: http://aisel.aisnet.org/bled2007/30/ (accessed: the 22nd September, 2014).

Tajfel, H. and Turner, J.C. (1979). An integrative theory of intergroup conflict. *The Social Psychology of Intergroup Relations*, 33(47), p. 74.

Tussyadiah, I.P. and Fesenmaier, D.R. (2009). Mediating tourist experiences: Access to places via shared videos. *Annals of Tourism Research*, 36(1), pp. 24–40.

Tuten, T.L. (2008). *Advertising 2.0: Social media marketing in a web 2.0 world*. London: Greenwood Publishing Group.

UNWTO. (2016). *Tourism highlights 2016*. Madrid: UNWTO.

Uysal, M., Gahan, L. and Martin, B. (1993). An examination of event motivations: A case study. *Festival Management and Event Tourism*, 1(1), pp. 5–10.

Valkenburg, P.M., Peter, J. and Schouten, A.P. (2006). Friend networking sites and their relationship to adolescents' well-being and social self-esteem. *Cyber Psychology and Behavior*, 9(5), pp. 584–590.

Vigneron, F. and Johnson, L.W. (1999). A review and a conceptual framework of prestige-seeking consumer behavior. *Academy of Marketing Science Review*, 1, pp. 1–15.

Webb, H.J. and Zimmer-Gembeck, M.J. (2014). The role of friends and peers in adolescent body dissatisfaction: A review and critique of 15 years of research. *Journal of Research on Adolescence*, **24**(4), pp. 564–590.

Xiang, Z. and Gretzel, U. (2010). Role of social media in online travel information search. *Tourism Management*, **31**(2), pp. 179–188.

Yürük, P., Akyol, A. and Şimşek, G.G. (2017). Analyzing the effects of social impacts of events on satisfaction and loyalty. *Tourism Management*, **60**, pp. 367–378.

Zajonc, R.B. (1980). Feeling and thinking: Preferences need no inferences. *American Psychologist*, **35**(2), pp. 151–175.

Zhou, C.N., Qiao, G. and Ryan, C. (2017). How might Chinese medium sized cities improve competitive advantage in the event tourism market? *Event Management*, **21**(1), pp. 109–118.

Zimmerman, J. and Ng, D. (2010). *Social media marketing all-in-one for dummies*. Hoboken: John Wiley & Sons.

9 The roles of social media in the promotion of traditional cultural tourism events in Indonesia

Desloehal Djumrianti

Introduction

The rapid development of communication and information technology has penetrated all fields of the tourism industry. Today, with the emergence of the digital technologies, the word of mouth information has extended beyond a limited group to the entire world. The promotional materials based on papers including newspapers, magazines, flyers, brochures and pamphlets; or electronic media, such as television, radio, or electronic billboard compete with promotional tools based on the Internet in distributing information and promotion of cultural events. As Madasu (2013:72) claims "new technologies have changed the priorities in terms of promotion as, previously, it was the enterprises that established the flow of communication and used technologies only as an instrument of support". Social media as a part of the digital technology revolution now connects many people to the opinions and recommendation of millions of people, including people who are interested in cultural events.

In addition, internet apps, the power of smart phone, and other mobile devices enable DMOs to use Facebook, Instagram and Twitter as more than just communication tools. Those social media have become increasingly popular in the tourism and travel industry, and as crucial tools for creating, introducing and promoting tourism events. For example, they have been used by DMOs of Jakarta, Bandung and Bali to promote cultural tourism events of their cities. The number of traditional culture events, such as traditional dance shows, traditional clothes festivals, and street food festivals were promoted by using social media, including Facebook, Twitter and Instagram. These social media are popular among young people in Indonesia; as reported by Hidayat (2016) on Liputan 6 news, Facebook is the most famous social media that has been used for many reasons at around 54.6 per cent of Internet users.

DMOs of Jakarta, Bali and Bandung use social media such as Facebook, Twitter and Instagram for 'hard sell' advertising, where they seem enthusiastic and aggressive in pushing potential customers to get involved in the traditional cultural events (Okazaki, 2010).

Therefore, to understand how Facebook, Twitter and Instagram serve as promotional media of DMOs of Jakarta, Bandung and Bali, the aim of this study is to investigate how social media is used in the promotional cultural events; social media as used as a source of information to gather the events; and the roles of Twitter, Instagram and Facebook in the promotion of traditional cultural events of three different cities.

Problem statement

In this digital era, as Internet technology enables DMOs to create promotion strategies more than the conventional paper-based ways. As Madasu (2013) claims, many tourism promotions can benefit more from word-of-mouth marketing. The communication through the Internet is able to reach potential customers in large scope. Some scholars agree that social networking sites (SNS), including Facebook, Twitter and Instagram, and so on are used in order to promote destinations (Digital Buzz Blog, 2017; Chung and Koo, 2015). Kaplan and Haenlein (2010) state they are not only becoming exceedingly widely adopted in the tourism and travel industries, but also other types of communication that are popular among Internet users, particularly young people. According to the Internet users' statistics in 2016, young people ages 18–29 are the highest number of Facebook users in USA (Greenwood et al., 2016). In addition, Salid (no date), CEO and co-founder of 'invesp', claims there are an increasing number of global online retail transactions in the last four years. In ten countries across the UK, Europe and Asia around 7.4 per cent on the average per year use online social media. Paquette (2013) believes that social media are effective as the marketing communication media. This, therefore, leads to some DMOs to trust social media and use them for other communication marketing, such as promotional tools of the traditional cultural events (Chatzithomas et al., 2014).

Therefore, this study is required to fill this gap in tourism research and to give detailed analysis to provide a comprehensive discussion of the use of social media in order to promote the traditional cultural events of Jakarta, Bandung and Bali; the role of Facebook, Twitter and Instagram as the information resources; and in the promoting of traditional cultural events in those cities.

Methodology/approach

This study is based on qualitative research, and the aim of the qualitative method is to provide insights into the problem or to help to develop ideas or hypotheses for potential quantitative research. Qualitative research allows the researcher to interpret the reality that is constructed by humans in the course of their actions. Also, it enables the researcher to collect deep and insightful data from a small sample (Creswell, 2003; Neuman, 2006).

There are two types of data in this study; the primary data is based on the discussion in the Focus Group Discussion (FGD) via Skype. Secondary research is based on the observation to the respondents through the social media that they used for six months (February–July 2016) by using Netnography approach. Data collection in netnography means "communicating with members of a culture or community"

(Kozinets, 2010:95). It provides guidelines for the adaptation of participant-obser-vation procedures to the contingencies of online community and culture that mani-fest through computer-mediated communications (Kozinets, 2010). This approach is considered to have some benefits compared to the conventional ethnography, such as it can save time and money. Ethnography can be very expensive and extremely time consuming. The reliability of the data has been a subject of debate as well. Some opinions express a concern for consumer behaviours to be skewed as they know they are being observed and thus might not act in the same manner as they normally would. Because of the surveillance method used in ethnography, the number of subjects that can be observed is greatly limited by time and money. This is where netnography truly shines. Netnography is also vastly more cost-effective than ethnographic studies (Wu and Pearce, 2014; Mkono and Markwell, 2014).

Although FGD were conducted via Skype, there were only 130 out of 200 respon-dents who were able to participate in this current study. They were grouped into thirteen users for each group online discussion. The discussion was more or less 60 minutes for each group discussion. As Frietas and colleagues (1998:1) define,

> Focus Group is a type of in-depth interview accomplished in a group, whose meetings present characteristics defined with respect to the proposal, size, composition, and interview procedures. The focus or object of analysis is the interaction inside the group. The participants influence each other through their answers to the ideas and contributions during the discussion.

Nagel and William (no date:10) claim "focus groups are valuable research tools and can capture information that will help to better tell story on the study topic". Thus, the FGD were used to gain the information about how social media are used as the promotion tools of cultural events of Jakarta, Bandung and Bali.

Around 200 respondents of this study are the users of social media and part of the online communities of Facebook, Twitter and Instagram. They are young peo-ple between 15 and 28 years old. Respondents were selected using simple random method, based on users who gave the comments on the Twitter and Instagram of each DMOs, and mutual friends on DMOs' official Facebook accounts.

Brief literature review

In establishing a context for this research project, several theoretical areas within the literature need to be understood. First, the study determined what are the SNS that have been used by DMOs in order to promote tourism and culture, followed by an understanding of the significance of the social media trends to promote traditional cultural events.

Social networking sites in the tourism industry

As mentioned earlier, some scholarly people agree that SNS are among the most widely adopted in the tourism and travel industries (Kaplan and Haenlein, 2010), such as many social media sites including Facebook, Twitter, Wayn, Airbnb, TripAdvisor, Instagram and so on are used in order to promote destinations (Digital Buzz Blog, 2017; Kong, 2010). Further, Kaplan and Haenlein (2010:61) define SNS or social media as "a group of Internet-based applications that build on the ideological and technological foundations of Web 2.0, and that allow the creation and exchange of user-generated content" (UGC). From this definition it can be underlined that the 'credibility' of social media is questionable, because anyone is freely able to produce any content in the site. The accuracy of information through the content of a site is probably not a hundred per cent trustworthy (Collier, 2008).

In addition, Xiang and Gretzel (2010) find that the development of advanced technology communication enables tourists to do more than just travel. The communication devices allow travellers to express and share their tourism experiences on social media, for example. A blog, vblog (video blog), or Youtube allows people to share information in accordance with their own interests, express their opinions, photos, videos, and ideas of a destination as much as they like (Chen et al., 2014; Dearstyne, 2007).

Similarly, Pan et al. (2007) argue that the emergence of TripAdvisor in 2000 has impacted on the way travellers search for tourism information. Like any other social media, TripAdvisor is not only to assist potential tourists in gathering travel information, but also tourists to post reviews and opinions of travel-related content and engage in interactive travel forums (Tripadvisor.com, 2017; Amaro et al., 2016). Today, social media is playing an increasingly important role as an information source for tourists. Many potential tourists use it to collect travel-related information (Tussyadiah and Fesenmaier, 2009). Additionally, the linking of social media with the search engine, Google, has enhanced the importance of social media in the online tourism domain (Xiang and Gretzel, 2010; Park et al., 2016).

Importantly, however, Park et al. (2016) claim that social media in the context of tourism is not merely used by travellers but it is also employed by government: for example, the use of Facebook by the Korean government to promote tourist destinations in the country. As the 'official' Facebook page, the content of this social media site can be viewed as accurate and reliable. Thus, it seems the issue of credibility of the content of various types of social media becomes blurred in this context. Xiang and Gretzel (2010) also argue that some tourists are not concerned with the credibility of the content of sites.

Hence, the various internet apps and smart devices not only allow tourists to share their feelings, experiences, ideas, and comments through words, photos, or videos; many other organisations including DMOs and other stakeholders use them to promote destinations and tourism products. The ways in which those narrate a place are through not only stories of meaning but of power (Bruner, 2005) that influence readers' (other potential tourists) images of a touristic place (Wong et al., 2016). For DMOs to establish a narrative "have tremendous consequences as they make meaning, shape action, mould tourist behavior, serve" to select which aspects of destinations are represented (Bruner, 2005:3). Therefore, the next part will review the way DMOs use official websites to construct narratives of their destinations.

Social media and young users

As Quan-Haase and Young (2010) claim, the most widely used forms of social media is an online activity in which friends or peers interact with each other in a social group using a central website or application to transmit messages. Additionally, Buckingham and Willet (2013) emphasise these messages can contain text, images, videos, links or other sharable media. Social networks allow users to create virtual approximations of their real-world social relationships and facilitate sharing of news and content. Their focus is usually on immediate, sharing-based casual interactions between acquaintances, though this can vary depending on the platform. Despite the differences between the social networks, there are three main characteristics of social networking in general: connecting, sharing and engaging.

Most of social media users are among young people, according to a study conducted by Folaranmi (2013). His survey on Facebook addiction level among undergraduates in selected Nigerian universities revealed that of the 994 students surveyed, 220 (22.1 per cent) stated their reason for Facebook addiction as 'meeting people'; for school work, 149 (15 per cent); dating, 134 (13.5 per cent); uploading, 113 (11.4 per cent); chatting, 194 (19.5 per cent); uploading pictures, 69 (6.9 per cent); messaging, 82 (8.2 per cent); and celebrity follow-up, 33 (3.3 per cent). However, the study found low addiction (1.6 per cent) particularly among university undergraduates in private universities, attributing the result to the low level of Internet access generally in Nigeria. Facebook was one of the examples of how social media that has been used by young people for many purposes. The popularity of the social media has been greatly enhanced by its flexibility, interactivity and ability to perform multiple roles in almost every sphere of life. Unlike the mainstream of the traditional media with their rigid regulations and time-wasting characteristics, the social media platforms are virtually free, instantaneous, open to all, and have little or no restriction (Folaranmi, 2013).

Results and discussion

There are around two hundred cultural events that are promoted in Jakarta's official Facebook, Twitter and Instagram in 2016. They include traditional dances and music shows, folk theatres, batik – traditional clothes festivals – Pantun Kampung Pela, Jakarta traditional culture festival, Jakarta street foods festival, weekly Betawi puppet shows, Betawi punya cerite exhibitions, and so on.

There was an equal number of use of the three social media as advertising tools; the information which is available on the Facebook people may also can find on Twitter and Instagram. There are various comments on three different social media. On the official Twitter and Instagram of Jakarta anyone may comment on their advertising. During the netnography on the Internet through Jakarta's social media, and the feedbacks on FGD, around 73 respondents answer normally; users place simple comments on Twitters or Instagrams. This also leads to UGC; any user may suggest the content of the advertising in their comments. On one hand, this may enrich the content of each advertisement (Migúens et al., 2008). On the other hand,

Pan et al. (2007) claim the UGC lead to less trustiness of the content itself. The involvement of social media users may change the purposes of the cultural advertisings (Amaro et al., 2011).

As users who use Facebook, however, are mutual friends of Jakarta's Tourism FB, comments of users are more specific and private. They may ask more detail about the events, such as how they could get involved in the events, the discount of ticket prices, and so on.

As Pan et al. (2007) argue, the emergence of social media has impacted on the way people search for tourism information, including cultural events. The social media is playing an increasingly important role as an information source for tourists (Amaro et al., 2011). Many potential tourists use it to collect travel-related information (Tussyadiah and Fesenmaier, 2009). Additionally, the linking of social media with the search engine, Google, has enhanced the importance of social media in the online tourism domain (Xiang and Gretzel, 2010; Park et al., 2016).

While, in Bandung, there are around 126 traditional cultural events that are promoted through the official Facebook, Twitter and Instagram of Bandung's DMO. Similarly, Twitter is one of the social media that is used by some users in order to gather traditional cultural events. Around 45 per cent of respondents used it to look for traditional events, such as Bandung food festival, Bike to Cook, traditional clothing – Batik hand painting and Batik Design Competition, Liga Seni Budaya Bandung. Most of them looked for the venues of events and ticket prices. However, around 30 per cent of social media users prefer to use Facebook to get detail of events. Normally, they communicate in the Facebook chat rooms with admin or directly to the events providers. Although the Instagram users who search for information on Bandung traditional events were only around 25 per cent, 10 per cent of them are also users of Facebook and Twitter. Because the content of promotion of traditional events of Bandung on Twitter, Facebook and Instagram were exactly the same, they use Instagram just see the comments of other users of an event.

Bali is a city in Indonesia which has a lot of traditional cultural events which are not only enjoyed by locals but also consumed by foreigners. Bali's DMO promoted the annual traditional cultural events through its official website, Twitter, Instagram and Facebook. They include Youth Hindus conference, Pesta Kesenian Bali (PKB) – Bali Arts Party, Kite festival, Kuta carnival, Denpasar festival, Ogohogoh festival, Ubud festival and so on. Normally, some young Balinese participate in several traditional cultural events, whether they are as dancers, singers, or as spectators. Some of these traditional events were free of charge, and provided as tourists commodities. Although these are part of Bali's annual cultural events, the venues of events normally are not the same. Therefore, the online communication tools such as social media were selected by local government to promote and inform the events. The study found that there are 40 per cent of respondents gather the event information through Twitter, followed by Facebook around 35 per cent, and Instagram more or less 25 per cent. Most of them use the social media to gather information about venues of events.

However, it was found that in Twitter and Instagram, the local governments cannot control the feedbacks from users, whatever they want to say. This will bring negative effect to the image of the traditional events that are promoted by the Twitter, Instagram or event to the government itself. However, it did not happen to Facebook.

Conclusion

Social media is one of online media that is used by local governments in order to promote traditional cultural events in Indonesia. They are Twitter, Facebook and Instagram. It was found that Twitter is the most favourite social media among young people in order to gather information related to the cultural events in three cities – Jakarta, Bandung and Bali – followed by Facebook and Instagram. Young people as users who got the information from official Twitters of Jakarta, Bandung, and Bali were not necessarily mutual friends of these governments. They could post comments and share events that were created by Twitter users. Therefore, unnecessary comments and feedback were overwhelming. However, some respondents prefer to use Facebook as this social media enables people to do live chat, is more private, the trustiness of the comments is higher, and it is less anonymous.

References

Amaro, S., Duarte, P. and Henriques, C. (2016). Travelers use of social media: A clustering approach. *Annals of Tourism Research*, **59**(1), pp. 1–15.

Bruner, E.M. (2005). The role of narrative in tourism. *Urbana*, **51**, pp. 1–22.

Buckingham, D. and Willett, R. (eds.). (2013). *Digital generations: Children, young people, and the new media*. Oxon: Routledge.

Chatzithomas, N., Boutsouki, C. and Hatzithomas, L. (2014). Social media advertising platforms: A cross-cultural study. *International Journal on Strategic Innovative Marketing*, **1**, pp. 74–90.

Chen, Y.C., Shang, R.A. and Li, M.J. (2014). The effects of perceived relevance of travel blogs' content on the behavioral intention to visit a tourist destination. *Computers in Human Behavior*, **30**, pp. 787–799.

Chung, N. and Koo, C. (2015). The use of social media in travel information search. *Telematics and Informatics*, **32**(2), pp. 215–229.

Collier, M. (2008). *This is why authority matters' argument is total BS*. Retrieved from: http://moblogsmoproblems.blogspot.com/2008/12/this-is-why-authority-matters-argument.html (accessed: the 10th November, 2017).

Creswell, J.W. (2003). *Research design: Qualitative, quantitative, and mixed approaches*. Thousand Oaks: Sage Publications.

Dearstyne, B. (2007, July). Blogs, mashup, and wikis: Oh, my Ready or not, Web. 2.0, a new generation of web-based service, is changing the way people work and the way records and documents are created, used, and shared. *Information Management Journal*, pp. 25–33.

Digital Buzz Blog. (2017). *Infographic: Social media statistic for 2013*. Retrieved from: www.digitalbuzzblog.com/infographic-social-media-statistics-for-2013/ (accessed: the 12th April, 2017).

Folaranmi, A.O. (2013). A survey of Facebook addiction level among selected Nigerian University undergraduates. *New Media and Mass Communication*, **10**, pp. 70–80.

Freitas, H., Mírian, O., Milton, J. and Oveta, P. (1998). The focus group, a qualitative research method. *Journal of Education*, **1**(1), pp. 1–22.

Greenwood, S., Perrin, A. and Duggan, M. (2016). Social media update 2016: Facebook usage and engagement is on the rise, while adoption of other platforms holds steady. *Pew Research Center Internet and Technology*. Retrieved from: www.pewinternet. org/2016/11/11/social-media-update-2016/ (accessed: the 20th November, 2017).

Hallet, W.R. and Kaplan-Winger, J. (2010). *Official tourism website: A discourse analysis perspective*. Exeter: Short Run Press, Ltd.

Hidayat, W.M. (2016). *3 social media favourite among internet users in Indonesia – 3 media social favorit pengguna internet Indonesia. Online News – Liputan 6*. Retrieved from: http://tekno.liputan6.com/read/2634027/3-media-sosial-favorit-pengguna-internet-indonesia (accessed: the 08th October, 2017).

Kaplan, A.M. and Haenlein, M. (2010). Users of the world, unite! The challenges and opportunities of social media. *Business Horizons*, **55**(1), pp. 27–31.

Kong, C. (2010). *The self-representation of regional and national identities: Comparing the translation patterns between China and Hong Kong tourism websites*. Retrieved from: www.gla.ac.uk/media/media_141051_en.pdf (accessed: the 10th November, 2017).

Kozinets, R.V. (2010). *Netnography: Doing ethnographic research online*. London: Sage Publication.

Madasu, P. (2013). Social media marketing and promotion of tourism. *Management Insight*, **IX**(1), pp. 71–80.

Migúens, J., Baggio, R. and Costa, C. (2008, May). Social media and tourism destinations: TripAdvisor case study. *IASK ATR2008 (Advances in Tourism Research 2008). Aveiro. Portugal*, pp. 26–28.

Mkono, M. and Markwell, K. (2014). The application of netnography in tourism studies. *Annals of Tourism Research*, **48**, pp. 266–291.

Nagel, B. and William, N. (n.d.). *Methodology brief: Introduction to focus group*. Retrieved from: www.mmgconnect.com/projects/userfiles/file/focusgroupbrief.pdf (accessed: the 12th September, 2017).

Neuman, L.W. (2006). *Social research methods: Qualitative and quantitative approaches*. Boston: Pearson Education, Inc.

Okazaki, S. (2010). Measuring hard sell vs soft sell advertising appeals. *Journal of Advertising*, **39**(2), pp. 5–20.

Pan, B., Litvin, S.W. and O'Donnell, T.E. (2007). Understanding accommodation search query formulation: The first step in putting "heads in beds". *Journal of Vacation Marketing*, **13**(4), pp. 371–381.

Paquette, H. (2013). *Social media as marketing tool: A literature review*. Retrieved from: http://digitalcommons.uri.edu/cgi/viewcontent.cgi?article=1001&context=tmd_major_papers (accessed: the 01st November, 2017).

Park, M., Naaman, M. and Berger, J. (2016). A data-driven study of view duration on YouTube. *Tenth International Conference on Web and Social Media* (ICWSM 2016). Cologne, Germany: May, 2016.

Quan-Haase, A. and Young, A.L. (2010). Uses and gratifications of social media: A comparison of Facebook and instant messaging. *Bulletin of Science, Technology and Society*, **30**(5), pp. 350–361.

Tripadvisor. (2017). *About Tripadvisor*. Retrieved from: https://tripadvisor.mediaroom.com/us-about-us (accessed: the 02nd November, 2017).

Tussyadiah, I.P. and Fesenmaier, D.R. (2009). Mediating tourist experiences: Access to places via shared videos. *Annals of Tourism Research*, **36**(1), pp. 24–40.

Wong, J.Y., Lee, S.J. and Lee, W.H. (2016). "Does it really affect me?" Tourism destination narratives, destination image, and the intention to visit: Examining the moderating effect of narrative transportation. *International Journal of Tourism Research*, **18**(5), pp. 458–468.

Wu, M.-Y. and Pearce, P.L. (2014). Appraising netnography: Towards insights about new markets in the digital tourist era. *Current Issues in Tourism*, **17**(5), pp. 463–474.

Xiang, Z. and Gretzel, U. (2010). Role of social media in online travel information search. *Tourism Management*, **31**, pp. 179–188.

10 Prominent and innovative tourism events in Peninsular Malaysia

Nor Aida Abdul Rahman

Introduction

The tourism industry plays an important role to develop and boost the country's economy. It not only contributes to social entities via job creation, but also supports other business sectors especially in transportation, food, clothing, crafts and gifts, manufacturing and also the information and technology industry. There are two types of tourist, namely local tourists and international tourists. Local tourists, or domestic tourists, can be defined as a resident of that country that travel within their country. On the other hand, international tourists or foreign tourists refer to the tourists who are travelling to different countries (outside their country). Both types of tourist are acknowledged as the key vehicle that boost the tourism industry of any country.

According to World Travel and Tourism Report published in 2017, the total "direct contribution of Travel & Tourism to GDP was USD2,306.0bn (3.1 per cent of total GDP) in 2016, and is forecast to rise by 3.8 per cent in 2017, and to rise by 4.0 per cent pa, from 2017–2027, to USD3,537.1bn (3.5 per cent of total GDP) in 2027". This reflects the importance of tourism events globally. Research in tourism events started in the early 1990s. As suggested by Getz (2008), developing events and a marketing plan to promote any destination is a key factor in attracting tourists to come to that place. Events are a motivator of tourism. Parties involved in tourism activity should plan properly and well document whatever events planned are identified in promoting any places. At present, with the increase of technology in business activity, all information is at everyone fingertips. The use of social media or digital marketing to promote events is vital to support tourism activity all across the globe.

In Malaysia, tourism events started gained popularity in 1990 when it first launched in 1990 with the theme 'Fascinating Malaysia, Year of Festival'. During that time, Malaysia received 7.4 million tourists in arrivals compared to 4.8 million tourists in 1989. At that time, Malaysia's Independence Day has been the most prominent tourism event compared to 83 other organised tourism events. After almost three decades, the number of tourist visits in Malaysia has hugely increased to 25.9 million arrivals in 2017 and is expected to reach 36 million tourist arrivals as outlined in the Malaysia Tourism Transformation Plan (MTTP)

2020. Malaysia is known as one Asian country that has its own uniqueness with multi-cultural people, colourful environment (flora and fauna), multi-religious nation, multi-cultural festivals such as Eid Mubarak, Chinese New Year, Deepavali, Christmas, Ramadhan and many more. It has its own natural attraction apart from the tourism events activities. This is aligned with what has been emphasised by Quinn (2010): That unique culture owned by country or events is the core factors to attract tourists.

Literature review

The evolution of tourism industry in Malaysia

From a review of past literature, the researcher could conclude that the strength of the Malaysian industry is led by its diversity of multi-racial society, multilingual, multi-religious, multi-cultural, multiple festival events, food varieties, affordable luxury events, varieties of nature and adventure, green tourism activity, rural tourism and many more (MIDA, 2013). All of these factors are identified as a key factor that boosts the tourism industry in Malaysia. Detailed explanation for each key factor is shown in Table 10.1. All of these factors are aligned with what been suggested by UNCTAD (2013). According to UNCTAD (2013), the main factor

Table 10.1 Contributing factors to Malaysia tourism industry

Key factor	Explanation
Multi-racial society	Malaysia is recognised as a country that has a multi-racial society. There are about 127 ethnic/subethnic groups in Malaysia; for instance Malay, Chinese, Indian, Peranakan, Iban, Kadazan, Minangkabau, Bugis, Kelabit, Serani, Dusun etc.
Multilingual	Malaysia also has varieties of dialects such as Malay, Tamil, Chinese, Mandarin, Punjab, Singh, Malayalam, Telugu, and Dusunic
Multi-religious	Islam, Buddhist, Hindu, Singh etc.
Multiple festival events	Chinese New Year, Eid Mubarak, Deepavali, Raya Haji etc.
Food varieties	Satay, rendang, coconut rice, char kuew tiaw, curry mee etc.
Affordable luxury events	Golfing, shopping, spa, cruising, diving etc.
Varieties of nature and adventure	25 national parks, rainforest, islands and beaches
Green tourism activity	Cycling, hiking etc.
Rural tourism activity	Homestay, agro tourism, railway tourism etc.

(Source: MIDA, 2013)

for the travel and tourism industry to aggressively develop is from its diversity sector which is recognised as tourism value chain.

As stressed by Giap et al. (2016), Malaysia tourism started as early as the 1970s. However, it was still underdeveloped at that time until the Malaysian government looked at the tourism industry as one of the most significant industries that generated the Malaysia economy in the 1990s. In the 1980s, Malaysia experienced slow growth in its commodity industry (rubber, palm oil). As emphasised by Mosbah and Al Khuja (2014), the collapse of primary commodity prices led Malaysia to recognise the immense potential of the tourism sector. Starting from that point, in 1990, all tourism planning and strategic planning has been crafted in Malaysia Plan. Malaysia Plan is recognised as a blueprint that is developed by the Malaysian government. It outlines comprehensive strategic plans and policies. Each master plan developed is for 5 years. Tourism activity was first introduced in the sixth Malaysia Plan policy in the 1990s. After 38 years, the Malaysia government has identified areas that it needs to focus on in establishing the tourism industry in Malaysia. At present, Malaysia is known globally as one of the best destinations to visit for both leisure and business. Malaysia's tourism industry not only has a direct impact on GDP, but it also relates with other industries such as logistics (Rahman, 2012), food, banking and other industries.

The evolution of the tourism industry in Malaysia can also be seen in parallel with the development of the Malaysia Plan (MP) from MP6 through MP11. Figure 10.1 shows the evolution of the tourism industry in Malaysia. All of the development plans for the tourism industry has been documented in the Malaysia Plan since sixth Malaysia Plan. Each of these master plans stated the key focus of tourism industry accordingly. As highlighted in each stage of the tourism development, it is important to note that innovation and creativity is a must

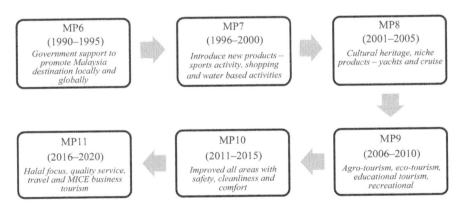

Figure 10.1 Tourism industry and Malaysia Plan 6–11

(Source: the author)

in order to maintain and increase the performance of the tourism industry. As mentioned by Drucker (2002), innovation is the core strategy for any business. In order to ensure the wellbeing of any companies in any sector, every business strategy should relate with innovative activity. In the tourism industry, every country should make their country image as unique and different from other country. Country branding is important to create demand and attract tourists. Branding is known as the image that represents any company, product or country (Rahman et al., 2014).

Tourism events in Malaysia: Creativity and innovation

Creativity of tourism events is important as it stimulates tourists to come and repeat their visit. Creativity of the tourism events becomes the key factor for tourism growth and prosperity in many countries (Rátz, 2017; Fagerberg and Godinho, 2004). For example, niche tourism or special interest tourism is a new phenomenon in the tourism field (Novelli, 2005). In Peninsular Malaysia, east and north region each has its own uniqueness. For instance, Terengganu and Kedah is recognised as a place for water activities. The shift of activity from land to water or sea activity stimulates many changes in the tourism industry. This innovative activity has increased the number of tourists and led to Malaysian economic development. Langkawi island, which located in Kedah is known as a place for yachting and cruise activity. Kapas island, Redang island and Perhentian island are located in Terengganu, the east region of Peninsular Terengganu.

Terengganu Tourism Department has introduced squid jigging activity since 2014 as one of the special interest tourism activities. Squid jigging is not new to Terengganu people, as it has been around for many generations already. However, it is started to be popularly introduced to tourists locally and globally to increase the number of tourists to visit Terengganu. The shift from land activity to sea activity is one of the innovative activities that attract tourist.

In east region of Peninsular Malaysia, squid jigging is one of the most popular tourism events in Terengganu. Since Malaysia has hundreds of islands, some of them have become a key attraction of local and foreign tourists. Squid jigging was introduced to promote Terengganu and the focus is at Kapas Island, Redang Island and Perhentian Island, all located in Terengganu. Squid jigging season runs from March to October each year and the best time to jig each month is during full moon. Tourists will experience jigging their own squid and experience different types of squid such as Sotong Torak (Mitre Squid), Sotong Jarum (Siboga Squid), Sotong Katak (Cuttlefish), Sotong Mengabang (Oval Squid) and Sotong Ketupat.

Since 2014, squid jigging has become an international festival that attracts many foreign tourists to come to Malaysia and Terengganu specifically. The participation of more than twenty countries globally each year shows the success of this innovative tourism event in Terengganu. Apart from squid jigging as a special attraction of tourism events in Malaysia, there is also another event that attracts tourist to come to Terengganu, for example, Rantau Abang place and turtles. According to Zakaria (2018:3), "Rantau Abang will be developed with replicas of the various types of turtles to invoke nostalgic feelings about the place which was once the best turtle watching spot in the country". Terengganu is expecting five million visitors in 2018 despite the global economic challenges. Tourist targets are from Singaporeans, Australians and ASEAN neighbour countries. In 2018, according to Chief Minister of Terengganu, Abdul Rahman (Bernama, 2018a), another special tourism event will be art and craft (Songket, Batik and brass carvings). This shows that innovative effort is highly important to create demand and attract tourists to come.

As discussed previously, special tourism events in north and east regions of Peninsular Malaysia are focused on water activities, while in southern and central region of peninsular Malaysia the focus is on non-water activity. Apart from shopping, leisure activity, hiking and sports, the prevalent tourism activity in the central region is largely focused on MICE activities. The latest world class MICE activity was held in Kuala Lumpur in April 2018. Since Malaysia is a leading country in World Halal industry, this annual event has brought many tourists from all over the world to Malaysia. The World Halal Conference (WHC) is an international thought leadership conference which gathers many top leaders in the Halal industry, academicians, logistics players, manufacturers, business leaders, scholars and other stakeholders. WHC is an annual event that provides a platform to further accelerate global Halal industry growth. Halal has become trending and branded to Malaysia and this innovative Halal event has successfully increased the number of tourists to Malaysia (Rahman et al., in press). Malaysia is known as Halal country with almost all of their restaurants being Halal. Malaysia is also known for Halal tourism as Malaysia provides Halal spa, Halal saloon, Halal flight menu, Halal banking, Halal hotel and Halal logistics (including Halal transport, warehouse and packaging).

In Malacca, tourism event activity is largely based on festivals as Malacca is known as a historical city in Malaysia and receives huge numbers of tourists every year. According to Bernama (2018b), Malacca has received 16.7 million tourists in 2017. As mentioned by Malacca's chief minister, Malacca is always the main spot for tourists as Malacca is well known as a historical city. He added that Malacca may be a small state but is immense in stature, where centuries of civilisation have shaped its foundation. The majority of tourists that come to Malacca are mainly from China, Singapore, Indonesia, Hong Kong, and Taiwan, followed by Western countries.

Tourism events in Malaysia: Mobile marketing

Internet or communication technology has helped many business players to succeed and sustain in their business. Internet made businesses and any other activity easy where the information is at our fingertips. The technology here consists of the Internet, technology or system used, digital system, social media and also mobile marketing (Lamberton and Stephen, 2016). Digitalisation and mobile marketing are becoming fundamental for online marketing strategies in tourism industry. Nowadays, social media is widely used as a platform to reach and engage with the customer (Pagani and Pardo, 2017; Singaraju et al., 2016). Social media is also vital in the tourism industry as the information needed is searchable to tourists. Social media imitates the major transformation of practice in marketing activities across the globe, regardless of what is their business, the industry, their type of businesses and the country they operate in, either local or international. The utilisation of Internet including social media such as Facebook, Instagram and Twitter to reach consumers is not a new phenomenon as mentioned by Rodriguez et al. (2012). In the tourism industry, social media helps the tourist a lot, especially with identifying places to visit, hotels, to understand the culture and much more. From the business provider perspective, tourism companies experience a lot of benefits as social media helps them to communicate effectively with their future customer. In fact, they are able to understand their future customer's preferences via online communication and also provide opportunities to make decisions in offering any tourism activity (Leung et al., 2013).

Research methodology

In this study, multiple qualitative case study method has been chosen. Qualitative methodology is the best method in exploratory research as it allows researchers to build the theory on the phenomenon studied (Rahman, 2015; Rahman, 2017). This study focuses on four cases of tourism events in Malaysia. All four cases came from east, north, south and central regions of Peninsular Malaysia, focusing on four main states in each region. These are Terengganu, Kedah, Kuala Lumpur and Malacca. Aligned with what has been suggested by Johnson (2006) and Yin (2018), a case study is the best method for research that relates to community engagement or community analysis such as tourism.

In order to understand prominent tourism events in Malaysia, the researcher uses qualitative content analysis and contextual analysis. Subsequent document review has been performed to provide deeper understand of tourism events in Malaysia. A series of keywords and keywords plus were used in getting the information and the findings were presented by controlled emerging themes. Themes and patterns across information were created and analysed.

Discussion

The discussion will be based on all four regions of Peninsular Malaysia in this study. The selection of states in this study is based on the tourist visit data to the identified place. Table 10.2 shows the main region and states in this study with a list of recognised and tourism events. Each of these tourism events has its own uniqueness and could stimulate tourists to come and visit Malaysia.

Table 10.2 Main region and main state selected in this study

Region	States	Identified tourism events
North	Kedah	Le tour de Langkawi – international cycling rate Langkawi international water – water sports competition Ironman Langkawi Malaysia – triathlon (starts with swimming, cycling and long running competition) Langkawi International Regatta Perdana & ASAF Sailing Cup Royal Langkawi International Regatta – sail boat competition Langkawi International Maritime & Aerospace Exhibition (LIMA) – aerospace and maritime showcase Langkawi International Laksa Festival – an annual food festival showcasing various preparations of Laksa (rice noodles) from all over Malaysia as well as many other Asian countries Langkawi Craft Festival Langkawi Nature Festival – birds, butterflies and wildlife Langkawi International Lawn Bowls (Mahsuri Cup)
East	Terengganu	Squid jigging Turtle Watching – Leatherback, Green, Hawksbill and Olive Ridley turtles Beautiful Terengganu Festivals International Lawn Bowl Terengganu Beautiful Terengganu Boat Parade Underwater Beach Clean Up at Redang Setiu Wetlands Eco Challenge International Gamelan Festival Terengganu International Eco & Marine Tourism Conference ASEAN Monsoon Casting Tournament Terengganu Seafarer Challenge Beautiful Terengganu International Judo Championship
Central	Kuala Lumpur	World Halal Conference Sepang Formula One Grand Prix Malaysia Technology Expo World Cancer Congress SenseAsia Conference National Art Gallery Malaysia Super Sale KL Biennale National Craft Day
South	Malacca	Masimugam Festival Melaka Festivals Mariamman Festival Festa Santa Cruz Festa San Pedro Dragon Boat Festival Malacca Historical City Day Medan Portugis Christmas Light

(Source: the author)

Conclusion

To conclude, the tourism industry in Malaysia has a strong potential to grow further as Malaysia is recognised as a country that has wonderful culture, a mixture of many religious, culture, language, activities and events. The stakeholders including policy makers need to make each event. All parties involved should use the advantage of information and technology and market it via social media for the most significant effort. A combination of old and new events is a good strategy as tourists always love to know the history of each events. Newly organised events are also important as an innovative effort in ensuring the wellbeing of the tourism industry in Malaysia.

From the research perspective, this writing could be used as a main reference to the researchers or tourism scholars to further explore the preceding list of tourism events. Scholars could explore further in terms of issues and challenges of each event and how each event helps to boost the Malaysian economy generally and the states particularly. This could be used as a basis to extensively research the challenges from many perspectives such as policy makers, tourism industry players, consumers, villagers and event organisers. This is aligning with what been suggested by Laing (2018) and Getz and Page (2016), which stress the lack of research on sustainability of festivals and events which reflects on challenges and impacts.

References

Bernama. (2018a). *New and upgraded tourist attractions*. Retrieved from: www.thestar.com.my/metro/metro-news/2018/01/04/new-and-upgraded-tourist-attractions-terengganu-out-to-draw-more-tourists-by-offering-unique-experie/ (accessed: the 09th June, 2018).

Bernama. (2018b). *More tourists visit Melaka*. Retrieved from: www.thestar.com.my/metro/metro-news/2018/02/01/more-tourists-visit-melaka-number-of-visitors-the-highest-seen-by-state-in-years/#WIfLam03AtxLrPJq.99 (accessed: the 09th June, 2018).

Drucker, P.F. (2002). *The discipline of innovation*. Retrieved from: https://hbr.org/2002/08/the-discipline-of-innovation (accessed: the 08th June, 2018).

Fagerberg, J. and Godinho, M.M. (2004). Innovation and catching-up. In J. Fagerberg, D. Mowery and R. Nelson (eds.) *The Oxford handbook of innovation*. Oxford: Oxford University Press, pp. 514–544.

Getz, D. (2008). Event tourism: Definition, evolution, and research. *Tourism Management*, **29**, pp. 403–428.

Getz, D. and Page, S.J. (2016). Progress and prospects for event tourism research. *Tourism Management*, **52**, pp. 593–631.

Giap, T.K., Gopalan, S. and Ye, Y. (2016). Drivers of growth in the travel and tourism industry in Malaysia: A geweke causality analysis. *Economies*, **4**(3), pp. 1–15.

Johnson, M.P. (2006). Decision models for the location of community corrections center. *Environment and Planning B: Urban Analytics and City Science*, **33**(3), pp. 393–412.

Laing, J. (2018). Festival and event tourism research: Current and future perspectives. *Tourism Management Perspective*, **25**, pp. 165–168.

Lamberton, C. and Stephen, A.T. (2016). A thematic exploration of digital, social media, and mobile marketing: Research evolution from 2000 to 2015 and an agenda for future inquiry. *Journal of Marketing*, **80**(6), pp. 146–172.

Leung, D., Law, R., van Hoof, H. and Buhalis, D. (2013). Social media in tourism and hospitality: A literature review. *Journal* of *Travel & Tourism Marketing*, **30**(1–2), pp. 3–22.

MIDA. (2013). *Policies, guidelines and potential tourism opportunities in Sabah*. Retrieved from: www.mida.gov.my/env3/uploads/events/Sabah04122012/MOTOUR.pdf (accessed: the 09th June, 2018).

Mosbah, A. and Al Khuja, M.S.A. (2014). A review of tourism development in Malaysia. *European Journal* of *Business* and *Management*, **6**(5), pp. 1–9.

Novelli, M. (ed.). (2005). *Niche tourism: Contemporary issues, trends and cases*. Oxford: Elsevier Butterworth-Heinemann.

Pagani, M. and Pardo, C. (2017, November). The impact of digital technology on relationships in a business network. *Industrial Marketing Management*, **67**, pp. 185–192.

Quinn, B. (2010). Arts festivals, urban tourism and cultural policy. *Journal of Policy Research in Tourism, Leisure & Events*, **2**, pp. 264–279.

Rahman, N.A.A. (2012). *The Car Manufacturer (CM) and Third Party Logistics Provider (TPLP) relationship in the outbound delivery channel: A qualitative study of the Malaysian automotive industry*. PhD thesis. Brunel University Library, London.

Rahman, N.A.A. (2015). *PhD Mosaic*. Kuala Lumpur: Lantera Kufi Enterprise.

Rahman, N.A.A. (2017). *388 need to know research terms*. Kuala Lumpur: MPWS Rich Publication.

Rahman, N.A.A., Melewar, T.C. and Sharif, A.M. (2014). The establishment of industrial branding through dyadic logistics. *Industrial Marketing Management*, **43**(1), pp. 67–76.

Rahman, N.A.A., Mohammad, M.F., Muda, J., Ahmad, M.F., Rahim, S.A., Majid, Z.A. and Noh, H.M. (in press). Linking Halal requirement and branding: An examination of Halal flight kitchen provider in Malaysia. *International Journal of Supply Chain Management*.

Rátz, T. (2017). "Be global, go local" – Innovation and creativity in the development of alternative guiding services in Budapest. *Journal of Tourism and Cultural Change*, **15**(5), pp. 476–489.

Rodriguez, M., Peterson, R.M. and Krishnan, V. (2012). Social media's influence on business-to-business sales performance. *Journal of Personal Selling and Sales Management*, **32**(3), pp. 365–378.

Singaraju, S.P., Nguyen, Q.A., Niininen, O. and Sullivan-Mort, G. (2016). Social media and value co-creation in multistakeholder systems: A resource integration approach. *Industrial Marketing Management*, **54**, pp. 44–55.

United Nations Conference on Trade and Development (UNCTAD). (2013). Sustainable tourism: Contribution to economic growth and sustainable development. *Proceedings of the Expert Meeting on Tourism's Contribution to Sustainable Development*. Geneva, Switzerland: 14th–15th March.

World Travel and Tourism Report. (2017). *Travel & Tourism Economic Impact 2017 World*, pp. 1–20. Retrieved from: www.wttc.org/-/media/files/reports/economic-impact-research/regions-2017/world2017.pdf (accessed: the 06th June, 2018).

Yin, R.K. (2018). *Case study research and applications: Design and methods*. Singapore: Sage Publication.

Zakaria, R. (2018). *Tourism activities set for huge boost in Visit Beautiful Terengganu Year*, pp. 1–6. Retrieved from: www.nst.com.my/news/nation/2018/01/320316/tourism-activities-set-huge-boost-visit-beautiful-terengganu-year (accessed: the 09th June, 2018).

11 National identity and dark tourism

Symbolising the 'Omor Ekushey February'

Azizul Hassan

Introduction

In the history of Bangladesh, cultural and political monuments offer significant influences. Among all of the political events, the Bengali Language Movement on February 21, 1952 resembles momentum in terms of its sensitiveness and values of the nation's identity. This is undoubtedly a valued episode of the Bengali nation that conveyed a common feeling and guided the nation for independence. The gradual realisation for rights by this nation finally stepped towards the independence of Bangladesh after a prolonged time period of two decades on December 16, 1971. Conceptually, the 'Omor Ekushey February' is a conventional dark tourism event but this study suggests a theoretical reshaping of dark tourism terminology that should not limit focus on death and disaster. The 'Omor Ekushey February' as the Bengali Language Movement both highlight the significance of an independent Bangladesh with her socio-cultural and political freedom (Chowdhury, 2018). It is important that as a nation, the Bengalis become able to feel the depth and richness of their culture. The preservation of sentiments and spirits of the 'Omor Ekushey February' is also a challenge and vice-versa. Thus, this study aims to outline calls for sentiment, architecture and planning to be seen as tools of national identity formation that emblem the 'Omor Ekushey February'. Also, this research summons a theoretical shift to attach peoples' perception towards a death tourism event.

Dark tourism – what is the actual 'Darkness'?

From a typical touristic viewpoint, the most commonly uttered term that is used in relation to monuments representing political or socio-cultural issues is 'Dark Tourism'. The actual meaning with centrality of 'Dark Tourism', also termed as 'Thana-tourism', is ambiguous, where this is typically concerned with visits to murder sites, battlefields and cemeteries apart from attractions of disaster and death (Frew and White, 2013). Dark tourism events are typically viewed as basic elements to form a type of tourism where the 'Omor Ekushey February' can be a conceptual example. Yet, the 'Omor Ekushey February' is an important element of Bengali history and a decisive component for leading the nation towards independence in terms of identity, heritage and nationality.

The psychological dimension of national identity arises from the consciousness of forming a group based on the 'felt' closeness uniting those who belong to the nation is confronted with an external and internal enemy-real or potential or imagined-threatening its people, its prosperity, its traditions and culture, its territory, its international standing or its sovereignty.

(Guibernau, 2008:12)

Dark tourism as the act of travel to sites *of* or sites associated *with* death has gained significant attention with media imaginations and academic scholarship. There is a growing body of literature on the (re)presentation and tourist experience of 'deathscapes' within contemporary visitor economies. As such, dark tourism is now a recognisable field of academic study, which include interdisciplinary perspectives of the 'darker side of travel' in sociology, anthropology, cultural studies, geography, thanatology, and business management.

(Institute for Dark Tourism Research, 2018)

Events in dark tourism are commonly attached with death, suppression and so on (Biran and Poria, 2012; Foley and Lennon, 2000). However, this is very unlikely that an event as 'Omor Ekushey February' can be able to detach emotions and sentiments of general peoples, both from within and beyond the Bangladesh geographical area. This event is more than a traditional happening of death but becomes a celebration where political and cultural activities are involved. Very often, the day is celebrated with processions, meetings and so on. The spirits and values that this event beholds are truly phenomenal that have passed on to millions of hearts. Dark tourism events represent and hold sentiments that generally move to fellow generations. Thus, from a practical manner, dark tourism events should be featured with emotions and exclusivity that the 'Omor Ekushey February' beholds. This is neither an event, nor even a dark tourism celebration but the spiritual event of a nation as related to their national identity, patriotism and pride (Willis, 2014).

The 'Omor Ekushey February' – the background

The 'Omor Ekushey February' as the Bengali Language Movement is an extraordinary event that experienced the caring and emotions of a nation to save and to establish the rights of her language. The country itself was passing through unbalanced situations coupled with visible domination by the non-Bengali speakers. This is a most common assertion that no other nations in the world have shed blood to save their language. However, this is also in fact right that no other country in the world was formed of two geographical landscapes having hundreds of miles of distance. This physical feature of a country of the then Pakistan as divided between the West and the East surpassed the seed of dominance and aggression of one part over the other. Language is the most sensitive element for development of humans where, this is also the most critical tool for conserving and representing the cultural heritage of both tangible and intangible nature. This is where the most generic feature of the Bengali Language Movement reclines and that is the emotional attachment of a nation for its language.

The socio-cultural and political history of Bangladesh is enriched having centuries-old traditions, customs, beliefs and norms (Rahman, 2003). At the same time, the Bengalis as a nation witnessed misinterpretation of their identity, culture and language in several occasions as intervened by power users (Scohel, 2018). In certain cases, such activities turned to ignite sparks of anger among the locals and forced the authorities to reconsider. The history of Bangladesh mostly supports the view where unexpected decisions by the rulers can lead to stand against the entire socio-administrative system as related to sentiments of the entire nation. Both morally and legislatively, the right is universal and comprehensive within a sovereign state nation when a person speaks and communicates in its own language as mother tongue.

Partition by the British in 1947 gave birth to two separate countries, India and Pakistan where the earlier had Muslim and the latter had Hindu majority. The state of Pakistan was parted into two: West Pakistan and East Pakistan, where East Pakistan became known as Bangladesh after getting independence on the December 16, 1971 followed by a nine months long liberation war (Rahman, 2000). Even having two separate parts, the central authority was practised by the West part of Pakistan. The socio-cultural distances between both parts of Pakistan were huge where, in fact the then East Pakistan had similarity with the West Bengal, which belonged to India due to the Hindu majority. The Bengali Language Movement, commonly known as the Language Movement, is an example that impassions the emotions of a nation for its language. This movement is more related to sentiment and emotions of a nation than as a political event. Still, the Bengali Language Movement was commonly viewed as a political movement in the then East Pakistan on the base of feelings for independence by the Bangladeshis.

According to Alhelal (1986), in 1948, the Language Policy was designed to impose Urdu as the national language for Pakistan. The movement was the outcome of a decision imbued by the West Pakistani rulers that at a later stage took the shape of a possession with the involvement of mass population. The demand for establishing Bengali as the official language in the then East Pakistan in all divisions of administration was the nerve of this movement. This subsequently diverged into allowing its use in currency, media, stamps, as the medium of education and above all as to allow the continuity to write in the Bengali script. Protests staged by students of several academic institutions and political activists, mainly from the Dhaka Medical College and the University of Dhaka. On February 21, 1952 a group of activists of political parties and mainly students of the Dhaka Medical College and the University of Dhaka came out in processions demanding the same right for the Bengali language as the Urdu. More than dozens of peoples were killed by the police when fire was opened on these demonstrators including Rafiq Uddin Ahmed, Abul Barkat, Abdus Salam, Abdul Jabbar, Shafiur Rahman, Ahi Ullah, Abdul Awal, an unidentified boy and few others (Scohel, 2018). Location of this incident was between the Ramna Park, the University of Dhaka and the Dhaka Medical College. This sparked the feeling to establish own rights, freedom and safeguarding language among the Bengalis that actually concluded with a war that led to an independent Bangladesh in 1971.

The 'Omor Ekushey February' and the Central Shaheed Minar

The Central Shaheed Minar structurally symbolises that in front of a crimson rising sun, a mother is shielding her children. The idea is unique representing the mother as standing for the victims against confrontation, suppression and aggression. The Ekushey February is the commemoration for those martyrs who lost their lives on February 21, 1952 to protest against the decision that imposed Urdu as the state language of Pakistan. The martyrs were killed by the Pakistan Police as a heinous act of brutalism that in fact led to the independence of Bangladesh in 1971. Followed by recognition of international communities, the Ekushey February (21st February) was declared as the 'World Mother Language Day' by the United Nations (UN) on February, 1999 (Banglapedia, 2017). The day is observed, remembered and solemnised each year with respect, honour and wreaths to souls of the martyrs where the main ground of such activities remains at the Central Shaheed Minar.

A series of attempts were made to construct the Central Shaheed Minar, a monument to remember the martyrs that experienced demolition and destruction from the rulers. However, in an independent Bangladesh, this monument clearly failed to keep apart from bureaucracy, corruption and politicisation, in terms of shaping it as a complex as actually designed on the initial design mapping. This was most likely the world's single monument erected for language movement. The international recognition was achieved from the UN through declaring February 21 as the 'International Mother Language Day'. Most notably, this declaration had support from Pakistan (Mjos, 2010).

The 'Omor Ekushey February' and a nation's celebration

Bangladesh as a country is mostly festive all over the year round where the participation of both private and governmental organisations are both culturally and socially influential. Throughout the year, numerous festivals are placed on different occasions as mainly the Pohela Boisakh (Bengali New Year), the Pohela Falgun (First Day of Spring), the Nabanna (First Day of Harvesting) and the Ekushey February (the 21st February) and many more (Kamol, 2009). Students from several academic institutions normally organise and arrange performances with the participation of peoples of all ages and segments. The demand for spaces to organise social and cultural activities on such festivals on a permanent basis is relevant and has always been pertaining. However, continuous efforts are required to find suitable places to accommodate such events and activities as part of the celebrations and festivals.

Dhaka is the capital of Bangladesh with limited spaces for recreation and limited availabilities of monuments, murals and similar. Within these limitations, the 'Omor Ekushey February' stands surpassingly high both to the locals and the international audience. This is a core dark tourist event of the country that represents Bangladesh in the global arena and is visited by tens of thousands of tourists every year. A reasonable form of maintenance of the Central Shaheed Minar is performed particularly on eve of the 21st February each year. The entire premise becomes wash, clean, decorated and adorned with colourful paintings and various designs as related to the sentiment of the day with the involvement of concerned authorities. The Faculty of Fine Arts of the University of Dhaka plays a crucial role for these purposes. The safety and security concerns are also raised at an expected level around the entire Central Shaheed Minar on the 'Omor Ekushey February'. The 'Omor Ekushey February' is the representation of a nation and positions high over decades. This is a national event of the country, offers importance to the nation and to all Bengalis in every part of the world. The interrelationship between the 'Omor Ekushey February' and the cultural heritage of Bangladesh is inseparable where the ground of an independent Bangladesh was laid by the 'Omor Ekushey February'. Thus, this cannot be an illusion that the 'Omor Ekushey February' as the Bengali Language Movement can stand for a comprehensive form to resemble the expression of socio-cultural and political identity of the Bengali as an independent nation (Bari, 1998).

Bangladesh as a geographical locale was under non-native rulers for centuries and the nation stood against them in certain times. This literally led to the independence of this country in 1971. This initiated the journey to build the Central Shaheed Minar (the Monument of Martyrs) that lasted for three decades and along with other issues accelerated the movement that at last established the equal status of Bengali with Urdu. Significance of the 'Omor Ekushey February' and the Central Shaheed Minar is enhanced when the little girl holding her mother's hand or the little boy riding on his father's shoulder comes very early in the morning to render respect to the language martyrs. This is the appeal of the 'Provat Feri' (Early Morning Possession) of the 21st February each year. In order to have an expanded 'Provat Feri', a cultural belt surrounding the Central Shaheed Minar is possible through involvement of academic institutions like the University of Dhaka, the Dhaka Medical College Hospital, and the Bangladesh University of Engineering and Technology. On the other side, the notable specialised institutions circled around the Central Shaheed Minar are the National Museum, the Bangla Academy, the Central Public Library, the Institute of Fine Arts, the Shishu Academy (the Academy for Children), the Teachers Students Centre (TSC) and few others. Apart from these, the Ramna Park and the Suhrawardy Uddyan (the Suhrawardy Park) are the natural luxuries. The involvement of all of these institutions can benefit the early morning procession to be performed in an organised manner.

In the 'Provat Feri', the 'Omor Ekushey February' passes the message to feel and realise depth of the Bengali language through engagement of millions of peoples regardless of gender, race or ethnicity. Each of these peoples is meant to become responsible to pass the glory of this language to every parts of the world with the concentration of safeguarding individuality, nationalism and identity. They are also believed to forward complete meaning of the Bengali Language Movement and to keep on establishing glory of the Bengali language in each part of the world. This is crucial to guide the future Bengali generations to become well versant about their own culture and to stay on similar directions as those for which their ancestors gave their lives. The 'Omor Ekushey February' stands as a lighthouse to protect the Bengali language from wrong influences of other languages and cultures (Guhathakurta and van Schendel, 2013). However, the Central Shaheed Minar as a complex might be more capable to serve the interests of diverse populations from different backgrounds to incorporate the interaction of modernity and authenticity of the 'Provat Feri' (Historical Places of Bangladesh Blog, 2018). From their remote past, the Bangladeshis have come closer to invaders, warriors and rulers from different backgrounds. However, the nation has never lost her identity to forces and retained the position upon which the culture and society is created. Severe linguistic interactions with foreign languages and cultures were brought by rulers themselves but, very hardly these were able to replace the Bengali language. The Bengalis managed to retain their glory for hundreds of years where the richness simply deepened with contributions of many Bengali language devotees.

The 'Omor Ekushey February' – resemblance with 'Darkness'

The visual symbolisation of cultural sensitivities is expressed through building monuments to reflect the emotions hidden behind each of the events related to culture, society or politics. The monument serves, therefore, to reinforce a natural nationalist sentiment. This sense is so prevailing that, even after years of independence, major cultural or socio-political activities centre around this monument. Bangladesh has centuries-old history in monument building that supports and covers the background of this country. Different political regimes have concentrated on building monuments with an aim to represent their ideologies and to remain in the minds of the visitors for the next several centuries. The base on which each of the monuments in Bangladesh was built visibly represents the engagement of tradition and artefacts as related to explore the general features of that specific time period.

The general history of Bangladesh is well enriched, followed by divergent political interests and the participation of the masses. This becomes evident in many times when the common mutual interests between the ruler and the ruling turn as conflicting and severely deteriorating. The generic reason for building monuments in any part of the world including Bangladesh is mostly tactical that serves particular purposes. The country is also said to be enriched in cultural heritage backed by the institutionalisation and enhanced spirit of nationality, identity and culture over generations. In fact, in many cases, appeals of some specific features of the Bangladeshi heritage have immersed into the global audiences regardless of their socio-political importance. A significance of righteousness of the Bengali culture appeared in diverse forms and covered many areas. In this particular case, the brilliance of richness that the country bestows spread over to audiences beyond the geographical boundary and evolves as truly international. Also, the richness and hidden significance of specific cultural events of the Bengali culture surpass the level of acceptance among many thousands of peoples involved with these. The 'Omor Ekushey February' is truly the event that is more than conceptually 'dark' where sentiments of a nation are involved. The strength of every Bengali added force to the Bengali Language Movement and building the Central Shaheed Minar. This followed a lengthy tussle that Bengali acquired having same status with Urdu. However, the nation never failed to recall contributions of those martyrs who were the main part of the Bengali Language Movement.

Conclusion

The conceptualisation and understanding of dark tourism are critical, in terms of its definition, complexities and practical aspects. This chapter concentrated on the particular case of the 'Omor Ekushey February' as a non-conventional dark tourism event and has offered extended analysis on its background and histories. What is conceptually dark cannot be 'dark' as always with the 'Omor Ekushey February' as an example. The attachment of peoples' sentiments and emotions are hardcore elements for popularising a certain object, place or monument as elements of dark tourism. In places where artefacts stand without emotional engagement of the masses, those can hardly resonate with people. This study suggests that dark tourism sites should be featured extensively with diverse factors and criteria rather than limiting them within specific frameworks. The study also suggests involving events and celebrations as generated from the example of the 'Omor Ekushey February' to help to keep the spirit alive. Dark tourism should be termed and viewed covering numerous aspects and perspectives to help spread sentiments, emotions and empathies. International recognition that the Bengali Language Movement received is simply unique and the 'Omor Ekushey February' is a visualisation of this. Sites that are termed as dark tourism sites need to work for achieving global recognition to ensure their presence in the global arena. Very few academic works have been done in dark tourism with the 'Omor Ekushey February' as the example. This was the main bottleneck of this study. Researches as based on this chapter can help to enhance and accelerate future studies on dark tourism.

The representation of a nation relies on the institutionalisation of her heritage and culture that help to influence the global cultural arena. Bangladesh with her centuries-old culture and the 21st February are tied up with sentiments and emotions where the event of the Bengali Language Movement becomes naturally able to create appeals to any person, regardless of geographical boundary or national identity. The reason is simple – that no known nation in this civilised world had to shed blood to save her language. However, an institutionalised form to celebrate the event can be helpful that will show the nation's feeling. Undoubtedly, the culture and language of the Bengalis are enriched where language solely acts as the most powerful element to safeguard both the tangible and intangible nature of heritage. This is a universal right to speak in mother language of a nation and this right is not expected to be taken away. Language is the major carrier of culture where the development and evolution of civilisations or cultures across the world have relied and have moved forward solely on their language. The lack of detailed and enriched literary source was the key limitation to elaborate opinions. More research can be carried out in the outlined areas.

References

Alhelal, B. (1986). *Bhasha andoloner itihash* (In Bengali). Dhaka: Bangla Academy.

Banglapedia. (2017). *International mother language day*. Retrieved from: http://bit.ly/1183sWQ (accessed: the 07th January, 2018).

Bari, M. (1998). *Ekushe February*. Retrieved from: http://bit.ly/1l4cdRT (accessed: the 07th January, 2018).

Biran, A. and Poria, Y. (2012). Re-conceptualizing dark tourism. In R. Sharpley and P. Stone (eds.) *The contemporary tourist experience: Concepts and consequences*. London: Routledge, pp. 62–79.

Chowdhury, P.K. (2018). *Bangla Academy, Dhaka's notes: The language movement and the Bangla Academy*. Retrieved from: http://on.fb.me/1ts43UG (accessed: the 07th January, 2018).

Foley, M. and Lennon, J. (2000). *Dark tourism*. London: Cengage Learning EMEA.

Frew, E. and White, L. (2013). Exploring dark tourism and place identity. In L. White and F. Frew (eds.) *Dark tourism and place identity: Managing and interpreting dark places*. Oxon: Routledge, pp. 1–10.

Guhathakurta, M. and van Schendel, W. (eds.). (2013). *The Bangladesh reader: History, culture, politics*. Durham, NC: Duke University Press.

Guibernau, M. (2008). *The identity of nations*. Oxford: Polity Press, p. 12.

Historical Places of Bangladesh Blog. (2018). *Shaheed Minar*. Retrieved from: http://bit.ly/1tL2xeL (accessed: the 07th January, 2018).

Institute for Dark Tourism Research. (2018). *Home*. Retrieved from: http://bit.ly/1ojcECP (accessed: the 07th January, 2018).

Kamol, E. (2009, February 20). Preserving the legacy. *The Daily Star Weekend Magazine*, Dhaka.

Mjos, O.J. (2010). *Media globalization and the discovery channel networks*. New York: Routledge.

Rahman, A. (2000). *Bhasha andoloner artho-samajik potobhumi* (In Bengali). Dhaka: University Press Ltd.

Rahman, M. (2003). *Bangladesher itihash: 1947–1971* (In Bengali). Dhaka: Somoy Prakashon.

Scohel, T. (2018). *Bangla language movement*. Retrieved from: http://bit.ly/1sheDvb (accessed: the 07th January, 2018).

Willis, E. (2014). *Theatricality, dark tourism and ethical spectatorship: Absent others*. Hampshire: Palgrave McMillan.

12 Anti-tourism against the commodification of culture

Varf Chal (pour snow in pit)/
Zan Shahi (Kingdom of Women)
ceremonies in the North of Iran

Amir H. Moghaddam

Introduction

Generally, social scientists, especially anthropologists studying tourism, are deeply concerned about the impacts of this phenomenon. A large part of the research and literature of anthropology of tourism has addressed the negative consequences of tourism on the host society (Greenwood, 1977; Nunez, 1989; Urry, 2011; Nash, 1989; Williams, 2009). Meanwhile, the transformation of the indigenous culture into a tourist attraction and its offering as a commodity for sale is a famous topic in the short history of anthropology of tourism. A classic example of this view can be seen in the critique of the Alarde ceremony in Basque by Greenwood (1977). In the work, Greenwood (1977) is not pleased with the municipality and institutions of Fuenterrabia city because in 1969 they turned the hundred years Alarde anniversary into a tourist attraction as a source of income for the city. He believed that the ceremony, which is a meaningful event within the cultural context of this city and has already performed functions such as social solidarity of Fuenterrabia, has become meaningless due to its monetisation, even though it kept its appearance. Greenwood (1977) uses the term 'Commodification of culture' or 'Local Color' in introducing this phenomenon and criticises it. He writes that proponents of traditional culture, social researchers and ethical philosophers have been complaining about the use and even abuse of the local colour for tourism (Greenwood, 1977:130).

According to Greenwood (1977), logically, anything for sale should be a combination of three factors: land, labour and capital. The characteristic of the capitalism system is that everything is priced and can be bought and sold. But this is problematic in cultural tourism. Greenwood (1977:131) writes: "We already know from worldwide experience that local culture [. . .] is altered and often destroyed by the treatment of it as a tourist attraction. It is made meaningless to the people who once believed in it". Greenwood (1977) sees anthropology as a knowledge that is not only appropriate for understanding the process of change and harm but is responsible for these traditions.

Although Greenwood (1977) points out that tourism imposes unimaginable cultural changes on people who had previously lost their balance through industrialisation, urbanisation, and inflation (p: 137), but it is clear from his point of view that he considers tourism is a cause and in fact, the main culprit of the change. In his view, it is assumed that the indigenous people change their culture based on what tourists like more. This process is described by Urry in his book 'The Tourist's Gaze' (1990, 3rd edition in collaboration with Larsen, Urry and Larsen, 2011). Urry (1990) used the term gaze to explain how to change the behaviour of indigenous peoples to be similar to the demands of tourists. The term commodification of culture is called 'Cocacolaisacion' by Nunez (1989). He borrows the concept from Mexican intellectuals who were concerned about changing the traditions of their indigenous people. But Nunez (1989:266) uses it to illustrate the similar concern of anthropologists about the consequences of tourists on the native culture of the host community.

Nash and Smith (1991:15) criticise this negative view and the contradictory method of the anthropologists. They believe that anthropologists collect tourism-related data and then review the changes that have been made in the host societies. But finally, they introduce these changes as a result of tourism, while they do not see or consider any other factors of change such as immigration, the media, industrialisation, training etc. Smith (1989:17) says "it is patently easier to blame a nameless, faceless foreigner who comes (and goes) than it is to address and solve fundamental problems". Crick (1989:338) believes that other societies have been influenced by the West for centuries even when tourism was not a concept yet defined. Mings (1978:343) warned even earlier that if anthropologists would not be able to fully understand the complexities involved in the development of tourism, and if all the benefits and costs of this phenomenon are not recognised within the framework of the appropriate space and their contemporary context, hearing any of these two claims of the 'Boom or Doom' factors of tourism will continue. Therefore, many anthropologists despise tourists for their consequences. This view sees indigenous people as passives who receive complete packages of modernisation without any resistance, even though indigenous people are active subjects that can accept or reject tourism.

Further research on commodification of culture has examined more dimensions. For example, Shepherd (2002) says that before we can talk about the commodification and transformation of authentic culture through tourism, we need to determine what is meant by the authenticity. McLeod (2006) also says that the relationship between tourism with the commodification of culture is very special and should consider factors such as destination policymakers and the type of destination. Roland (2010) shows that in Cuba, hosts benefit from some kind of commodification of culture for building an image they want to portray of Cuba. Even Pröschel (2012) defends one type of commodification of culture. He believes that if cultural products such as handicrafts can be commodificated, provided that we do not trade the entire culture, this commodity can also maintain the cultural identity of that society alive and bring it economic benefits. In fact, Pröschel (2012) believes that in the process of commodification of culture, the host community sell only the part that they want, and this does not mean that the whole of culture has been commercialised. But as it will be showed here, sometimes the values of one part of a culture, like a ceremony for indigenous people, are so prominent that if they feel tourism can harm it, they prefer their ceremony to tourism and its resulting income. Here an example of such behaviour against tourism in the north of Iran is examined.

The data obtained in this chapter was gathered by the author studying all papers and newspaper notes about the ceremonies. In 2013, after coordinating with field goalkeepers, the author succeeded in taking the part of a spectator in the male ceremony (participant observation) and talked to indigenous people during it (deep interview). But for the feminine ceremony that was held at the same time and there was no possibility in taking part as a male researcher, it was helped by research conducted by a female researcher's thesis.

Ask villagers against tourists

The village of Ask (which sometimes is called Ab-Ask), situated eighty kilometres northwest of Tehran, the capital of Iran, near Damavand Peak, the tallest peak of the Middle East (5671 metres). This village is located on a steep hillside slope, and on the other side it reaches the valley that flows through the river Haraz. Therefore, the main way to access the village is from a bridge built on the river and connecting the village to the Haraz road. This is the main road between Mazandaran in one side and Tehran and other areas of Central and South of Iran in the other side. In other words, this road is the most touristy road of Iran, because the Caspian Sea and the Hyrcanian forests of Mazandaran are the main destinations for domestic tourism in Iran. Still, Ask villagers strongly resist the arrival of tourists when setting up their traditional ceremonies. In this village, two separate ceremonies are celebrated every year in the same day: the 'Barf Chal' (Pour Snow in the Pit) by the men and 'Zan Shahi' (Kingdom of Women) by the women.

Barf Chal (Pour Snow in the Pit) ceremony

Barf Chal in Persian translates to 'Pour Snow in the Pit'. The Pour Snow in the Pit has a long-standing root in Iran. In the central and desert cities of Iran, in the winter, people gather large clean snow and ice fragments and pour them into the architectural structures made for this purpose, known as the 'Yakh Chal' meaning Ice Pit. They then close the door of the structure. In the summer, when the weather is warm, they open the doors of these Yakh Chals and use its cold water (for more data, see: Zandieh et al., 2012; Niroumand et al., 2012). To this day in the Persian language, a refrigerator is still called a Yakh Chal.

In the village of Ask, the Barf Chal ceremony continues. This ceremony is held traditionally at least in recent decades, on the second Friday of the Ordibehesht (one of the Iranian months, which is similar to the months of April and May). In the middle of Ordibehesht, the weather becomes warm, so they pour snow in the pit, before the snow melts. Of course, if snowfall is little in winter or the weather is so warm in the spring, they will hold the ceremony sooner to have enough snow for pouring. For example, due to the low snowfall in the winter of 2012, the ceremony was held in 2013 Farvardin month (March and April). Even if there is no snow in the year, the people will go to the ceremony and clean the ancient road and also the snow pit will be cleaned and dredged (Mirmoradi, 1990:40), because it is necessary to hold this ceremony in any circumstances.

The ritual is held as follows: a few days before the ceremony, the villagers decide on its time. One day before the ceremony, a person uses the speaker of the mosque and reminds the people that they must prepare their daily meals to go to the Barf Chal. Early in the morning, the elders of the village walk in the alleys and by their singing, other men are informed that they must leave the village. All men gather in the field square with dishes filled with cooked food by their women the previous night, accompanied by Chavoshi, which commonly is a type of Persian religious singing, and leave the village.

For nearly two hours, they have to walk in the mountains to reach the place of the Barf Chal. This place is located near the Damavand mountain (the highest peak in the Middle East and an important mountain in Iranian mythology). A historical pit/well there is 10 metres deep and 7 metres in diameter. The well is covered and has one trapdoor. Nearly five hundred metres away from this well, there is a field where snow of winter is still visible. The men go there, and each one cuts off large cubes of compressed and frozen snow, lays it on his shoulders and carries to the well and dumps it through the trapdoor. One of the elders also sings Chavoshi (Persian religious song). When everyone puts their snow pieces into the pit, they close the trapdoor. This snow and ice is used as cold water for drinking in the summer by the people farming or grazing their sheep near there.

This ceremony is believed to date to as late as six hundred years ago.[1] However, at that time, the villagers decided to delve a big pit and throw snow in it to save water in the summer. But wherever they delved, they encountered rock due to the region being very mountainous. Seyed Hassan Wali, whose tomb is now near the village of Ask (Niyak village) and is a shrine for the people of the region, was informed of the problem and went to help them. Seyed Hassan said to them that if he were to place the tip of his cane anywhere, there will be without rock and cliff and they can delve easy, provided that every year, when they want to pour the snow in it, the people of the village of Ask as well as the people of the village of Niyak should feed their guests.[2] The people of Ask ultimately accepted his condition as respect to the sacredness of Seyeds, who are thought to be descendants of the Prophet of Islam. So Seyed Hassan drew a 7-diameter circle with his cane which then the people dug into a well with a depth of 10 metres without dealing with rock or stone. Since that year, the ceremony has been held annually with the conditions that have been laid by Seyed Hassan. On this day, when the people come to each other, the sentence 'Your revenge with Seyed Hassan Wali' keeps alive his memory and emphasises the sacredness of the ceremony.

After the end of the snow pouring, at the same time as the noon prayer, a man goes on a roof of the snow pit and says Azan. Those who pray are reading their prayers. Lunch tablecloths are then set. The lunch brought by each man is much more than his own need. They give the rest to those who come as guests and even invite guests to their lunch. Because they believe that the lunch of that day is blessed due to Sayed Hassan, the number of passengers and guests is not important, and lunch is always enough. People of the nearby Niyak village also participate in the ceremony. The people of Niyak village generally host the guests with bread, cheese, walnuts and sometimes honey. Men usually stay there a while longer because they do not have permission to enter the village until afternoon.

Women cannot take part in the Barf Chal ceremony. If a woman is in the ceremony, she breaks its sanctity. On the other hand, they believe that if a woman is present in the Barf Chal, until the next year that the ceremony will be held, she will have many bad experiences. In fact, women attend the other ceremony called Zan Shahi which is held in the village.

Zan Shahi (Kingdom of Women) ceremony

The Zan Shahi (which in Persian means Kingdom of Women) ceremony was held in many places in ancient Iran.[3] It was held in at least seven other places until a few decades ago (Rahmani and Farahzad, 2014:16–17). Today, this tradition continues in the village of Efus, and the Ask village. The patterns of these ceremonies are very similar to each other.

In general, one woman becomes king for one or several days; she choses some ministers and soldiers for herself, and all her commands must be done. The roots of this ceremony in Iran can also be found even before Islam. Nizami Ganjawi, the Persian poet of 12th century in his *The Seven Beauty* book, where the history of the Sassanid Empire is recounted, refers to the 'Kingdom of Women in the Spring'[4] (Nizami, 1936:318). If we accept that such ceremonies were rooted pre-Islam, then the age of six hundred years should not be true for the ceremony of the Zan Shahi (Kingdom of Women) and its history is more than six hundred years. However, the male Barf Chal ceremony was probably added to the Zan Shahi ceremony six hundred years ago (Farahzad, 2013).

At the Zan Shahi ceremony in the village of Ask, one of the women of the village becomes Shah or king. This woman must have features that include: beauty, experience (and therefore not too young), healthy and respected by other women. For over twenty years now, one of the women in the village held this position and is re-elected every year. Before her, her sister had the position until her death. On the morning of the ceremony and after all the men went to Barf Chal ceremony, the women of the village who adorned themselves, rejoicing and applauding, walk until they reach the front of the Shah Zan or Woman King's house. The Shah Zan, who dresses similarly to a king, comes out and goes with them to the Tekyeh of the village, which is a sacred place, and sits on the throne of the kingdom. She then chooses two women as her right-hand and left-hand ministers.[5] A young woman also plays the role of bride. Around twenty to thirty of the agile girls of the village declare readiness to be soldiers. The soldiers guard with their sticks, and sometimes the guns all over the village to be sure that no man can enter the village. They even close all the entrance paths to the village. If a man comes to the village for whatever reason or is left in the village, women find him and take him to the Shah Zan. Usually they beat the stranger man badly with sticks on the order of the Shah and sometimes even without her permission. No man over the age of five should be in the village, except patients and those who are too old and unable to go to the

Barf Chal. These men should stay in their houses and close all of doors and windows. A few years ago, a vendor man who did not know about the ceremony entered the village, was arrested and beaten by women, and imprisoned in a stable. Eventually, when the men returned in evening, he was freed.

Following the election of the ministers and other officials, the Shah Zan/King Woman, together with other women, go to the homes of those who've had a member of the household recently die. The king and other women conveyed condolences and asked them to take off the black dress (mourning dress in Iran). The landlord woman also serves the king and other women. They also go to the homes of women who are sick and visit them. If a girl has just had a wedding, the symbolic bride congratulates her.

The Shah Zan/King Woman also listens to women's complaints from other women on this day, treats them fairly and eventually reconciles them. All women should listen to her orders. If someone fails to comply with her orders, she will face punishment, which is usually not physical. Instead, she rides a donkey through the village while the other women boo her in the village, while the other women boo her. Sometimes she has to buy cookies for Shah Zan and other women (Farhadi, 2002:178). Sometimes Shah Zan commands funny things and forces the others to do it to make the women happy.

At noon, the women's ceremony is over, the Shah Zan thanks the women, and apologises for her behaviour if she causes anybody irritation. Then women go to their homes and eat lunch. If a woman from another place has come to this ceremony, she will also be invited to lunch. Because this is a holy day for women, many of them vow to this day for the acceptance of their wishes. So they cook food and gift them to each other or to the guests. In the evening when men return to the village from Barf Chal, normal life returns.

Changes in these two ceremonies

Several changes have occurred today in these ceremonies. In the men's Barf Chal ceremony: first, no one else goes to the venue of Barf Chal on foot from the village, but they drive their cars from the Haraz road. When the author wanted to attend the ceremony in 2013, he walked the mountain path himself to know how many people go to the Barf Chal on foot on the traditional way. But contrary to what he had heard that some people still walk this way, he did not see anyone along the way. If someone had gone before the author, it was a very rare exception. Another change is the way of carrying the snow to the pit. While many Askian men still carry their snow pieces with their hands, the main part of the snow is carried with a few pickup trucks to the pit. Therefore, instead going and coming several times between the source of snow and the pit, each man usually goes one or two times and the rest of the snow is brought by the pickup trucks. The third transformation relates to the use of speakers in the ceremony. The one who usually manages the Barf Chal and accompanies the snow carriers with the Chavoshi songs, now uses the speaker to reach out his voice to everyone.

Some changes have also occurred in the Zan Shahi/ Kingdom of Women ceremony. At least two of the following changes are due to photography and video recording. In some rural communities in Iran, women remain sensitive to having their photos be taken by foreigners. The Woman King of Ask said in an interview (Farahzad, 2013) that photographing and video recording of the women in this ceremony would cause their villages to be dishonoured. This photography or video recording may be performed by young villager girls or by guest women coming from elsewhere. First of all, Askian women now have more veils in the ceremony, unlike in the past. Although their veils are more free than other days, but some women, especially middle-aged and elder ones, avoid excessive freedom whereas it seems that they have not had such restrictions in the past. The second transformation in the Zan Shahi ceremony is the removal of the symbolic bride that took place a few years ago. In this part, a girl who had not yet been married, dressed her bride cloth to find husbands for her and other unmarried girls, and would have been with the woman king during the day. Because the bride's clothes are also very thin and open and of fear of photography and video recording, this part of the ceremony has also been removed. Another change that affects both Barf Chal and Zan Shahi ceremonies is the change or oblivion of some of the functions of these ceremonies. Some researchers argued about functions of these ceremonies (Farahzad, 2013; Farhadi, 2002, 2006). Anthropologists usually interpret these ceremonies and rituals as a tool which society uses to support its basic values and principles and protect its moral system (Hamilton, 2002:146). Along with these functions of solidarity and etc. the Barf Chal and the Zan Shahi also had other functions. For example, in the Barf Chal, saving snow and using its water in the summer was one of the main obvious functions of the ceremony. But now, due to the existence of a water flask, as well as the rapid transfer of water from the village to the fields by car, this function has been very dimmed. In the Zan Shahi ceremony, some functions were like empowerment in a patriarchal society, the preparation to take care the village in the absence of men, and the struggle against bandits. But nowadays, patriarchy doesn't have the same form as the past, nor are the dangers of bandits attacking the village and threatening the women and children prevalent.

But the most important change that is focused on here is related to both the Barf Chal and the Zan Shahi, and that is the change in their time. Unlike the other changes mentioned previously, and more because of the arrival of technology to the village, the change of time of the ceremonies is the only change that has occurred due to the presence of tourists. Of course, before the tourists arrived, there were minor examples in the change of the time of the ceremonies. For example, they held them a week later in 1989, because one of the villagers who was resident in the United States of America had a problem to arrive in time for the ceremony. Basically, on the day of the ceremony, most of the village people who live in other cities come to the village. Or as mentioned previously, if the snowfall is small in a year, the ceremonies were held earlier. But these were exceptions.

Keeping the ceremonies from tourists

The main reason for changing the time of the ceremonies is preventing them from being attended by tourists. About twenty years ago, the ceremonies were opened to tourists. The Askian people at first had no problem with the presence of tourists in their ceremonies, provided they did not disrupt the process of holding them. But the tourists were not without trouble. In the Barf Chal ceremony, the main problems that tourists created were: first, women tourists liked to be present in this manly ceremony whereas in Askians' view, women were not allowed to attend this ceremony. That is why Askian men are very sensitive to the presence of women tourists. If women tourists try to take part in the Barf Chal, Askian men try to stop them by closing the way or shooting snowballs at them. So similar to the Zan Shahi, Barf Chal is a single gender and each of them is forbidden for another gender of tourists. The second problem with the presence of tourists in the Barf Chal is related to their excessive participation in the ceremony. Some tourists like to participate in this ceremony by carrying the snow, but some indigenous men in conversation with the author said that they had taken this ceremony from Seyed Hassan, and that this is their responsibility to uphold. Of course, when the number of tourists is small, no problem arises. But if a large number of tourists arrive and all of them want to participate in the ceremony, there is nothing left for many of the Askian men to do. The third problem was the turmoil caused by the presence of tourists, which caused difficulties in organising the ceremony. Crowded tourists were in the way of those who carried the snow or were disturbing the ceremony by gathering near the snow pit.

However, there are some exceptions to this mild hostility towards this alien presence, as the author was able to obtain permission to attend the ceremony in 2013, after coordinating with the village elders. Every year Mazandaran's local broadcasting and other television programmes provide a report of the ceremony. Of course, they cannot attend the Zan Shahi ceremony and Askian women do not allow them to enter the village because as noted previously, photography and video recording of women is prohibited on this day. There are, of course, exceptions to the women's Zan Shahi ceremony, too. Women who have coordinated with the village before the ceremony can attend it. But the main reasons why female tourists are not allowed to be present in the Zan Shahi ceremony and why Askians conceal the history of holding these ceremonies from tourists are: firstly, female tourists came to the village on the grounds of the freedom derived from the rule of women on this day and behaved in a deconstructive manner to the ceremony. Even though during the Zan Shahi ceremony a sort of anti-structure is formed, as Turner and Turner say (1991:129), there is a structure within the anti-structure. All the positions, behaviours, punishments etc. are identified in the framework of a structure that is different from the structure of everyday life in the Ask village. In the Zan Shahi ceremony, whatever the Shah Zan / woman king orders, the other women have to execute. But the tourist women were practically outside of this framework. For example, they were gathered in a corner of the village square and danced and rejoiced with their car music at a very loud volume, so much that it sometimes overwhelmed the ceremony and severely disrupted it. Second, tourism is nowadays integrated with cameras and photography and some researchers do research work about this relation (Gillespie, 2006; Gogoi, 2014; Ye and Tussyadiah, 2011). The tourist likes to take photos of everything that is interesting. But as shown previously, the women of this village are not willing to be photographed themselves and their ceremony on this day.

To avoid these troubles from tourists, for a few years these ceremonies have been hidden from the eyes of tourists. The villagers no longer hold these ceremonies on the second Friday of the Ordibehesht month and change its time to the middle of the week, so that less tourists have the chance to attend it (in Iran Friday is the weekend day, not like Western countries where the weekend is Saturday and Sunday). But they do not care about it being in the weekend, so they hide its time. For example, they rumour that the ceremonies be held on Tuesday, but when tourists arrive at the village or the place of the Barf Chal on the Tuesday, they find that the ceremony has been held on Monday and is over.

Conclusion

In contrast to Greenwood's (1977) view about commodification of culture in tourism that believes people sell their culture as a commodity to tourists, in Barf Chal (Pouring Snow in the Pit) and Zan Shahi (Kingdom of Women) economic gain is not the only aspect that is considered, but the villagers themselves also use some part of their economic assets to provide a vow and food. In Bourdieu's (1986) language, if we claim that social capital is in the service of economic capital in the commodification of culture, then in Zan Shahi and Barf Chal it is an economic capital that serves a social capital. Because, according to Bourdieu, the types of capital are capable of change. The greatest capital that the Barf Chal and Zan Sahi create for the indigenous people is social capital, not economic. This type of capital especially focuses on the solidarity of intergroup relationships rather than outgroup relationships. Here, the economic capital is spent for social capital, which indigenous spend on holding ceremonies, cooking food etc. and trying to invite others to their tablecloths to eat with them. In the meantime, everything that puts the social capital in jeopardy, will be set aside.

Both of these ceremonies are holy and religious for the people of Ask village. At least two reasons for this sacredness can be counted: First, the water was considered a sacred element in both ancient Persia and after Islam, especially after the expansion of Shi'ism in the 16th century. Water supply to others and in the memory of Imam Hussein, who is the third Shiite Imam Hussein [. . .] was martyred with thirty lips, is very valuable in Shiite and Iranian culture, which is a land with little rainfall. Therefore, many water-related ceremonies are also sacred. Second, according to local narratives, Seyed Hassan, a religiously respected person, ordered the Barf Chal ceremony, so it is religious ceremony (Farhadi, 2002:174). According to the indigenous people, not holding these ceremonies is impossible as it will cause drought and famine and Seyed Hassan will be miffed with them (Farahzad, 2013:38).

Along with the reasons of sanctity mentioned previously, there are many signs of sanctity in these two ceremonies. In the Barf Chal ceremony, songs such as Chavoshi songs which always display religious topics; reminding the name of Seyed Hassan Wali and asking help from him to carrying the snow pieces; believing in the blessing of their tablecloths because of Seyed Hassan Wali etc. In the Zan Shahi ceremony, the years in which the ceremony coincides with the month of Muharram, which Imam Hussein was martyred in (who is highly respected by Shiites) instead of ordinary and comedy theatre, a Ta'ziye, a kind of religious theatre is held to remind of the events of the martyrdom of Imam Hussein. Also, in the years of the war between Iran and Iraq, where many Iranian youths were martyred (and the martyr is a sanctity concept), in the honour of the families of the martyrs, there was a change in the ceremony (Farhadi, 2002:174). Prayers for such needs as the health of patients, the marriage of girls who do not have a bridegroom, birthing of a baby for infertile couples, and similar problems related to the sanctity of this day.

But the behaviours of tourists can endanger the sanctity of this ceremony and prevent the satisfaction of Seyed Hassan Wali or prevent the fulfilment of their vows and prayers. As Graburn (1983:21) says, tourism is a 'Ritual Inversion', and many tourists are abandoned in moral terms through a journey that is liminal to the ritual. Despite their anti-structural situations, the ceremonies of Barf Chal and Zan Shahi are sacred. The people of the Ask village, who saw the social freedoms of tourists in their province of Mazandaran (the most famous domestic tourist destination) also have experienced the disturbance tourists cause to their ceremonies in the previous years. So they protect the sanctity of their ceremonies against the behaviours of tourists. In fact, if Grauburn calls tourism as a ritual inversion, because of the anti-tourism position of Barf Chal and Zan Shahi, these ceremonies can be regarded as ritual inversion, too. While the northern regions of Iran, especially the Mazandaran province, is the main domestic tourism destination of Iran, and every village and city in this province is trying to attract more tourists and gain from their economic benefits, in the Barf Chal and Zan Shahi ceremonies, this process is completely inverse to what is done by a village in a very touristic region. They ignored hundreds or thousands of tourists who were likely to participate in this ceremony, while they could gain the economic interests of them by commodification their culture.

Therefore, tourism has not played a very significant role in the changes to these two ceremonies in the past years, but they have been transformed independently of tourism more due to technological impacts. The only change caused by tourism in these ceremonies is the changing of its time in order to escape the intrusion of tourists.

Notes

1 Given that the name of this village in historic sources has been referenced more than a thousand years ago (in the travel writing of Ibn Hawqal (1987) in the 10th century and in *The History of Tabaristan* by Ibn Isfandiyar (1941) in the 13th century), the historicity of this event becomes more acceptable.
2 The emphasis on guests in this narrative can be a reference to travellers and pilgrims who used the ancient road of Mazandaran to other parts of Iran, which was passing through the area.
3 Max Gluckman shows a similar feminine ritual among the Zulu tribe in Africa. He believes that this inversion of ritual includes a kind of rebellion against the ruling order (Gluckman, 1954). These are part of the inversion rituals and, as Turner and Turner (1991) say, anti-structural.

150   *Amir H. Moghaddam*

4 Since Nizami referred to this celebration for five days, this ritual seems to have been
followed by a ritual such as Mir Nowruzi, which was held in Nowruz for five days. Mir
Nowruzi was a normal person who elected to the kingdom, and even the real king was
forced to follow his orders (Ghazvini, 1944).
5 Also at the Mir Nowruzi ceremony, which is alive and held in Mahabad in western Iran
yet, two ministers of the right hand and left hand are elected by the interim Shah (Maroufi,
2000: 68).

References

Bourdieu, P. (1986). Forms of capital. In J. Richardson (ed.) *Handbook of theory and research for the sociology of education.* Westport: Greenwood, pp. 241–258.

Crick, M. (1989). Representations of international tourism in the social sciences: Sun, sex, sights, savings and servility. *Annual Review of Anthropology*, **18**, pp. 307–344.

Farahzad, Y. (2013). *Women's ceremonies in Iran: Case study of kingdom of women.* Thesis of Master of Art. Islamic Arts Department, University of Art of Isfahan, Isfahan, Iran.

Farhadi, M. (2002). The kingdom of women in the Ask village. *Journal of Women Research*, **3**, pp. 163–182.

Farhadi, M. (2006). Typologies of traditional assistances and cooperation in Iran. *Journal of Social Sciences and Humanities*, **Special Issue: Social Researches**, pp. 13–60.

Ghazvini, M. (1944). Mir-e Nowrouzi. *Yadegar Monthly*, **1**(3), pp. 13–16.

Gillespie, A. (2006). Tourist photography and the reverse gaze. *Ethos*, **34**(3), pp. 343–366.

Gluckman, M. (1954). Rituals of rebellion in South-East Africa. *Frazer Lecture, 1952.* Manchester: Manchester University Press.

Gogoi, D. (2014). A conceptual framework of photographic tourism. *International Journal of Research in Applied, Natural and Social Sciences*, **2**(8), pp. 109–114.

Graburn, N. (1983). The Anthropology of tourism. *Annals of Tourism Research*, **10**(1), pp. 9–33.

Greenwood, D.J. (1977). Culture by the pound: An Anthropological perspective on tourism as cultural commoditization. In V. Smith (ed.) *Hosts and guests: The Anthropology of tourism.* Pennsylvania, PA: University of Pennsylvania Press, pp. 129–138.

Hamilton, M. (2002). *The sociology of religion: Theoretical and comparative perspectives.* Oxon: Routledge.

Ibn Hawqal (1987) (2nd edition). *The travel writing of Ibn Hawqal: Iran in Surat-al Arz book.* (translator and editor by J. Shoar). Tehran: Amir Kabir.

Ibn Isfandiyar (1941). *The history of Tabaristan* (edited by A.E. Ashtiyani). Tehran: Kalale Khawar.

MacLeod, D. (2006). Cultural commodification and tourism: A very special relationship. *Tourism Culture & Communication*, **6**, pp. 71–84.

Maroufi, S. (2000). Mir-e Nowrouzi ceremony in Kurdistan. *Monthly Book Review of Art*, **29** and **30**, p. 68.

Mings, R.C. (1978). The importance of more research on the impact of tourism. *Annals of Tourism Research*, **5**(3), pp. 340–345.

Mirmoradi, H. (1990). A report from Ab Ask village. *Journal of the Growth of Social Science Education*, **3**, pp. 38–43.

Nash, D. (1989). Tourism as a form of imperialism. In V. Smith (ed.) *Hosts and guests: The Anthropology of tourism.* Philadelphia: University of Pennsylvania Press, pp. 37–52.

Nash, D. and Smith, V. (1991). Anthropology and tourism. *Annals of Tourism Research*, **18**, pp. 12–25.

Niroumand, H., Zain, M. and Jamil, M. (2012). The earth refrigerators as earth architecture. *International Journal of Environmental Science and Development*, **3**(3), pp. 315–318.

Nizami, G. (1936). *The seven beauties* (edited by V. Dastjerdi). Tehran: Armaghan.

Nunez, T. (1989). Touristic studies in Anthropological perspective. In V. Smith (ed.) *Hosts and guests: The Anthropology of tourism*. Philadelphia: University of Pennsylvania Press, pp. 265–279.

Pröschel, N. (2012). *Commodification and culture: How can culture be economically used without selling it out?* Bachelor Thesis in Tourism and Hospitality Management. Modul Vienna University, Vienna.

Rahmani, J. and Farahzad, Y. (2014). From ethnographic film to pseudo-documentary: Women City film review. *Journal of Cultural Studies & Communication*, **15**(26), pp. 7–30.

Roland, L.K. (2010). Tourism and the commodification of Cubanidad. *Journal of Tourist Studies*, **10**(1), pp. 3–18.

Shepherd, R. (2002). Commodification, culture and tourism. *Journal of Tourist Studies*, **2**(2), pp. 183–201.

Smith, V. (1989). Introduction. In V. Smith (ed.) *Hosts and guests: The Anthropology of tourism*. Philadelphia: University of Pennsylvania Press, pp. 1–17.

Turner, V. and Turner, E. (1991). *The ritual process: Structure and anti-structure*. New York: Cornell University Press.

Urry, J. (1990). *The tourist gaze: Leisure and travel in contemporary societies*. 1st ed. London: Sage Publications.

Urry, J. and Larsen, J. (2011). *The tourist gaze*. 3rd ed. London: Sage Publications.

Williams, E.L. (2009). *Anxious pleasures: Race and the sexual economies of transnational tourism in Salvador, Brazil*. PhD thesis in Cultural and Social Anthropology Department. Stanford University, Stanford, CA.

Ye, H. and Tussyadiah, I. (2011). Destination visual image and expectation of experiences. *Journal of Travel and Tourism Marketing*, **28**, pp. 129–144.

Zandieh, M., Khaleghi, I. and Rahgoshay, R. (2012). Iranian vernacular architecture: Notable example of a thermal mass. *International Journal of Architectural Engineering & Urban Planning*, **22**(1), pp. 51–59.

13 Visitor routes in Old City of Damascus with implications and strategies for improvements

Dimah Ajeeb

Introduction

Cultural routes have gained wide recognition over the last decades for their contribution to social, cultural, economic and regeneration principles of cities and destinations. In definition, a cultural route is a

> physical, tangible section in space defined by an inventory of tangible and intangible cultural and historical elements connected by a theme, concept or definition as well as by the identification of sites of existing cultural heritage linked in a dispersed, linear or regional structure creating a marked and interpreted continuous whole within the unified context of the route.
>
> (Androić et al., 2013:9)

Cultural thematic routes are categorised based on geographical extents to: Local such as (Literally Dublin), regional (the Wine Route in Hungary), national (From the Alps to the Baltic Sea in Germany), or International (Silk Road) (Richards, 2007).

It is argued that the development of a successful thematic route extends far beyond the mere selection of a theme, alignment of tangible (physical structures) and intangible (culture) elements to it, and its promotion. The successful design and sustainable delivery of such projects are very challenging (Richards, 2007). This study suggests that the EU's Municipal Administration Modernisation's (MAM) thematic routes project has been limited to the mere identification of themes and physical elements and to modest promotion. This study however suggests that a successful thematic route project is subject to a carefully designed management and promotional structure and mechanism. To prove this, the study will look into the MAM project of thematic visitor routes in the Old City of Damascus, identify the opportunities and weaknesses, and suggest proposals to overcome the project's shortages based on lessons derived from successful international case studies on similar projects of cultural tourism in old city centres.

Literature review

MAM project to Syria

MAM, 2005–2009, is the EU's project to Syria for devolution, institutional reform, and local governance and delivery (BMB Mott MacDonald, n.d.). The project delivered a comprehensive framework and seventeen action plans including: Decentralised Governance, Institutional Development, Financial Resources Management, Local Development, Urban Planning and Informal Settlements, Old City of Damascus, and Public-Private Partnerships (BMB Mott MacDonald, n.d.). The Action Plan No. 10, 'the Old City of Damascus', was given the following objectives: i. Integrated sustainable development, regeneration and conservation plan for the old city with consideration to unique heritage and culture; ii. One Stop Shop for municipal services; and iii. a framework to promote tourism activities (EU Neighborhood Info Centre, 2009; EuropeAid, n.d.; Michelmore and Trusiani, 2005).

MAM's framework for tourism promotion in the Old City of Damascus

For the world's earliest inhabited city with its unique history and monuments, which go back to Century 11 BCE, the Aramean City, the Roman Empire, Omayyad and Ottoman eras (Doughman, 2007), the development of Damascus cultural tourism was one of MAM's priorities. Figure 13.1 represents the development of the Old City of Damascus through the centuries.

However, MAM was faced by the challenging governance and planning arrangements of the Old City: "The Directorate of the Old City forms part of the Governorate of Damascus and is supported by other directorates with regard to issues such as the provision of services and traffic control, but the fragmentation of decision making has hindered the development of holistic management policies. The Directorate has capacity in staffing, but effective management of the Old City is restricted by deficiencies in planning tools and lack of clarity about who holds real responsibility. In the case of Damascus, the failure to develop comprehensive strategies for the Old City is due to insufficient inter-sectoral coordination. Planning is seen in terms of land-use planning rather than a holistic plan for conservation, information and development, from the conservation of a single house to the whole Old City and its context within the wider city" (Michelmore and Trusiani, 2005:3).

In response to such challenges, MAM designed an integrated Conservation and Development Plan for the Old City of Damascus that is separated from the wider Development Plan of the City of Damascus (Michelmore and Trusiani, 2005). This action is with high importance to the Old City as it opens real opportunities for devolved governance arrangements and local decision making. This in turn creates an optimal environment to carefully consider the unique historical, physical and

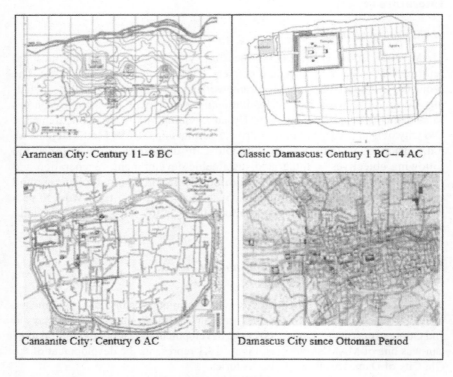

Aramean City: Century 11–8 BC	Classic Damascus: Century 1 BC – 4 AC
Canaanite City: Century 6 AC	Damascus City since Ottoman Period

Figure 13.1 The Development of Old City of Damascus
(Source: Doughman, 2007)

local identity of the Old City so to run a sustainable and effective management and development of its cultural tourism.

MAM examined the tourism practices in the Old City to identify shortages and to propose actions for development. In terms of shortages, MAM realised that the Directorate of the Old City has no tourism department, there was no single visitor centre for tourism guidance and information, the maps on local remarkable attractions were privately produced and printed rather than being officially prepared, and the official website of the city lacks information and a practical welcoming agenda. In addition, there was no official system of directional signs that would help visitors to walk through the Old City (Michelmore and Trusiani, 2005).

To overcome these shortages, MAM aimed at

1   Providing the local and international visitors with tourist promotional and information materials through two centres for tourism services.
2   Working towards the implementation of the following priority actions:

   i   Promote Old Damascus conservation through tourism.
   ii Preparation of a Tourism Action Plan for the Old City.

iii   Preparation of visitor routes in the Old City and buffer zone.
iv   Implement a system of directional signage.

Figure 13.2 is a summary of MAM's priority actions in relation to tourism, each with its plans, means and outcomes. As the figure indicates, there was no proposal to assign a dedicated local management team that helps to ensure a successful and sustainable delivery of MAM's priority actions, including the visitor routes project. Thus, this study suggests that MAM's Tourism Action Plan for Old Damascus and its visitor routes projects would face challenges to successfully deliver their initial aims and objectives.

The design, implementation and outcomes of MAM's visitor routes

MAM designed six routes with various interesting themes: Old Damascus Highlights (live examples of the numerous eras the city has witnessed), Classical Route (Displays the Greek, Roman and Hellenistic periods in the city), Essential Old

Priority Action	Plan	Pilot Area	Means	Outcome
Promote Old Damascus conservation through tourism.	Regeneration plan for a pilot area for replication on a wider scale in the Old City. Initiate development, conservation and crafts promotion activities through the historic areas.	Souq al-Atiq including a redesign of linkages between the urban areas. Comprehensive regeneration and tourism plan for Souq Sarouja.	Provision of experience in survey and the preparation of development proposals to be shared with stakeholders in Damascus and the other cities through a training workshop.	Training on preparation of proposals on rehabilitation of historic market areas including: documentation of historic structures, economic and social analysis, financing urban regeneration (tourism development, public-private partnership); public realm improvements.
Preparation of a Tourism Action Plan for the Old City	Preparation of a plan that will form part of the overall Conservation Management Plan of Old City	Identify tourism activities to be implemented in Souq Sarouja.	Overview for the Syrian national tourism industry to inform the specifics of tourism in the Old Cities	Promote the growth of national tourism with respect to the Old Cities, community participation, the promotion of private investment, public/private partnership.
Preparation of Visitor Routes in the Old City and buffer zone	To be publicised through one-page guides which will be available in hotels, museums information centres, etc.	The routes are: -Islamic pilgrimage route -Christian pilgrimage route -Cultural heritage route -Souqs route -Crafts route.	Visitor Routes help to lead visitors between the buffer zone and the walled city.	Publications on the city's cultural heritage (rof self-guided visitors). The routes will promote tourism more widely and will promote sustainable economic development through diversification and the promotion of local crafts.
Implement a system of directional signage	Utilizing standard "brown-and white" signs to tourism attractions.	Old City of Damascus.	Design bilingual signage in Arabic and English to tourism attractions.	Promote tourism within the two governorates. Strengthen the links between the Old City and the modern city.

Figure 13.2 MAM's Tourism Priority Actions

(Source: developed by author from Michelmore and Trusiani, 2005)

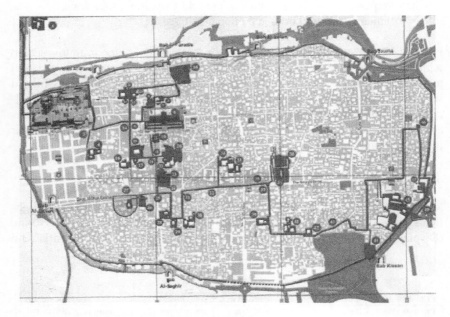

Figure 13.3 Part of MAM's Old Damascus Highlights route
(Source: MAM, n.d.)

Damascus (a short visit route runs through a number of important buildings and locations), Spiritual Old Damascus Route (identifies the religious landmarks), Traditional Souqs (bazzars) Route, and Hand Craft Route (The Syria Times, 2012; Tishreen Newspaper, 2010). Figure 13.3 is a map of part of MAM's Old Damascus Highlights Route.

Although MAM's visitor routes project is valuable not just to Damascus City itself but to the World heritage, the project's implementations have been limited to cosmetic instalments of two info kiosks and nine electronic screens at multiple sites in the Old City. The screens are intended to map the six characterised tourist routes, supported by photos and explanatory information represented by three languages: Arabic, English and French (EU Neighborhood Info Centre, 2009; EuropeAid, n.d.). In addition, a limited number of paper brochures on the project were printed. At the local level, very few knew or heard about the project, so it is not surprising that the project is unrecognised internationally, especially because seldom could any materials be found online about it. Thus, this study suggests that no concerted social or economic development has resulted from this project. The study also suggests that the shortage in the project implementations and outcomes is due to the failure in assigning a dedicated management and promotional team which could help to ensure an effective and sustainable delivery of the project's aims and plans.

Methodology

This study took a comparative case study approach to examine the practices and outcomes of MAM's visitor routes project to the Old City of Damascus and to derive lessons for improvements. Examining the extent to which MAM's visitor routes project was successful has not been studied before and so a qualitative approach was considered most appropriate as it allows the author to look in depth into various cases and then draw a single set of 'cross case conclusions' (Yin, 2013). The qualitative approach also helps the author to examine a variety of phenomena in relation to the proposed study (Flick, 1998).

Three international case studies have been examined: Walk London (London, UK), League of Historical and Accessible Cities (LHAC) (Mulhouse, France), and the Croatian Thematic Routes (Croatia). The case studies have been chosen on the basis of their renowned success in implementing successful and sustainable thematic tourist routes projects. Looking into successful international projects helps to provide insights into the strengths and weaknesses of MAM's project as well as to derive lessons for improvements and effective outcomes.

Findings

Case study 13.1: Walk London (London, UK)

Walk London is 390 miles of seven routes across the capital. The routes are: The LOOP Walk, Capital Ring Walk, Green Chain Walk, Lea Valley Walk, Thames Path Walk, Jubilee Walkway and Jubilee Greenway Walk (Walk Unlimited, n.d.-b). Figure 13.4 represents one of the project's tourist maps, the Bloomsbury area.

Routes management and promotion formed the core elements of the project to ensure its sustainable delivery and effective outcomes. The initial part of routes management was to assign a dedicated management team which in turn integrated the 33 London Boroughs in the project. The management team also involved managers for each route in addition to two professionals, all working together to ensure a successful delivery of projects' aims and plans (Walk Unlimited, n.d.-b). The management team had then developed a survey system and a route management system in collaboration with survey software experts Exegesis. Like the management team, the 33 Boroughs have access to these two systems in addition to a web interface so that they can plan how they can participate in the project as well as to report their activities to the project (Walk Unlimited, n.d.-b). To ensure the project's consistency between all participants, a design guide has been set to unify practices and elements such as signage and the identification of individual assets and their significance.

With regards to route promotion, Walk Unlimited promoted 'Walk London' through different channels including social media, underground posters, festivals and events, postcards, digital promotion through Time Out, web interactive layered maps, and related websites and newsletters (Walk Unlimited, n.d.-b). Paper and online promotion included information such as the length of each route, the start

158 *Dimah Ajeeb*

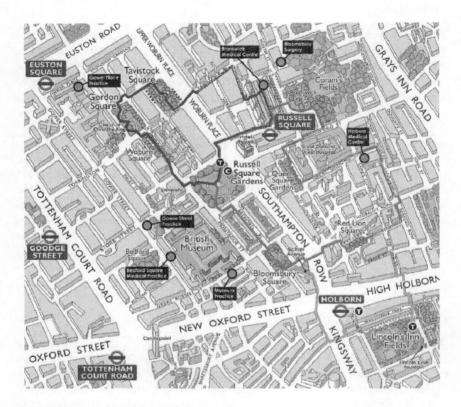

Figure 13.4 Bloomsbury tourist map
(Source: Walk Unlimited, n.d.-a.)

and end points, waymakers discs installed in the pavements, 158 pdf maps/leaflets for individual sections along the routes, interactive panels, downloadable audio guides, and a phone number provided in transportation hubs to provide audio information about wayfinding. Promotional arrangements also included the city's key players such as Transport for London and the Boroughs to publicise Walk London in their mappings and promotional materials. With such intensive management and promotional efforts, Walk London has successfully met and implemented all its 3,000 plans in January 2012 (Walk unlimited, n.d.-b).

Case study 13.2: League of Historical and Accessible Cities (LHAC) (Mulhouse, France)

The European Foundation Centre's Disability Thematic Network set a project in different European cities to enhance the accessibility of routes in historical cities for disabled people. In Mulhouse, a city in eastern France, apart from its overall governance arrangements, the project established its own governance structure and arrangements to enhance the implementation of the project's aims and objectives. In doing so, and under public–private partnership mode of governance, a multidisciplinary working group was formed. The group consists of four foundations: the Ministry of Culture, an architectural firm, an expert in applied research on disability, and a communication agency; each was expected to contribute with advisory, management and implementation roles in accessibility issues from its own experience, norms and network relationships (Ambrose et al., 2013). The working group itself brought into actions other key stakeholders such as "various accessibility and disability experts . . ., associations of people with disabilities. . . ., Mulhouse Tourism Office and Mulhouse Sud Alsace Museums" (Ambrose et al., 2013:24).

The project gains success for its outcomes such as the new pedestrian signage that provides navigating, touristic and red thread which indicates a variety of street furniture that impeded easy movement along the routes. In parallel, the project developed an open data site to inform about the city's accessible sites, and a radio frequency identification technology to improve the interconnectivity of the routes. A diagnostic tool has been developed and offered free by the city of Mulhouse, which uses a "colour-coded image of a key to indicate the accessibility levels of buildings, public spaces, shops, and hotels" (Ambrose et al., 2013:25). In addition, the city produced a methodological guide about accessibility requirements aimed at businesses, contractors, architects and other entities. Furthermore, a tourist guide highlighting the accessibility aspect in Mulhouse was published by the tourism office (Ambrose et al., 2013:25).

Inspired by the effective management arrangements and promotion outcomes, Mulhouse has been considered a successful project that can provide lessons to other historical cities in delivering equal rights and opportunities to integrate disabled people in social life through tourist routes projects.

Case study 13.3: Croatian Thematic Routes (Croatia)

In 2007–2009, the Croatian Thematic Routes programme was proposed as part of the European cultural routes initiative. Thematic routes were considered a way to identify, preserve and promote the unique Croatian cultural heritage and identity. Funded by the EU, the programme aimed at a variety of plans including; i. the promotion of tourism in less developed sites along with the enhancement of well-being and job opportunities for local people; and ii. the promotion of regional tourism products through the identification, design and implementation of a single tourist theme which links different areas at different spatial scales (sites, municipalities, cities and counties) (Androić et al., 2013).

Acknowledging the difference in spatial scale between MAM's project in the Old City of Damascus (city) and the Croatian Thematic Routes programme (regional), the key strength of the Croatian project is that it has been rooted and developed by a variety of local stakeholders: local and regional authorities, tourist institutions (educational, cultural and scientific) and local people (Androić

Figure 13.5 Croatian Thematic Cultural Routes
(Source: Androić et al., 2013:55)

et al., 2013). For the creation and development of thematic routes, the programme set 'minimum requirements' for regions' proposals to be accepted and funded including i. the identification of at least two sites of cultural or natural values; ii. the provision of at least three various types of accommodation as hotel, camp, private accommodation; iii. the provision of tourist services (belvedere, parking lots, sanitary facilities) and information points along the thematic routes; iv. the provision of at least five hospitality services (restaurants, pubs, hostels, vineyard cottage); and v. the ability to fund the proposed project e.g. not to request funds and investments of more than 50 per cent of the total cost of the project, and the ability of the project to attract co-funding of different local, national and international bodies (Androić et al., 2013). Although financing sounds critical in this project, as it is not entirely funded by a specific authority or organisation, this study considers the fifth requirement a good opportunity for routes' management team to seek collaborations and partnerships with other bodies to ensure sustainable funding and thus sustainable management and delivery of the project. Figure 13.5 is the Croatian Routes map.

Discussion and analysis

Based on the comparison developed between the plans, practices and outcomes of MAM's visitor routes project with those of the three international case studies identified before, it would be beneficial to spot areas of weaknesses in MAM's project and propose suggestions for development and effective outcomes.

Weaknesses in MAM's project

First of all, and most importantly, there was no dedicated management and promotion team for Damascus visitor routes project which helps to ensure a sustainable implementation and effective outcomes of the project. Secondly, although public–private partnership was one of the core 17 Action Plans of MAM's project to Syria and that private funds were integrated in MAM's proposals to conserve Old Damascus through tourism, neither public–private partnership, nor collaborations with private funds were established in Damascus visitor routes. Thirdly, there was no suggestion for involving volunteers in the project's operation and delivery at the time of the crucial needs to seek plans that helps in cost efficiency and savings.

Suggestions for effective development and outcomes

For effective management, promotion and delivery of visitor routes, Richards (2007) identifies the needs to have i. sustainable funds, preferably private funds; ii. compact coordinating body for the delivery of efficient marketing and the meeting of a variety of visitors' interests; and iii. the involvement of volunteers in the operation of routes and its physical assets and in theme- related events. Hardy (2003) adds the values of community involvement and infrastructure. This study suggests that for a successful design, management, delivery and outcomes of visitor/cultural routes projects, a dedicated management team should be assigned and empowered with full authorities and responsibilities to manage and promote the routes through integrating different strategies including the ones mentioned previously by Richards (2007) and Hardy (2003).

It is highly important that such key projects establish their own governance structure and arrangements to enhance the implementation of projects' aims and objectives. In the case of Old Damascus, this could be reached through the delegation of routes management to the local authority of the Old City of Damascus and authorising it with full responsibility to set its own management system for the project. The local authority of the Old City should in turn form a dedicated management team, 'a multidisciplinary working group', similar to that of Mulhouse project. Exercising a full spectrum of authorities, the management team itself should set a public–private partnership under which it can integrate and manage key stakeholders and associations, act as an advisory, managing, and delivery body of the plans, ensure sustainable funding, and collaborate with local and regional authorities, local stakeholders, private entrepreneurs and companies, relevant institutions (cultural, educational, scientific, financial), tourist organisations, other stakeholders at international, national and local levels, and the local people. The management team should also assign managers for each route in addition to local people representatives, volunteers, urban designers, architects, professionals and experts in different themes i.e., heritage, hand crafts, history and religions. In addition, it should set a design guide to ensure consistency in current and future development of the project. Similar to the Walk London project, all integrated bodies and associations should have access to management systems through web interface so that they can record their activities, informed by others' plans and contributions, and make collaborations with each other and with rational parties.

The governance of the Croatian cultural routes should be perceived as a very challenging and complicated task. Not just because of the constraints applied by the political context and governance arrangements of the country of Croatia itself, but also for the constraints applied by the wider different political and governance arrangements of the other participating EU countries in the project (Androić et al., 2013). In spite of this complex and critical governance landscape, there was a way to manage a successful governance and implementation of tourist routes between all participating countries through the 'cooperation policy' which has been set and placed as a core element to manage routes' governance and outcomes. Given that the cooperation policy achieved success in such a complex and challenging governance landscape in the Croatian project, there is no doubt that this policy can achieve promising outcomes in much less complicated governance arrangements such as the ones of Damascus visitor routes.

The clear delegation of tasks to the different parties involved in routes management is very essential for a successful implementation of thematic routes. While MAM's project in Damascus did mention this importance, it did not clarify the structure and mechanism of achieving it. The Croatian project, however, although it covers a much bigger spatial scale than the Damascus project does and it involves more challenging partnerships between different EU partners, each with its own agenda, preferences and plans, it still represents a much stronger and higher level of governance arrangements, clearer delegation of authorities and responsibilities, and the fostering of shared interests, business collaboration, and the change in behaviour to the benefits of the sider success of the project (Androić et al., 2013). Figure 13.6 identifies the set of tasks assigned to each of the involved partners which in turn helps to ensure a successful and sustainable implementation of the project.

In terms of routes promotion, MAM's project should be widely publicised locally and internationally and through different channels. The project is known by very few of the professionals in Syria. The author became aware of this project by a word of mouth and there were no printed or online data or information about the project even in the related institutions such as the Directorate of the Old City of Damascus and the Ministry of Tourism. The author, after intensive communication with professionals at different governmental, administrative and educational units ended up with a brochure of the project, which was one of the last two copies available.

No doubt that attractively designed and coded brochures are vital for the promotion of Damascus visitor routes; however digital promotion, websites and newsletters, collaborations with key services such as transportation hubs and travel agencies, universities, libraries, universally designed audio guides in different languages, web interactive layered maps, social media, and the other cultural and social venues for promotion can by far enhance the popularity of the routes and attract the visitors.

Partners?	What can be expected from them?
Scientific institutions (archives, historic, social, musical institutes, etc)	Provide high quality scientific background to the theme Provide data for evaluation of resources and attractions Interpretation and presentations
Heritage institutions (museums, galleries, music and concert halls etc)	Provide high quality scientific background to the theme Provide data for evaluation of resources and attractions Interpretation and presentations
SMEs: Hospitality and restaurants	Contracting. Added value on the route, thematically appropriate for various visitor segments (i.e. Roman Emperors Route – occasional Roman dinners, events, culinary workshops ...)
SMEs: Accommodation	Provide an offer on the route, thematically appropriate for various visitor segments (for cyclists–offer BIKE & BED on the Roman route). Contracting.
DMCs, Travel agents, Tour operators	Provide assistance in assessing the route resources for tourism purposes. Offer packages organized for target groups (school children, students, specific groups: team building, foreign markets, archaeo lovers, artists. Contractual relationship.
DMOs, NTOs	Support the promotional activities, financial support.
Development agencies	Organizational support, project preparation, funding sources
Local associations (folk, fishermen, women)	Participation in creating activities and events, and the associated structural content
Artists, prominent scientists, entrepreneurs	Participation in creating activities and events, and the associated structural content
Educators, teachers, guides and animators	Elaboration of content and interpretation for targeted educational groups, social groups ...

Figure 13.6 The tasks of the involved partners
(Source: Androić et al., 2013:21)

A major lesson that could be derived from the Croatian project is that it was initially designed to have international character and appeal to attain the project's sustainability and uniqueness. The Croatian project aimed to "exceed the local and regional level of routes, establish new partnerships, address new users and get included in the international tourism offer" (Androić et al., 2013:726). An example of this is the Roman Emperors Route in which Croatia acts as a partner in a wider network of other European destinations that offer the same cultural and heritage product. This networking of cultural landscape between those different EU destinations meant to enhance partners' relations, people mobilities, an exchange of ideas and experiences, social and cultural communications, and a promotion of job opportunities, education and sustainable development. Damascus's visitor routes project was to be with more effective impacts if it was designed in collaboration with similar thematic routes in wider geographical contexts to attract a wider international recognition and interests. The wider geographical contexts such as the historical centres of the other Syrian cities: Aleppo, Homs, Lattakia, or historical cities from neighbouring counties such as Lebanon and Jordan. This is a strategy claimed to "promote regional identity and collective memory" (Androić et al., 2013:14).

Theme-related events for Damascus visitor routes will not be limited to attract international visitors but also the local ones. Involving local communities in theme-related events helps to generate jobs and enhance sustainable local economic development. Living history events is something worth looking into in the Croatian project and to derive lessons to the Syrian one. The Croatian project is well known for its different famous living past events such as Museums of Hrvatsko Zagorje, which initially meant to produce entertaining and educational events similar to the real ones that took place in the past in Zagorje in the 16th century or late Middle Ages. Although such living history events face critics in terms of the needs to add fake information or assumptions to fill the gaps in the past story which in turn do not provide the total truth of the past, there are still benefits of such events to bring the attention, interests and profits to local people and the industry itself.

Whilst both the Syrian and the Croatian projects share the importance of introducing local crafts to visitors in Hand Craft Route in Damascus and the Traditional Workshops in Croatia. Still, the Croatian project represents stronger promotion and facilities: multimedia venues (e.g. auditorium with 120 seats and an LCD projector); urban design instalments (e.g. arranged promenades and benches, arranged trails, and promenades in the park with benches), facilities for the disabled (e.g. toilets); and a wide variety of interesting events (e.g. museum night, anniversary of the Croatian–Slovene Peasant Revolt, International Museum Day, Meetings for Rudi, Medieval Tournament, Summer at Castle Oršić, Advent Fair at Oršić, Triennale) (Androić et al., 2013:26). Implementing such traditional craft events and facilities to Damascus Hand Craft Route, for example, can add much to its popularity, usability and urban design, social and economic regeneration.

'Theme processing' is a principle emphasised in the Croatian thematic routes that the values of a route extend beyond the scientific research or historical stories to include a wider spectrum of integrated values such as emotional, moral, intellectual experiences, and social. In this regard, Androić et al. (2013) claim that,

> the theme must encompass general human experiences, problems, viewpoints, solutions . . . (e.g. the route with the Roman heritage theme will deal with the lives of women or the housing solutions in Imperial Rome etc.). However, to make the route memorable and recognisable, it is necessary to mark and emphasise the basis for theme interpretation. It is only with the directed interpretation that the theme forming process becomes long-lasting in the recipient's mind.
>
> (Androić et al., 2013:14)

Although MAM's routes integrate a variety of life aspects and values, the focus was intensively based on scientific and physical elements. This study suggests that a city such as Damascus, with its deep-rooted history and a wide variety of successive civilisations, when integrating theme processing values to its visitor routes project, it can deliver a global recognition and a fruitful and life-long memorable experience.

Conclusion

MAM's thematic visitor routes in Old Damascus is highly valuable as it represents the city's rich cultural, civil and historical assets to the world. MAM examined a variety of challenging governance and planning arrangements of the Old City of Damascus including; the lack of local decision making, local governance, clear delegation of responsibilities, and the lack of inter-sectoral coordination. MAM suggested that the success of any development plan in the Old City of Damascus, including the visitor routes project, is subject to devolution, institutional reform, and effective local governance and delivery, as well as to the implementation of MAM's holistic plan for regeneration, conservation and development for the Old City. This study however suggests that, apart from MAM's devolution and modernisation of municipal administration and its holistic plan for development, the failure in the successful implementation and outcomes of MAM's visitor routes is due to the lack of dedicated management and promotion team and to the lack of clear delegation of tasks to the different parties involved in routes' management.

Based on a comparative case study approach, in which three international case studies have been examined to derive lessons on their success in thematic routes projects, this study concludes that creating a dedicated management and promotion team that is separate from the overall management and governance team of the city itself, is key to succeed the project. The management team should be assigned with full authorities and clear responsibilities to manage and promote the routes, create its own governance structure and arrangements, integrate and manage key stakeholders and associations, make collaborations with interested and relative bodies, set the norms and design guide for the project, and monitor a sustainable and effective implementation of the project's plans and objectives. Subject to a successful implementation of the core principles mentioned previously, the cooperation policy, public–private partnership, sustainable funds arrangements, volunteers and community involvement, theme-related events, intensive promotional activities, the creation of international appeal, networking of cultural landscape and theme processing have all proven their efficacy in successful management and delivery of thematic routes projects.

References

Ambrose, I., Balmas, S., Barragán Iturriaga, A., Medina Higueras, M. and Orejas, M. (2013). *Accessible routes in historical cities: Best practice guide.* European Foundation Centre, ASBL. Retrieved from: www.accessibletourism.org/?i=enat.en.reports.1487 (accessed: the 14th October, 2017).

Androić, M., Horjan, G., Klarić, V. and Nevidal, R. (2013). *Managing visitors on thematic cultural routes handbook.* Retrieved from: www.fpdd.bg/userfiles/files/Handbook%20 Thematic%20Cultural%20Routes%20adopted%20for%20Danube%20project.pdf (accessed: the 09th June, 2017).

BMB Mott MacDonald (n.d.). *Municipal administration modernization project, Syria.* Retrieved from: www.extranet.ecbmb.nl/iddnet/download.asp?file=Docs/Projects/ BMB/2010%20LG403MAM.doc. (accessed: the 11th December, 2016).

Doughman, M. (2007). The development of Old Damascus Wall "Current situation and preservation principles". *The 2nd International Forum for Rehabilitation of Islamic and Arab Cities*. Damascus, Syria: Damascus University.

EU Neighborhood Info Centre. (2009). *EU project showcases local development activities in old Damascus*. Retrieved from: www.euneighbours.eu/mainmed.php?id_type=1&id=19701. (accessed: the 14th December, 2016).

EuropeAid. (n.d.). *Governance and institutional reform*. Retrieved from: http://ec.europa.eu/europeaid/documents/case-studies/syria_mam_en.pdf (accessed: the 12th May, 2017).

Flick, U. (1998). *An introduction to qualitative research*. London: Sage Publications.

Hardy, A. (2003). An investigation into the key factors necessary for the development of iconic touring routes. *Journal of Vacation Marketing*, **9**(4), pp. 314–330.

MAM. (n.d.). *Visitor routes in Old City of Damascus- Old Damascus highlights* [Brochure]. Damascus, Syria.

Michelmore, D. and Trusiani, E. (2005). *Municipal administration modernisation project-case study: Old Damascus*. Retrieved from: www.yumpu.com/en/document/view/40700020/damascus-syria-old-city-a-case-study-2005pdf-building-/3 (accessed: the 13th December, 2016).

Richards, G. (2007). *Cultural tourism: Global and local perspectives*. London: Psychology Press.

The Syria Times. (2012). *Old Damascus visitors routes project*. Retrieved from: http://syriatimes.sy/index.php/archaeology/167-old-damascus-visitors-routes-project (accessed: the 13th May, 2017).

Tishreen Newspaper. (2010). *Tourist guide signboards to easily explore Old Damascus*. Retrieved from: http://archive.tishreen.news.sy/tishreen/public/read/207187 (accessed: the 12th May, 2017).

Walk Unlimited. (n.d.-a). *Examples of maps*. Retrieved from: www.walkengland.org.uk/uploads/file/Dr%20Maps%20examples/BLOOMSBURY.pdf (accessed: the 09th November, 2017).

Walk Unlimited. (n.d.-b). *Route management*. Retrieved from: www.walk.co.uk/route-management.asp (accessed: the 09th November, 2017).

Yin, R.K. (2013). *Case study research: Design and methods*. London: Sage Publications.

14 Northern tourism

A comparative analysis of the national parks of the northern territories of Canada and the Arctic regions of Sakha Republic (Yakutia), Russia

Elena Egorovna Totonova

Introduction

In recent years, tourism has been playing an increasingly important role all over the world due to the growing impact of this sector on the global economy. This also results in the growing popularity of adventure, ecological and exotic tourism in the global tourism industry, which facilitated the development of tourism in the countries of the Arctic Basin: the US, Canada, Iceland, the Nordic countries and Russia.

Over the recent decades, regions of the North with their picturesque landscapes and unique nature have become the focus of growing tourist activity. The tourist markets of the developed nations see a shift in consumer pattern towards more active forms of recreation. The share of active tourism keeps growing with extreme and exotic tours to far away, 'unexplored' destinations becoming more and more popular.

Certain geo-political processes, growth of currency rate against the Russian ruble, and a number of other reasons have led to the increasing popularity of domestic tourism. The current world economy situation has resulted in the growing attraction of Russian holiday-makers to the distant and less-known areas of the country. Hence, the northern regions began to offer exclusive tourist routes which became particularly attractive (given their considerable cost) in the context of global tourist market development.

The system of natural reserves is swiftly being developed in the Sakha Republic (Yakutia) as well as in Russia in general. There are three levels of such reserves: federal, regional and municipal.

On the vast territory of Yakutia preserved ecologically clean areas contributed to the creation in 1994 for the setup of a natural reserves system (Ytyk Kere Sirder). The republic's reserve system (officially given the status of national heritage) is presented by two federal reserves, 125 republican-level SPNAs (specially protected natural areas) and 95 municipal ones (Ministry of Nature Protection of the Republic of Sakha [Yakutia], 2016). The Artctic coast of the republic is part of the SPNT system as well. The SPNTs are of unique environmental, research, cultural and recreational value where land use is completely or partially banned. Doubtlessly, the development of SPNTs is a new form of landscape and environment preservation.

Thus, the republic is capable of offering quite a variety of adventure/extreme tourism possibilities on the Russian market. Therefore, grows the relevance of detailed analysis of market specifics and potential growth perspectives against the urge to minimise negative outcomes and high costs of territorial development.

Review of the literature

Since the problems of the relationship between industries and regions turned out to be the focus of research i.e. the issue that for decades has been developed both from the perspective of the industrial markets theory and numerous theories of regional development, one must admit that the problem has been explored quite well regarding its theoretical aspect (Granberg, 2000; Luzin et al., 1996; Vishnevskiy and Demyanenko, 2010).

However, if analysing not the industry itself, but the tourism industry, and not all regions but the regions of the Arctic and northern Canada (Grenier, 2009), it is seen that the level of investigation of this problem, at least in Russian economic science, remains fairly low. In this regard, when carrying out an in-depth study of the northern territories, first it is necessary to identify the system of factors that influence the development of tourism and its impact on the specific economy of the North. Therefore, our study of the northern territories was based on a comprehensive approach which included the analysis of natural, social, ethnographic, environmental and economic factors affecting the development of tourism and changing the course of the North's development. When considering works dedicated to the territorial management of Canada's North economy, special attention should be paid to the works of Hamelin (Hamelin, 2002) and Rea (Rea, 1968).

Methodology of this study is based on the fundamental works of Russian and international scientists considering the problems of the formation of industrial markets, including the markets of tourist services, as well as the research on the issues of regional development, including the problems of economic development of the northern regions. Of special note are the works of both Russian and international researchers dedicated to the principles of the regional policy development, also in relation to the northern regions. The economic data were summarised and studied through the methods of economic analysis, economic-statistical methods, methods of survey, interview, comparative economic and statistical analysis, geographical demarcation, zoning, the study of international practices and expert assessments.

The tourist market of Sakha Republic (Yakutia)

The market for tourist services in Sakha Republic (Yakutia) began to develop relatively recently, which is explained by geographical distance from the main tourist centres and underdeveloped transport infrastructure. According to data for 2013,

83 travel agencies operated in the republic, of which 4.8 per cent worked as a tourist operator, 54 per cent as a tourist agent, 6 per cent combined both forms of activity, and 34.9 per cent of travel agencies engaged in sightseeing activities. The volume of revenue from the provision of paid tourism services in 2013 showed a significant increase – 433.2 million rubles. As compared to 2005, it grew by 60 per cent. The average number of employees of tourist firms was 356 people, without external part-time employees and workers who performed work under civil law contracts (see Table 14.1).

Table 14.1 The development of tourism in Sakha Republic (Yakutia) in 2005–2013

	Number	*2005*	*2006*	*2007*	*2008*	*2009*	*2010*	*2011*	*2012*	*2013*
Number of total tourists	In thousands	15,2	18,1	17,4	24,3	19,6	27,0	27,5	32,5	37,1
Domestic tourists	In thousands	6,7	6,7	5,8	12,9	8,5	8,3	9,7	9,8	8,7
Inbound tourists	In thousands	0,5	0,3	0,2	0,2	0,1	0,2	0,2	0,2	0,4
Outbound tourists	In thousands	8,03	11,1	11,5	11,2	10,9	18,5	17,6	22,7	26,3
Number of total tourism enterprises	Unit	33	43	43	43	43	66	64	74	83
Number of employees	In thousands	136	194	183	217	225	361	358	354	356
Paid tourism services volume	Million Ruble	122,1	125,3	173,0	201,6	208,7	231,4	261,6	276,4	433,2
Percentage from the previous year	%	110,2	108,3	102,5	96,2	91,7	106,4	110,0	105,7	–
Contribution to the budget	Million Ruble	10,7	86,7	95,4	137,9	142,8	153,7	162,9	163,0	169,8
Share in GDP	%	0,006	0,042	0,039	0,045	0,045	0,048	0,05	0,05	–
The volume of funds of the consolidated budget of the entity aimed at the development of tourism	Million Ruble	5,4	5,7	5,05	8,4	8,4	17,3	34,4	44,6	97,4

(Source: Republic of Sakha, 2016)

The most common in the number of specialisations of tourist operators is out-bound tourism (74.9 per cent); domestic tours offer 24.2 per cent of firms. Analysis of the dynamics of tourist flows for 2005–2013 showed a clear predominance of outbound tourism over the inbound, which was facilitated not only by the opening of the Iron Curtain, but also the economic crisis of the 1990s and low customs duties that forced tourist firms to engage in light business-shop tour. According to the data for 2013, the number of tourists who travelled abroad was 26.3 thousand people.

Inbound tourism in Yakutia was developed at the beginning of 'Perestroika', when the republic was visited by up to 1.8 thousand tourists a year. During the economic crisis, the number of tourists fell sharply to 60 visits. Currently there is a stable development of inbound and domestic tourism in the country. According to data for 2013, the republic was visited by 3 thousand foreign tourists, which is 66 per cent less than in the similar 2005 (4.7 thousand tourists). The republic mostly is visited by tourists from Germany (26.4 per cent) and China (23.8 per cent).

Foreign tourists in Yakutia prefer extreme tours. Trips to the village of Oimyakon (the tour route 'Pole of Cold') to Verkhoyansk for the ascent to the sacred mountains of Kisilyakh and the national parks 'Lena Pillars' and 'Buluus' (Totonova, 2011).

Event tourism is developing dynamically in Yakutia. Tourists are attracted by the festival 'Journey to the Pole of Cold', 'Ysyakh National Holiday', 'Diamond Week of Yakutia', 'Winter Begins with Yakutia', and gastronomic festival 'Taste of Yakutia'. The traditional festival 'Winter Begins with Yakutia' has a rich pro-gramme; it includes a fur festival, an international festival of children's creativity, and a festival of 'Stroganina'. According to tradition, Father Frost from Great Ustyug comes as a symbol of the cold – for the Yakut winter.

One of the most prominent types of event tourism in the Republic of Sakha (Yakutia) is the 'Ysyakh National Holiday'. Culture of Yakutia is a 'mirror' of its history and national traditions. Since ancient times the peoples of the north piously revere and protect their customs. Traditionally, since the beginning of the XII century, in the middle of summer Yakutia celebrates the rebirth and renewal of nature and the northern sun meeting – Ysyakh or Yakut New Year. Feast is a sym-bol of unity and friendship of all indigenous peoples of the North. All residents of the republic go on the summer solstice, to sing to northern nature and thank her for her generosity and kindness (The national tour operator 'Satal tour', 2018).

Recently, with the rise in price of air transport in the republic. Domestic tourism has been growing. Five to six years ago, Yakut tourist firms were mainly engaged in outbound tourism. Now there is a development of domestic tourism. New tourist routes are opening in the regions of the republic. The most popular tourist routes in the republic are cruises to the Lena Pillars, Hunting and fishing tours, the festival 'Pole of Cold', visits to specially protected areas (national parks, 'Ust-Lensky' Nature Reserve), as well as the cultural and educational programme 'Yakutsk and its environs'. In the field of domestic tourism, the priority areas are weekend tours, event-based tourism and activities aimed at the development of social tourism, the organisation of youth tourism, and recreation of the elderly. The domestic tourism market in the republic is seasonal with a peak in July and early August. At that time, sales of weekend programmes in the vicinity of the city of Yakutsk, cruises along the Lena River and rafting along the rivers of the republic grow sharply. The internal tourist market is represented by vacationers from the republic. Among most residents of cities in recent years, there has been a trend of increasing demand for the tourist product of the republic from Russian tourists represented by residents of such large cities as Moscow, St. Petersburg, Yekaterinburg, Novosibirsk etc. According to the State Statistics Committee of Sakha Republic (Yakutia), in 2013, the number of tourists who stayed in Russia on travel company tickets amounted to 8.7 thousand people or 24.5 per cent of the total number of tourists served. The most attractive for tourists were Krasnodar Territory (21.3 per cent), Moscow (10.6 per cent), and Altai Territory (4.7 per cent). The share of domestic tourism accounted for 61 per cent of the total number of tourists (Republic of Sakha, 2016).

In recent years, the number of hotels, quality and service level have been increasing in the republic. The number of rooms in the republic is 157 units of collective accommodation facilities. The leading position in the market of Yakut hotels is occupied by hotels with a small number of rooms (20 rooms and 30 beds). Out of thirty-two available hotels in Yakutsk, those in the 3 Star category are the Yakut branch of JSC 'Hotels ALROSA', 'Polar Star', 'Tygyn Darkhan', and 'Sterkh'. According to data for 2013, hotels and collective accommodation facilities received revenues from the services provided in the amount of 225.9 million Ruble, mainly due to the sale of rooms and from the sale of vouchers (courses). The average number of employees of collective accommodation facilities was 1.7 thousand people (2013), the average number of part-time employees – 119 people (Totonova, 2011).

The hotel market serves primarily business travellers (business and professional purposes – 80 per cent) as well as those travelling for personal purposes (19.9 per cent) etc. Among the people placed in hotels and similar accommodation facilities Russians predominate – 90.3 per cent of the far abroad – 1.6 per cent. In addition to Yakutsk, the city of Mirny (12 units), Vilyuisky region (11 units), Neryungri and Tomponsky regions (5 units) have sufficient market capacity (Republic of Sakha, 2016).

Today the Republic of Sakha attracts foreign tourists due to the novelty and exotic component of the proposed tourist product. However, the advertising and marketing component in the promotion of the tourist product is quite costly for the subjects of tourist activity and reduces the opportunities for large-scale positioning of the tourist potential of the republic.

For the further development of tourism in the country, four types of transport are important: aviation, automobile, railway and water. The level of development of any of them is determined by the density of the network of trails, their quality, and the level of rolling stock and the specifics of the organisation of transportation. In the total volume of passenger turnover on interurban traffic, air transport is more important (more than 90 per cent), and with the putting into operation of an international airport and the development of international air routes. The importance of air transport is growing rapidly (Totonova, 2016).

In connection with this, it is urgent to study the existing resource potential of tourism for targeted investments in profitable projects to stimulate the development of the tourism industry in the municipal formations of the Republic of Sakha (Yakutia).

Tourist resources of the Arctic

The Arctic coast of Yakutia is of unique environmental, climatic, historical, cultural and economic significance. When studying the specifics of cultural and economic development of Yakutia's Arctic regions one cannot but notice a drastic differentiation among these regions. The Anabarsky, Allaikhovsky, Bulunsky, Nizhnekolymsky, Ust-Yansky regions are based on reindeer-herding, hunting, cage fur-farming and fishing. All of them are to some degree characterised by selective natural resources, focal manufacturing and a marked economic disproportion decreasing the production effectiveness (Totonova, 2014c).

In the given situation service industry is viewed as the key to small-business development, particularly tourism which has the potential of leading to progress (Luzin et al., 1996). Tourism has a potential of entrepreneurial attraction without large-scale investments (unlike manufacturing, for example) and is the number one industry in terms of job creation. Given the overall potential and present under-development of tourism it is particularly relevant to focus on the investment in the sphere.

Arctic regions of the Republic Sakha (Yakutia) form an arctic-tundra area of even lands which consists of mountainous regions in its south-eastern part and takes up a wide strip of coastal parts in the north of the republic. Bulunsky region treated within the frame of the given analysis as a sample object of tourist development study serves as the Arctic 'Gate' of the Republic (river port, sea port and airport). All of the islands and northern parts of the coastal area are occupied by the arctic deserts (little-developed territories with sharply continental climate and solid permafrost with frozen soil depth as thick as 500 m). Geographic zones of arctic deserts are sharply pronounced here – tundra and northern taiga. Even land is presented by lacustrine-alluvial plains with northern taiga landscapes, dominating lakes and marshy lands (Gukov, 2010).

Today's coasts of East-Siberian and Laptev seas washing the Bulunsky region mostly consist of 'Arenaceous-argillous' soft sediments containing a large amount of ice. When the latter thawed fossils of pre-historic animals were discovered: mammoths, woolly rhinoceros, musk oxen and horses. In 1799, a local hunter named Osip Shumakhov came upon the first known mammoth fossils. The tusks were bought by the St. Petersburg Kunstkamera for 8600 Rubles. Waters of Lena concave the banks and gradually erode the ancient isles of the East-Siberian and Laptev seas with average speed of up to 6 metres per year. Researchers believe that the isles were once part of the ancient Arctide plain (Gukov, 2010). When ice wedges thaw, the cone-shaped forms – Baijarakhs – grow on the cliff slopes. Thermokarst processes lead to formation of large lakes.

Culture and lifestyle of the indigenous peoples is worth special mentioning. Cultural tourism includes all its types aimed at discovery and education. These programmes are based in the introduction and study of cultural and natural heritage in all its diversity. Tourism development promotes preservation of local cultures and traditional lifestyles. Products of such ethnographic tours are oriented at educating visitors on the traditional lifestyle, handicraft, ethnic cuisine, and traditional land use (Totonova, 2014a). To promote visits a combination of various types of tourism is practiced (cultural and ecotourism). The tours dwell on busy activity schedule and low-cost housing. These tours are popular among both international and domestic visitors.

Northern tourism: A comparative analysis of the national parks of the northern territories of Canada and the Arctic regions of Sakha Republic (Yakutia)

One of the tasks of the comparative analysis of the development of protected areas in Canada and Russia is to identify new changes that could affect the development of the territory (Totonova, 2014c). For a more detailed study of the impact of tourism development on the local economy, the author conducted a comparative analysis of the two protected areas of Canada and Russia. The author selected the National Park Tuktut-Nogaid of the Northwest Territories and the Nature Reserve of the 'Ust-Lensky Bulunsky' region of Sakha Republic (Yakutia), located on the coast of the Arctic Ocean and are respectively administered by the Parks of Canada and the Ministry of Natural Resources and Ecology of the Russian Federation. Specific protected areas of Canada and Russia have similar natural and climatic conditions, but they have different opportunities for socio-economic development and institutions that affect the behaviour of the local population.

In the Republic of Sakha (Yakutia), as well as across Russia, the networks of specially protected natural areas of three levels are developing at a rapid pace: federal, regional and municipal. The huge territories of the Republic of Sakha (Yakutia) with ecologically clean nature contributed to the creation in 1994 of a system of specially protected natural areas (Ytyk Keré Sirder). The system of specially protected natural areas of the republic includes two state nature reserves of federal importance, 125 specially protected natural territories of national importance (six natural parks, 74 resource reserves, one state nature reserve, twenty-six unique lakes, one protected landscape, and seventeen nature monuments) and ninety-five local–municipal significance. The Arctic coast of the republic is covered by a network of protected areas (Ministry of Nature Protection of the Republic of Sakha [Yakutia], 2016).

The largest state natural reserve 'Ust-Lensk' (located in the Bulunsky region) was established in 1986 to preserve and explore the natural complexes of the Lena Delta (an area of 1433 thousand hectares). This is one of the largest rivers in the world. The territory of the 'Ust-Lensky' nature reserve is divided into two sections: Delta (delta of the Lena River, part of the Laptev Sea basin) and 'Sokol' (the northern part of the Verkhoyansk mountain system and the Lena River). Here, under special protection are populations of wild reindeer, Laptev walrus, snow ram, narwhal, spawning ground of whitefish, and a place of mass nesting of waterfowl migrating birds. To study and carry out monitoring of the biological resources of the Lena Delta in 1995. the International Biological Station 'Lena-Nordenskiold' was established which is one of the world's biosphere reserves (89 bird species).

The peculiarity of the Bulun region where the natural park is located has ethnographic, historical and cultural potential of the Northern people of Yakutia. Scientific and ecological tourism is offered for acquaintance with the nature of the Arctic in the reserve (observation of the animal world, hiking routes). The main measure of tourism in protected areas is the registration of the number of visitors (organised and unorganised) but such data the state nature reserve 'Ust-Lensky' provides only in the form of its report 'On the results of the activities of the federal state budget institution' which is administered by the Ministry of Natural Resources and Ecology of the Russian Federation. As a result, the statistics bodies of Sakha Republic (Yakutia) do not take into account tourists visiting the Ust-Lena State Nature Reserve (Totonova, 2014a).

According to the State Reserve 'Ust-Lensky' (2014), data provided by the Scientific Department of the 'Ust-Lensky' State Nature Reserve and administrated by the Ministry of Natural Resources and Ecology of the Russian Federation, 24 ecological trails were recorded. In 2009–2012, Ust-Lensk State Nature Reserve was visited by 590 tourists, of which 172 are foreign tourists (see Table 14.2). Information about the attendance of the reserve may indicate an approximate value of visits to unorganised tourists as there is no systematic recording of data on the arrivals of tourists and sightseers. These data give little information about the quality of the services provided and the income received by the reserve.

However, one cannot but agree with Alexandrova (Alexandrova, 2010) that many of the programmes of visiting national parks and reserves, planned as ecotourism have flaws and misses. These programmes do not provide for the active involvement of their participants in environmental activities. Unfortunately, tourist activities in the Ust-Lensk State Nature Reserve are in embryo. The management and employees of the nature reserve realise that ecotourism is a developing direction in the tourism of Sakha Republic (Yakutia) and the reserve is of great interest to tourists as the natural territory of the Arctic which has enormous resources of biological and landscape diversity. Among the reserve's employees there are disagreements between supporters of the development of ecological tourism and conservationists who view ecotourism as having a negative impact on security activities. However, the development of the nature reserve is not considered in the

Table 14.2 Number of tourists who visited Ust-Lena State Nature Reserve

Year	Total number of tourists	Foreign tourists (within total number of tourists)
2009	230	60
2010	230	60
2011	95	40
2012	37	12

(Source: The State Reserve 'Ust-Lensky', 2014; The Report about the Results of the Activity of the Federal State-Financed Organization. Being Administrated by the Ministry of Natural Resources and Ecology of the Russian Federation. The State Natural Reserve "Ust-Lensky". Tiksi. Bulunsky region. the Republic of Sakha (Yakutia). 2014. [in Russian]. (Report not published))

regional context which could help to reach agreement and take into account the interests of the parties: the reserve, the local population, the local administration, and the republic. Each side lives and acts in its own direction and as a rule, the interests of the local population interested in preserving their ancestral habitats are unaffected (Totonova, 2014c).

The types of tourist services offered in the northern national parks have some differences from other regions which depend on the remoteness of the territory, climatic conditions, and transport accessibility. Canadians believe that the main goal of developing ecological tourism in protected areas is to promote knowledge of environmental problems and protect it and ecotourism serves as a powerful educational tool that disseminates information about the objects of ecological tourism and the value of the natural heritage, as well as the development of the local population (Totonova, 2009).

The Tuktut-Nogaid National Park (16,000 sq. Km), located 170 km from the Arctic Circle is a fairly 'young' park with undeveloped infrastructure. The park was created in 1996 at the insistence of indigenous peoples in order to protect the animal kingdom, in particular, the Caribou population. In the park, there are ancient Dorset culture sites which are archaeological monuments (300). For the short Arctic tourist season (July and August), tourists are offered an ecological (hiking, bird watching, and wild animals-musk oxen, caribou, bears), scientific, historical and cultural (acquaintance with the culture and history of the local population) tourism (Rapport sur l'état du parc national du Canada Tuktut Nogait, 2011).

Mostly in Tuktut-Nogaid, independent tours of tourists predominate which advance online applications and agree on their visit to the park. At the same time, an individual programme is developed for each tourist arriving in the park. Northern parks have a high cost of the offered individual tourist services and therefore attract physically prepared and financially secured tourists. Thus, 88 per cent of tourists who come to Tuktut-Nogaid are men aged 25–35. The only mode of transport with which you can come to this remote park is air transport (seaplane) (Rapport sur l'état du parc national du Canada Tuktut Nogait, 2011).

Types of modern tourist services in northern national parks have some differences from other regions depending on the remoteness of the area, weather conditions and transport accessibility. Canadians believe that the main goal of developing ecological tourism in protected areas is to protect the environment and ecotourism.

Therefore, the growth in prices for the tourist services in northern parks is largely influenced by the dynamics of tariff changes for airlines as the average distance travelled per tourist is reduced, the total number of tourists served and the volume of tourist flow. However, the development of air transport, the emergence of modern aircraft and the development of small aircraft ensure the possibility of rapid arrival in remote settlements and transport accessibility of the northern territories.

The cost of a trip to the park Tuktut-Nogai which is located 170 km from the North Pole is quite high and costs 30 thousand dollars per person. According to the data of 2011, Tuktut-Nogai was visited by only one tourist whose expenses amounted to 30 thousand dollars. At the same time in 2007–2011, there was a decrease in the number of arriving tourists which is explained not only by high transport costs but also by northern climatic conditions (strong wind and so on) (see Table 14.3).

A comparative analysis of the two protected areas shows that, despite the fact that the Canadian national park Tuktut-Nogai was established as a biological reserve for the conservation of the migrating Caribou population, it is also designed for the development of ecologically controlled tourism in the park. Due to the collision with the Russian Ust-Lena nature reserve, Tuktut-Nogaid offers the largest number of various tourist routes but has limited transport accessibility for tourists. It is possible to reach the national park by seaplane from the village Polatuk in the Northwest Territories only if the weather conditions are stable. The 'Ust-Lensky' nature reserve in comparison with Tuktuk-Nogai has good transport accessibility with the use of the local airport and the sea port of Tiksi (see Table 14.4). If we compare tourist traffic, then of course the Canadian park has much less attention than the Russian reserve but the types of individual tourist services provided by small aircraft are much larger. At the same time, the costs to Canadian tourists who are visiting Tuktut-Nogai are greater than in the Russian reserve.

The development of tourism in the national parks of northern Canada takes into account specific features, climate, the presence of permafrost, the sensitivity of nature to the anthropogenic impact and sparsity of the territories, and the

Table 14.3 The number of tourists visiting Tuktut-Nogai

2007	2008	2009	2010	2011	Total
6	6	4	2	1	19

(Source: Rapport sur l'état du parc national du Canada Tuktut Nogait, 2011)

Table 14.4 A comparative analysis of the two protected areas Tuktut-Nogai and the 'Ust-Lensky' nature reserve

	Tuktut-Nogai	*The 'Ust-Lensky' nature reserve*
Number of local population	Polatuk 313 people	Tiksi 5063 people
Types of tourism	scientific, ecological, historical, cultural and extreme tourism	ecological, scientific
Types of transportation	air (seaplane)	air, water
Number of tourists	4	146
Touristic expenditure	US$120 thousand	110 thousand Ruble.

(Source: the author)

development of a strategic plan for the development of the park facilitates obtaining support in the Department of Finance and at other levels of government. Also, the strategic plan of parks allocates work for the organisation and aims to represent all natural regions, rather than duplicate the already presented ones, helping to maximise the effectiveness of financial and human resources (Affaires autochtones et développement du Nord Canada, 2016).

Of course, tourism like no other sector of the economy depends on the ecological wellbeing of the natural environment but it cannot be said that its functioning will ensure the preservation of ecosystems in a pristine condition (Shimova, 2013). Canada has a unique experience in the development of ecological tourism in national parks and tourism is a reliable source of income not only for protected areas but also for indigenous people. The development of ecotourism in Canada is seen as a mechanism for self-financing of national parks, so the economic component prevails in this area of activity.

Given the Canadian experience in organising tourism activities in the national parks of the northern territories, it is necessary to develop research programmes that provide systematic information not only about the number of tourists but also about the quality of the services provided. At the same time, recreational opportunities should be combined with protection of the reserve's resources. The question arises of developing research methods to obtain regular, systematic information about visitors to the reserve for planning not only tourist but also security activities (throughput). Therefore, the Canadian national parks use the division of the recreational area into separate zones in order to control the permissible level of attendance of tourists. At the same time, joint planning and management of recreational opportunities of the national park with the local population on a systematic basis are used (Totonova, 2009).

For the development of the national park system as a resource for the development of northern tourism, there is a greater degree of involvement of indigenous people, local communities entitled to own these lands than for traditional tourism. Currently, in the development strategy of the north of Canada, tourism is seen not only as a source of income for the local population but also as a way of rational, careful use of the northern nature. For example, the National Park Tuktut-Nogai provides a permanent work for two to five people in the local community, and during the short tourist season attracts 25–35 people from neighbouring indigenous communities for temporary work. Consequently, the national park Tuktuk-Nogai contributes to the employment of the local population, although it mainly provides seasonal work for indigenous people (Rapport sur l'état du parc national du Canada Tuktut Nogait, 2011).

Unlike the Canadian national parks that offer seasonal employment to the indigenous population, the 'Ust-Lensky' nature reserve provides the local population with permanent jobs and wages (see Table 14.5). In the staffing of the reserve, a low-skilled labour force prevails which has a low salary. So, the administration of the reserve conducts planned upgrading of its personnel (in various forms).

The 'Ust-Lensky' State Nature Reserve which has been operating since 1986 has its own material and technical base with a book value of 16.6 million Rubles (2013), spends about 2.1 million Rubles to purchase inventories for their activities (fuel and lubricants, inventory, spare parts, medicines, products etc.). In the nature

Table 14.5 The number of staff members of the Ust-Lena State Nature Reserve and the average monthly salary

	The number of staff members	Average monthly wage (in Rubles)
Staff related to the core staff	16	33297
Staff related to administrative and management personnel	6	105716
Employees belonging to other staff	20	32162
Total	42	43102

(Source: The State Reserve 'Ust-Lensky', 2014; The Report about the Results of the Activity of the Federal State-Financed Organization. Being Administrated by the Ministry of Natural Resources and Ecology of the Russian Federation. The State Natural Reserve "Ust-Lensky". Tiksi. Bulunsky region. the Republic of Sakha (Yakutia). 2014. [in Russian]. (Report not published)).

reserve, there is a gradual wear and tear of the material and technical base which is also helped by specific Arctic conditions. But if you compare with the national parks of the Northern territories of Canada, directing the received investments in the development of the main fund, then they are directed to current expenses in the 'Ust-Lensky' nature reserve (The State Reserve 'Ust-Lensky', 2014).

The volume of paid services rendered to visitors of the 'Ust-Lensky' State Nature Reserve is also different from those of Canadian parks. If the transport costs prevail in the structure of the volume of paid services in the northern parks of Canada (the service of tourists within the parks), then in the 'Ust-Lensky' national park, the services of patrolling the territory of the reserve and environmental education work conducted in the schools of the Bulunsky region are leading. Schoolchildren of secondary educational institutions of the region are the main visitors of the museum of the reserve for which an impressive list of ecological and educational works is being conducted. Most of the services provided to schoolchildren are provided free of charge.

The inspectors of the reserve carry out protection throughout the territory of the nature reserve. Weak material and the technical base does not allow to provide transportation services to tourists on the vast territory of the reserve and a small number of vehicles are involved in patrolling the territory. To increase the efficiency of inspector activity, the effectiveness of the reserve activity is assessed on the basis of generalised indicators. The reserve administration plans to use the cordons of inspection to provide tourist accommodation services in order to increase the receipt of extra-budgetary funds from the services rendered.

The types of ecological tourism that are most suitable for the nature conservation activities of the 'Ust-Lensky' reserve are excursions for cruise ship tourists on specially equipped ecological paths, animal watching and scientific tourism. Therefore, in order to inform visitors, the system of signposts is being established along the entire long border of the reserve. It is planned to organise parking places.

The main work of environmental education is aimed at promoting the 'Ust-Lensky' nature reserve and creating effective links with the community, which contribute to the dissemination of information on the activities of the reserve (see Table 14.6) in the Bulunsky region, on the basis of general education institutions, as part of the environmental education work. According to the Ministry of Nature Protection of the Republic of Sakha (Yakutia) (2016), there were six day camps, two 24-hour tent camps with a total coverage of 345 children from low-income and disadvantaged families, nine camps day stay and two round-the-clock tent camps in Tiksi, Taimylyr village, Bykovsky village, Kyusyur village and Nayba village (The State Reserve 'Ust-Lensky', 2014).

The Canadian National Park Tuktut-Nogaid also actively cooperates with the younger generation of the village Polatuk. During the summer school holidays, the park organises excursions and summer camps in the park but in comparison with the 'Ust-Lensky' reserve, Tuktut-Nogaid does not have such a wide coverage of children's environmental education work because of the smaller number of settlements nearby and accordingly the local population.

The difficult accessibility of the territory, poorly developed road infrastructure and the material and technical base of the park as well as a small staff of the scientific department, complicated at the moment the implementation of effective scientific recommendations for the development of tourism in the territory, as well as the development of ecotourism. Weak technical equipment of the inspection service and cordons and the lack of cross-country vehicles (in the off-season) also hamper the development of tourism.

In connection with this, the main problem of the development of the state natural reserve 'Ust-Lensky' is the strengthening of the material and technical base, for example, the construction and renovation of cordons, the renewal of equipment etc. To implement the development plan, a set of measures is needed to structurally change the material and technical base of the natural reserve, improving the tourist infrastructure, as well as a management plan capable of giving a new impetus to the development of ecological tourism in the territory of the Bulunski region.

Development of tourism is also hindered by the lack of collective accommodation facilities in the village Tiksi, lack of interest of investors in the construction of hotels, and shortage of personnel. According to the statistics bodies of the Republic of Sakha (Yakutia), in 2014 a total of 2516 people were served by collective means of the Bulunsky region who on average spent 5.4 nights which is 49 per cent more than in 2012. But in the official statistical data on the collective means of accommodation of the Bulunsky region, only information on the hotel 'Arktika' is present, and the remaining means of collective accommodation facilities are not taken into account. For example, in the territory of the village Tiksi operates departmental collective accommodation facilities (housing and communal services – 20 beds, Polar Geospace Observatory – 22 places, 'Ust-Lensky' reserve – 8 beds) which are not taken into account in the compilation of statistical data. In addition, there are two individual entrepreneurs engaged in the provision of accommodation services (mini-hotels) whose prices are quite high – 3 thousand Ruble – that provide their services for accommodation and unregistered entrepreneurs whose services are in demand in the summer. The existing catering enterprises in the village Tiksi is the restaurant 'North' (60 seats), the bar 'North'

(25 seats) and the cafe 'Asia' (22 seats). The services that most correspond to the standards (personnel, menu, prices and service level) provide customers with the newly opened 'Asia' café (Totonova, 2016).

The development of tourism in the nature reserve faces the following problems:

i   Expensive transport services. underdeveloped infrastructure;
ii   The lack of qualified specialists in the field of ecological tourism;
iii Conducting research and effective monitoring of the activities of the reserve; and
iv   the disunity of stakeholders and participants.

Disorganised rest unlike organised rest does not demand lands for new construction of hotels. Placing and service of tourists are realised within the populated areas (rented accommodation, departmental and private hotels, café, eateries etc.). Placing of independent tourists is possible out of the populated areas, especially in summer in well-equipped places. It is accompanied by the action of significant local seasonal recreational loads on the natural complexes and reservoirs in the adjacent accommodation of tourists and also by difficultly controlled withdrawal of natural resources.

The natural reserve 'Ust-Lensky' can develop ecological tourist products and offer the services. Herewith the tourism should be developed in order to save the best that local people have and to bring out the things demanding improvement. For example, the state and local authorities are interested in the social development, the attraction of investments in development of the infrastructure, and the reserve is interested in the improvement of quality of services. The development of tourism must be accompanied by strict control by the ecologists with considering of capacity of the territory of the natural reserve. The main tasks are:

i   Guaranteeing of charging mechanisms for visiting the natural reserve;
ii   Development of public-private partnership (PPP) which promotes the creation of alternative sources of income for local population and the organisation of new workplaces;
iii Planning, monitoring and progress of scientifically based approach for development of ecological tourism.

(Totonova, 2016)

The development of tourism in the natural reserve depends on a complex approach to planning and its development management. The expected state of the natural reserve in future should be reflected in the plan with the most effective and real ways to achieve it. In a certain sense, the plan of tourism development in the reserve is needed for maximising benefits over minimising expenses. At the same time, as the Canadian experience shows, it is necessary to develop the network partnerships between participants of the tourist market in the 'Ust-Lensky' reserve (municipal society Bulunsky region, entrepreneurs and indigenous peoples). The development of the local government allows to solve jointly the ecological problems and promotes the emergence of new workplaces and coordination of activity of all participants.

Tourist service analysis

When resources for infrastructure development in Bulunsky region (where the 'Ust-Lenskiy' nature reserve is located) are insufficient, natural conditions and resources allow for advancement of ecotourism, cruise travel as well as sports, ethnographic, experiential, fishing, and hunting tourism. Despite that tourism doesn't take a significant part in Bulunsky region's economy, the local administration's interest to the development of tourism as a new income source and to the expansion of local businesses is gradually increasing. The most informative factor of tourism's part in the economy of the town of Tiksi is the tourist expense multiplier. The author reviewed the tourist expenses in Tiksi as the multiplying factor.

As the data in Table 14.6 show, the amount of an unorganised tourist's expenses in Tiksi on tourist services in seven days is 68,300 rubles on average. The average expense amount for a business trip to Tiksi is calculated without a departure from the town, because Russian Federation's border area begins there and a permit is needed for every departure. The average expense amount of an organised tourist with a tourist package tour is 95,000 Ruble. In setting up the travel product by tour operators, costs of tourist's individual expenses (without the costs of air travel to Tiksi), equipment and group expenses (cargo delivery, engine mechanic's wage, instructor's services, fuel product costs, dampening of utilised vehicles, income tax and pension fee) are taken into account.

Most of the business tourist expenses (58.5 per cent) in Tiksi are comprised of transportation charges whereas the same charges for an organised tourist from Yakutsk amount to 53 per cent. The rest of the expenses are comprised of servicing

Table 14.6 Average consumer costs of tourist services in Tiksi Bulunsky region in 2015

Types of expenses	Days of stay	Service costs in 1 day (RUB)	Total amount (RUB)
Transportation charges (Yakutsk-Tiksi-Yakutsk)			40000
Accommodation	7	3000	21000
Lunches in restaurants	7	350	2450
Food costs	7	500	3500
'Arctic' museum tour	1	200	200
Private museum tour	1	200	200
Costs of souvenirs made by local businesses			1000
Total	7	68350	

(Source: the author's expert evaluation following the results of an academic trip to Tiksi in August, 2015)

costs by auxiliary personnel (engine mechanic, instructor, accompanying inspector) during the tour. The difference of the developing tourist business in the Arctic is that 50–60 per cent of tourist expenses are taken by transportation charges and they completely depend not even on the quality of the provided transport services but on price policy and the state of logistics in Yakutian airlines. As Canada's experience shows, extensive state aid and investments in Arctic transport system development are required for solving this issue and further progress of tourism (Totonova, 2016).

The research conducted by the author shows that small hotels housing organised tourists in the town's residential areas have the most rapid penetration in the region's tourist service market. The largest personal income increase is influenced by extra sales of services involving housing tourists in individual accommodation facilities or residential areas during the summer season with the beginning of summer scientific research expeditions and also by providing tourist escorting services (engine mechanics, instructors without corresponding permits). Part of the extra personal income is spent on buying goods and services and with the increasing sales of goods made by local businesses, the local sales volume increases as well.

Conclusion

Canada's experience on developing national parks in northern territories may be used on business development of the 'Ust-Lenskiy' state nature reserve. For example, in order to efficiently manage the reserve, a creation of economic and institutional conditions with due account for Arctic first nations' gathered experience and a drawing-up of a new, internationally standardised management plan of the 'Ust-Lenskiy' state nature reserve is required. When drawing-up a strategic nature reserve management plan, the Canadians evaluate the historic, cultural, socio-economic and natural resource potential of the reserve, then explore the long-term development factors. Studying the market allows for exploring shortcomings of activities and factors affecting further development, consequently allowing for working out a proper policy for further development.

Taking into account many years of experience regarding tourism development in Canada's northern territories, we suggested the following ways for developing tourism in the municipalities of the Republic of Sakha (Yakutia) (Totonova, 2014b):

i   Development of tourist zoning is one of the research and area analysis methods. Factoring in the designated natural, social and economic aspects, zoning allows for planning the development of certain forms of tourism and concurrent tourist infrastructure with due account for natural resource management. Designated tourist zones of different levels may be under consideration as a scientific basis for forming a geographically differentiated development strategy for the tourism of the Republic of Sakha (Yakutia).

ii Creation of civic tourism development centres serving as a coordination centre of tourism industry enterprises and their partners in order to increase the tourism management efficiency of municipalities. Creation of tourism development centres should be aligned with, on one hand, achieving the strategic goals of the administration and on the other hand, supporting local business owners. The goal of the creation is to proceed to coordinating the activities of all organisations included in the tourism industry enterprise network.

iii Usage of territorial marketing tools: A municipality's marketing involves analysing and implementing a solution of marketing tasks directly on a region and community level, which means that a search for new tools for efficient reforming of a regional development strategy is being conducted. Territorial marketing is becoming one of the regional management tools, the use of which leads to socio-economic growth by means of optimal resource and territorial potential management.

Working-out of a tourism development strategy allows for creating a tool for forming a modern, highly efficient and competitive tourist complex that provides a significant contribution to the economy of Northern regions. The following priority guidelines for investing institutional, material and financial resources should be chosen by the regions during the development of functional strategies for developing a Northern tourist complex:

- formation of a modern marketing strategy for promoting a tourist product on domestic and international markets;
- advancement of tourist infrastructure based on creating conditions for attracting state and private investments;
- improvement of the regional tourist business management system;
- priority ranking of tourism industry development on a regional level from state authorities;
- creation of a local personnel training system.

Therefore, a tool for cooperation between government, regional and municipal institutions and tourist businesses is a most effective method of tourism management in the North. Network relations between tourist businesses and state authorities give an opportunity to improve the work of travel agencies by means of implementing scientific planning methods, forming an effective relations system between small and medium tourist businesses and government agencies.

Despite the differences in the historical development of Northern territories of Canada and Arctic regions of the Republic of Sakha (Yakutia), there are similar problems when it comes to the development of these specific territories. The research of the tourism development in the Northern territories of Canada and Arctic regions of the Republic of Sakha (Yakutia) conducted by the author shows that a comparative analysis is difficult. Because both areas have different socio-economic advancement levels, if Canadian Northern territories are showing rapid progress in tourism development, contributing to economic diversity, then the same development in Republic of Sakha (Yakutia)'s Arctic regions is taking a rather 'informal' approach linked with undeveloped infrastructure and a lack of qualified personnel. The development of the 'informal' tourism sector in Republic of Sakha (Yakutia)'s Arctic regions is enabled by a lack of local regulating institutions and a coherent economy management coordination in the North on federal, regional and municipal levels.

References

Affaires autochtones et développement du Nord Canada. (2016). *Home* (In French). Retrieved from: www.ainc-inac.gc.ca (accessed: the 05th January, 2018).

Alexandrova, A.Yu. (ed.). (2010). *The geography of tourism*. Moscow: KNORUS, p. 235.

Granberg, A. (2000). *Osnovy regionalnoj ekonomiki (foundations of regional Economy)* (In Russian). Moscow: State University.

Grenier, A.A. (2009). Conceptualisation du tourisme polaire: Cartographier une expérience aux confins de l'imaginaire (In French). *Téoros*, **28**(1), pp. 7–19.

Gukov, A.Y. (2010). Russian Arctic reserves: Problems and ways of solving them. *Conference proceedings*. Tiksi, Republic Sakha (Yakutia), pp. 3–13.

Hamelin, L.-E. (2002). *Discours du Nord* (In French). Retrieved from: http://lehamelin. sittel.ca/pdf/Documents/1484-2_DiscoursNord.pdf (accessed: the 05th January, 2018).

Luzin, G.P., Lazarev, E.E., Selin, V.S. and Shirokova, L.N. (1996). *Methodology of geographical demarcation for labor force management in the Northern Regions*. City Apatity: Apatity, p. 124.

Ministry of Nature Protection of the Republic of Sakha (Yakutia). (2016). *Home* (In Russian). Retrieved from: https://minpriroda.sakha.gov.ru/ (accessed: the 05th January, 2018).

The National Tour Operator 'Satal tour'. (2018). *Home* (In Russian). Retrieved from: http:// satal-tour.ru/portfolio-view/prazdnik/ (accessed: the 05th January, 2018).

Parcs Canada. (2011). *Rapport sur l'état du parc national du Canada Tuktut Nogait (2011)* (In French). Retrieved from: https://bit.ly/2rIazwq (accessed: the 05th January, 2018).

Rea, K.J. (1968). *The political economy of the Canadian North: An interpretation of the course of development in the Northern Territories of Canada to the early 1960's*. Toronto: University of Toronto Press.

Republic of Sakha. (2016). *The territorial body of the Federal State Statistics Service for the Republic of Sakha [Yakutia]* (In Russian). Retrieved from: www.sakha.gks.ru (accessed: the 05th January, 2018).

Shimova, O.S. (2013). *The foundations of sustainable tourism*. Minsk: New Knowledge, p. 198.

The State Reserve 'Ust-Lensky'. (2014). *The Rapport State Natural Reserve "Ust-Lensky", Tiksi, Republic of Sakha [Yakutia]* (In Russian). Retrieved from: www.ustlensky.ru (accessed: the 05th January, 2018).

Totonova, E.E. (2009). *Tourism development in Northern Canada*. Yakutsk: Yakutsk State University Publishing House, p. 194.

Totonova, E.E. (2011). The modern tendencies of tourism development in Republic of Sakha (Yakutia). *Economics*, 7, pp.432–434.

Totonova, E.E. (2014a). Arctic regions of Republic Sakha (Yakutia) and market adjustment perspectives. *Concept*, 9, pp. 111–115.

Totonova, E.E. (2014b). *The role of local self-government bodies in the formation of the system of tourism management of the Republic of Sakha (Yakutia)*. Retrieved from: www. uecs.ru/uecs62-622014/item/2755-2014-02-15-06-32-28 (accessed: the 05th January, 2018).

Totonova, E.E. (2014c). *The using of the experience of development for the National Parks on the North Territories of Canada in the Republic of Sakha (Yakutia)*. Retrieved from: ://qje.su/regionalnayaekonomikairazvitie/ispolzovanieopytarazvitiyanatsional-nyhparkovsevernyhterritorijkanadyvrespublikesahayakutiya (accessed: the 05th January, 2018).

Totonova, E.E. (2016). *Tourism in the North of the Republic of Sakha (Yakutia): The experience of geographical modeling*. Yakutsk: Publishing House of NEFU, pp. 188.

Vishnevskiy, D.S. and Demyanenko, A.N. (2010). Macroeconomic zoning as a method of strategic analysis: The Russian Far East. *Spatial Economics*, **4**, pp. 6–31.

Index

Page numbers in italic type indicate figures and page numbers in bold type indicate tables.